The Treatises of St. Cyprian

The Life and Passion of Cyprian

St. Cyprian

Life and Passion of Cyprian

© Lighthouse Publishing 2023

Written by: Cyprian (AD 200 - 258)
Translated by: Rev. Ernest Wallis, Ph.D.(1820 – 1910)
Updated into Modern U.S English: A.M. Overett (b.1960)

All rights reserved. Without limiting the rights under copyright reserved above, no part of this publication may be reproduced, stored in a retrieval system, or transmitted, in any form or by any means (electronic, mechanical, photocopying, recording or otherwise), without the prior written permission of the copyright owner of this book.

Published by
Lighthouse Publishing
SAN 257-4330
228 Freedom Parkway
Hoschton, GA 30548
United States of America

www.lighthousechristianpublishing.com

The Treatises of Cyprian.

Treatise I.
On the Unity of the Church.

Argument.—On the Occasion of the Schism of Novatian, to Keep Back from Him the Carthaginians, Who Already Were Not Averse to Him, on Account of Novatus and Some Other Presbyters of His Church, Who Had Originated the Whole Disturbance, Cyprian Wrote This Treatise. And First of All, Fortifying Them Against the Deceits of These, He Exhorts Them to Constancy, and Instructs Them that Heresies Exist Because Christ, the Head of the Church, is Not Looked To, that the Common Commission First Entrusted to Peter is Contemned, and the One Church and the One Episcopate are Deserted. Then He Proves, as Well by the Scriptures as by the Figures of the Old and New Testament, the Unity of the Church.

1. Since the Lord warns us, saying, "Ye are the salt of the earth," and since He bids us to be simple to harmlessness, and yet with our simplicity to be prudent, what else, beloved brethren, befits us, than to use foresight and watching with an anxious heart, both to perceive and to beware of the wiles of the crafty foe, that we, who have put on Christ the wisdom of God the Father, may not seem to be wanting in wisdom in the matter of providing for our salvation? For it is not persecution alone that is to be feared; nor those things which advance by open attack to overwhelm and cast down the servants of God. Caution is easier where danger is manifest, and the mind is prepared beforehand for the contest when the adversary avows himself. The enemy is more to be feared and to be guarded against, when he

creeps on us secretly; when, deceiving by the appearance of peace, he steals forward by hidden approaches, whence also he has received the name of the Serpent. That is always his subtlety; that is his dark and stealthy artifice for circumventing man. Thus from the very beginning of the world he deceived; and flattering with lying words, he misled inexperienced souls with an incautious credulity. Thus he endeavored to tempt the Lord Himself: he secretly approached Him, as if he would creep on Him again, and deceive; yet he was understood, and beaten back, and therefore prostrated, because he was recognized and detected.

    2. From which an example is given us to avoid the way of the old man, to stand in the footsteps of a conquering Christ, that we may not again be incautiously turned back into the nets of death, but, foreseeing our danger, may possess the immortality that we have received. But how can we possess immortality, unless we keep those commands of Christ whereby death is driven out and overcome, when He Himself warns us, and says, "If thou wilt enter into life, keep the commandments?" And again: "If ye do the things that I command you, henceforth I call you not servants, but friends." Finally, these people He calls strong and steadfast; these He declares to be founded in robust security upon the rock, established with immoveable and unshaken firmness, in opposition to all the tempests and hurricanes of the world. "Whosoever," says He, "heareth my words, and doeth them, I will liken him unto a wise man, that built his house upon a rock: the rain descended, the floods came, the winds blew, and beat upon that house; and it fell not: for it was founded upon a rock." We ought therefore to stand fast on His words, to learn and do whatever He both

taught and did. But how can a man say that he believes in Christ, who does not do what Christ commanded him to do? Or whence shall he attain to the reward of faith, who will not keep the faith of the commandment? He must of necessity waver and wander, and, caught away by a spirit of error, like dust which is shaken by the wind, be blown about; and he will make no advance in his walk towards salvation, because he does not keep the truth of the way of salvation.

3. But, beloved brethren, not only must we beware of what is open and manifest, but also of what deceives by the craft of subtle fraud. And what can be more crafty, or what more subtle, than for this enemy, detected and cast down by the advent of Christ, after light has come to the nations, and saving rays have shone for the preservation of men, that the deaf might receive the hearing of spiritual grace, the blind might open their eyes to God, the weak might grow strong again with eternal health, the lame might run to the church, the dumb might pray with clear voices and prayers—seeing his idols forsaken, and his lanes and his temples deserted by the numerous concourse of believers—to devise a new fraud, and under the very title of the Christian name to deceive the incautious? He has invented heresies and schisms, whereby he might subvert the faith, might corrupt the truth, might divide the unity. Those whom he cannot keep in the darkness of the old way, he circumvents and deceives by the error of a new way. He snatches men from the Church itself; and while they seem to themselves to have already approached to the light, and to have escaped the night of the world, he pours over them again, in their unconsciousness, new darkness; so that, although they do not stand firm with the Gospel of Christ, and with the

observation and law of Christ, they still call themselves Christians, and, walking in darkness, they think that they have the light, while the adversary is flattering and deceiving, who, according to the apostle's word, transforms himself into an angel of light, and equips his ministers as if they were the ministers of righteousness, who maintain night instead of day, death for salvation, despair under the offer of hope, perfidy under the pretext of faith, antichrist under the name of Christ; so that, while they feign things like the truth, they make void the truth by their subtlety. This happens, beloved brethren, so long as we do not return to the source of truth, as we do not seek the head nor keep the teaching of the heavenly Master.

4. If anyone consider and examine these things, there is no need for lengthened discussion and arguments. There is easy proof for faith in a short summary of the truth. The Lord speaks to Peter, saying, "I say unto thee, that thou art Peter; and upon this rock I will build my Church, and the gates of hell shall not prevail against it. And I will give unto thee the keys of the kingdom of heaven; and whatsoever thou shalt bind on earth shall be bound also in heaven, and whatsoever thou shalt loose on earth shall be loosed in heaven." And again to the same He says, after His resurrection, "Feed my sheep." And although to all the apostles, after His resurrection, He gives an equal power, and says, "As the Father hath sent me, even so send I you: Receive ye the Holy Ghost: Whose soever sins ye remit, they shall be remitted unto him; and whose soever sins ye retain, they shall be retained;" yet, that He might set forth unity, He arranged by His authority the origin of that unity, as beginning from one. Assuredly the rest of the apostles were also the

same as was Peter, endowed with a like partnership both of honor and power; but the beginning proceeds from unity. Which one Church, also, the Holy Spirit in the Song of Songs designated in the person of our Lord, and says, "My dove, my spotless one, is but one. She is the only one of her mother, elect of her that bare her." Does he who does not hold this unity of the Church think that he holds the faith? Does he who strives against and resists the Church trust that he is in the Church, when moreover the blessed Apostle Paul teaches the same thing, and sets forth the sacrament of unity, saying, "There is one body and one spirit, one hope of your calling, one Lord, one faith, one baptism, one God?"

5. And this unity we ought firmly to hold and assert, especially those of us that are bishops who preside in the Church, that we may also prove the episcopate itself to be one and undivided. Let no one deceive the brotherhood by a falsehood: let no one corrupt the truth of the faith by perfidious prevarication. The episcopate is one, each part of which is held by each one for the whole. The Church also is one, which is spread abroad far and wide into a multitude by an increase of fruitfulness. As there are many rays of the sun, but one light; and many branches of a tree, but one strength based in its tenacious root; and since from one spring flow many streams, although the multiplicity seems diffused in the liberality of an overflowing abundance, yet the unity is still preserved in the source. Separate a ray of the sun from its body of light, its unity does not allow a division of light; break a branch from a tree,—when broken, it will not be able to bud; cut off the stream from its fountain, and that which is cut off dries up. Thus also the Church, shone over with the light of the Lord, sheds forth her rays over

the whole world, yet it is one light which is everywhere diffused, nor is the unity of the body separated. Her fruitful abundance spreads her branches over the whole world. She broadly expands her rivers, liberally flowing, yet her head is one, her source one; and she is one mother, plentiful in the results of fruitfulness: from her womb we are born, by her milk we are nourished, by her spirit we are animated.

6. The spouse of Christ cannot be adulterous; she is uncorrupted and pure. She knows one home; she guards with chaste modesty the sanctity of one couch. She keeps us for God. She appoints the sons whom she has born for the kingdom. Whoever is separated from the Church and is joined to an adulteress, is separated from the promises of the Church; nor can he who forsakes the Church of Christ attain to the rewards of Christ. He is a stranger; he is profane; he is an enemy. He can no longer have God for his Father, who has not the Church for his mother. If anyone could escape who was outside the ark of Noah, then he also may escape who shall be outside of the Church. The Lord warns, saying, "He who is not with me is against me, and he who gathered not with me scattered." He who breaks the peace and the concord of Christ, does so in opposition to Christ; he who gathered elsewhere than in the Church, scatters the Church of Christ. The Lord says, "I and the Father are one;" and again it is written of the Father, and of the Son, and of the Holy Spirit, "And these three are one." And does anyone believe that this unity which thus comes from the divine strength and coheres in celestial sacraments, can be divided in the Church, and can be separated by the parting asunder of opposing wills? He who does not hold this unity does not hold God's law, does not hold the faith of

the Father and the Son, does not hold life and salvation.

7. This sacrament of unity, this bond of a concord inseparably cohering, is set forth where in the Gospel the coat of the Lord Jesus Christ is not at all divided nor cut, but is received as an entire garment, and is possessed as an uninjured and undivided robe by those who cast lots concerning Christ's garment, who should rather put on Christ. Holy Scripture speaks, saying, "But of the coat, because it was not sewed, but woven from the top throughout, they said one to another, Let us not rend it, but cast lots whose it shall be." That coat bore with it a unity that came down from the top, that is, that came from heaven and the Father, which was not to be at all rent by the receiver and the possessor, but without separation we obtain a whole and substantial entireness. He cannot possess the garment of Christ who parts and divides the Church of Christ. On the other hand, again, when at Solomon's death his kingdom and people were divided, Abijah the prophet, meeting Jeroboam the king in the field, divided his garment into twelve sections, saying, "Take thee ten pieces; for thus saith the Lord, Behold, I will rend the kingdom out of the hand of Solomon, and I will give ten scepters unto thee; and two scepters shall be unto him for my servant David's sake, and for Jerusalem, the city which I have chosen to place my name there." As the twelve tribes of Israel were divided, the prophet Abijah rent his garment. But because Christ's people cannot be rent, His robe, woven and united throughout, is not divided by those who possess it; undivided, united, connected, it shows the coherent concord of our people who put on Christ. By the sacrament and sign of His garment, He has declared the unity of the Church.

8. Who, then, is so wicked and faithless, who is so

insane with the madness of discord, that either he should believe that the unity of God can be divided, or should dare to rend it—the garment of the Lord—the Church of Christ? He Himself in His Gospel warns us, and teaches, saying, "And there shall be one flock and one shepherd." And does anyone believe that in one place there can be either many shepherds or many flocks? The Apostle Paul, moreover, urging upon us this same unity, beseeches and exhorts, saying, "I beseech you, brethren, by the name of our Lord Jesus Christ, that ye all speak the same thing, and that there be no schisms among you; but that ye be joined together in the same mind and in the same judgment." And again, he says, "Forbearing one another in love, endeavoring to keep the unity of the Spirit in the bond of peace." Do you think that you can stand and live if you withdraw from the Church, building for yourself other homes and a different dwelling, when it is said to Rahab, in whom was prefigured the Church, "Thy father, and thy mother, and thy brethren, and all the house of thy father, thou shalt gather unto thee into thine house; and it shall come to pass, whosoever shall go abroad beyond the door of thine house, his blood shall be upon his own head?" Also, the sacrament of the Passover contains nothing else in the law of the Exodus than that the lamb which is slain in the figure of Christ should be eaten in one house. God speaks, saying, "In one house shall ye eat it; ye shall not send its flesh abroad from the house." The flesh of Christ, and the holy of the Lord, cannot be sent abroad, nor is there any other home to believers but the one Church. This home, this household of unanimity, the Holy Spirit designates and points out in the Psalms, saying, "God, who makes men to dwell with one mind in a house." In the house of God, in the Church of Christ, men dwell with one mind, and continue in concord and simplicity.

9. Therefore also the Holy Spirit came as a dove, a simple and joyous creature, not bitter with gall, not cruel in its bite, not violent with the rending of its claws, loving human dwellings, knowing the association of one home; when they have young, bringing forth their young together; when they fly abroad, remaining in their flights by the side of one another, spending their life in mutual intercourse, acknowledging the concord of peace with the kiss of the beak, in all things fulfilling the law of unanimity. This is the simplicity that ought to be known in the Church, this is the charity that ought to be attained, that so the love of the brotherhood may imitate the doves, that their gentleness and meekness may be like the lambs and sheep. What does the fierceness of wolves do in the Christian breast? What the savageness of dogs, and the deadly venom of serpents, and the sanguinary cruelty of wild beasts? We are to be congratulated when such as these are separated from the Church, lest they should lay waste the doves and sheep of Christ with their cruel and envenomed contagion. Bitterness cannot consist and be associated with sweetness, darkness with light, rain with clearness, battle with peace, barrenness with fertility, drought with springs, storm with tranquility. Let none think that the good can depart from the Church. The wind does not carry away the wheat, nor does the hurricane uproot the tree that is based on a solid root. The light straws are tossed about by the tempest, the feeble trees are overthrown by the onset of the whirlwind. The Apostle John execrates and severely assails these, when he says, "They went forth from us, but they were not of us; for if they had been of us, surely they would have continued

with us."

10. Hence heresies not only have frequently been originated but continue to be so; while the perverted mind has no peace—while a discordant faithlessness does not maintain unity. But the Lord permits and suffers these things to be, while the choice of one's own liberty remains, so that while the discrimination of truth is testing our hearts and our minds, the sound faith of those that are approved may shine forth with manifest light. The Holy Spirit forewarns and says by the apostle, "It is needful also that there should be heresies, that they which are approved may be made manifest among you." Thus the faithful are approved, thus the perfidious are detected; thus even here, before the day of judgment, the souls of the righteous and of the unrighteous are already divided, and the chaff is separated from the wheat. These are they who of their own accord, without any divine arrangement, set themselves to preside among the daring strangers assembled, who appoint themselves prelates without any law of ordination, who assume to themselves the name of bishop, although no one gives them the episcopate; whom the Holy Spirit points out in the Psalms as sitting in the seat of pestilence, plagues, and spots of the faith, deceiving with serpent's tongue, and artful in corrupting the truth, vomiting forth deadly poisons from pestilential tongues; whose speech doth creep like a cancer, whose discourse forms a deadly poison in the heart and breast of everyone.

11. Against people of this kind the Lord cries; from these He restrains and recalls His erring people, saying, "Hearken not unto the words of the false prophets; for the visions of their hearts deceive them. They speak, but not out of the mouth of the Lord. They say to those

who cast away the word of God, Ye shall have peace, and everyone that walketh after his own will. Everyone who walketh in the error of his heart, no evil shall come upon him. I have not spoken to them, yet they prophesied. If they had stood on my foundation (substantia, ὑποστάσει), and had heard my words, and taught my people, I would have turned them from their evil thoughts." Again, the Lord points out and designates these same, saying, "They have forsaken me, the fountain of living waters, and have hewed them out broken cisterns which can hold no water." Although there can be no other baptism but one, they think that they can baptize; although they forsake the fountain of life, they promise the grace of living and saving water. Men are not washed among them, but rather are made foul; nor are sins purged away but are even accumulated. Such a nativity does not generate sons to God, but to the devil. By a falsehood they are born, and they do not receive the promises of truth. Begotten of perfidy, they lose the grace of faith. They cannot attain to the reward of peace, since they have broken the Lord's peace with the madness of discord.

12. Nor let any deceive themselves by a futile interpretation, in respect of the Lord having said, "Wheresoever two or three are gathered together in my name, there am I in the midst of them." Corrupters and false interpreters of the Gospel quote the last words, and lay aside the former ones, remembering part, and craftily suppressing part: as they themselves are separated from the Church, so they cut off the substance of one section. For the Lord, when He would urge unanimity and peace upon His disciples, said, "I say unto you, That if two of you shall agree on earth touching anything that ye shall ask, it shall be given you by my Father which is in

heaven. For wheresoever two or three are gathered together in my name, I am with them;" showing that most is given, not to the multitude, but to the unanimity of those that pray. "If," He says, "two of you shall agree on earth:" He placed agreement first; He has made the concord of peace a prerequisite; He taught that we should agree firmly and faithfully. But how can he agree with anyone who does not agree with the body of the Church itself, and with the universal brotherhood? How can two or three be assembled together in Christ's name, who, it is evident, are separated from Christ and from His Gospel? For we have not withdrawn from them, but they from us; and since heresies and schisms have risen subsequently, from their establishment for themselves of diverse places of worship, they have forsaken the Head and Source of the truth. But the Lord speaks concerning His Church, and to those also who are in the Church He speaks, that if they are in agreement, if according to what He commanded and admonished, although only two or three gathered together with unanimity should pray—though they be only two or three—they may obtain from the majesty of God what they ask. "Wheresoever two or three are gathered together in my name, I," says He, "am with them;" that is, with the simple and peaceable—with those who fear God and keep God's commandments. With these, although only two or three, He said that He was, in the same manner as He was with the three youths in the fiery furnace; and because they abode towards God in simplicity, and in unanimity among themselves, He animated them, in the midst of the surrounding flames, with the breath of dew: in the way in which, with the two apostles shut up in prison, because they were simple-minded and of one mind, He Himself was present; He

Himself, having loosed the bolts of the dungeon, placed them again in the market-place, that they might declare to the multitude the word which they faithfully preached. When, therefore, in His commandments He lays it down, and says, "Where two or three are gathered together in my name, I am with them," He does not divide men from the Church, seeing that He Himself ordained and made the Church; but rebuking the faithless for their discord, and commending peace by His word to the faithful, He shows that He is rather with two or three who pray with one mind, than with a great many who differ, and that more can be obtained by the discordant prayer of a few, than by the discordant supplication of many.

13. Thus, also, when He gave the law of prayer, He added, saying, "And when you stand praying, forgive, if you have anything against any; that your Father also which is in heaven may forgive you your trespasses." And He calls back from the altar one who comes to the sacrifice in strife, and bids him first agree with his brother, and then return with peace and offer his gift to God: for God had not respect unto Cain's offerings; for he could not have God at peace with him, who through envious discord had not peace with his brother. What peace, then, do the enemies of the brethren promise to themselves? What sacrifices do those who are rivals of the priests think that they celebrate? Do they deem that they have Christ with them when they are collected together, who are gathered together outside the Church of Christ?

14. Even if such men were slain in confession of the Name, that stain is not even washed away by blood: the inexpiable and grave fault of discord is not even purged by suffering. He cannot be a martyr who is not in

the Church; he cannot attain unto the kingdom who forsakes that which shall reign there. Christ gave us peace; He bade us be in agreement, and of one mind. He charged the bonds of love and charity to be kept uncorrupted and inviolate; he cannot show himself a martyr who has not maintained brotherly love. Paul the apostle teaches this, and testifies, saying, "And though I have faith, so that I can remove mountains, and have not charity, I am nothing. And though I give all my goods to feed the poor, and though I give my body to be burned, and have not charity, it profited me nothing. Charity is magnanimous; charity is kind; charity envies not; charity acts not vainly, is not puffed up, is not easily provoked, thinketh no evil; loveth all things, believeth all things, hopes all things, endures all things. Charity never fails." "Charity," says he, "never fails." For she will ever be in the kingdom, she will endure forever in the unity of a brotherhood linked to herself. Discord cannot attain to the kingdom of heaven; to the rewards of Christ, who said, "This is my commandment, that ye love one another, even as I have loved you:" he cannot attain who has violated the love of Christ by faithless dissension. He who has not charity has not God. The word of the blessed Apostle John is: "God," saith he, "is love; and he that dwelleth in love dwelleth in God, and God dwelleth in him." They cannot dwell with God who would not be of one mind in God's Church. Although they burn, given up to flames and fires, or lay down their lives, thrown to the wild beasts, that will not be the crown of faith, but the punishment of perfidy; nor will it be the glorious ending of religious valor, but the destruction of despair. Such a one may be slain; crowned he cannot be. He professes himself to be a Christian in such a way as the devil often feigns himself to be Christ, as the Lord Himself forewarns us, and says, "Many shall come in my name, saying, I am Christ, and shall deceive many." As he is not Christ, although he deceives in respect of the name; so neither can he appear as a Christian who does not abide in the truth of His Gospel and of faith.

15. For both to prophesy and to cast out devils, and to do great acts upon the earth is certainly a sublime and an admirable thing; but one does not attain the kingdom of heaven although he is found in all these things, unless he walks in the observance of the right and just way. The Lord denounces, and says, "Many shall say to me in that day, Lord, Lord, have we not prophesied in Thy name, and in Thy name have cast out devils, and in Thy name done many wonderful works? And then will I profess unto them, I never knew you: depart from me, ye that work iniquity." There is need of righteousness, that one may deserve well of God the Judge; we must obey His precepts and warnings, that our merits may receive their reward. The Lord in His Gospel, when He would direct the way of our hope and faith in a brief summary, said, "The Lord thy God is one God: and thou shalt love the Lord thy God with all thy heart, and with all thy soul, and with all thy strength. This is the first commandment; and the second is like unto it: Thou shalt love thy neighbor as thyself. On these two commandments hang all the law and the prophets." He taught, at the same time, love and unity by His instruction. He has included all the prophets and the law in two precepts. But what unity does he keep, what love does he maintain or consider, who, savage with the madness of discord, divides the Church, destroys the faith, disturbs the peace, dissipates charity, profanes the sacrament?

16. This evil, most faithful brethren, had long ago begun, but now the mischievous destruction of the same evil has increased, and the envenomed plague of heretical perversity and schisms has begun to spring forth and shoot anew; because even thus it must be in the decline of the world, since the Holy Spirit foretells and forewarns us by the apostle, saying, "In the last days," says he, "perilous times shall come, and men shall be lovers of their own selves, proud, boasters, covetous, blasphemers, disobedient to parents, unthankful, unholy, without natural affection, truce-breakers, false accusers, incontinent, fierce, hating the good, traitors, heady, high-minded, lovers of pleasures more than lovers of God, having a sort of form of religion, but denying the power thereof. Of this sort are they who creep into houses, and lead captive silly women laden with sins, which are led away with divers lusts; ever learning, and never coming to the knowledge of the truth. And as Jannes and Jambres withstood Moses, so do these also resist the truth; but they shall proceed no further, for their folly shall be manifest unto all men, even as theirs also was." Whatever things were predicted are fulfilled; and as the end of the world is approaching, they have come for the probation as well of the men as of the times. Error deceives as the adversary rages more and more; senselessness lifts up, envy inflames, covetousness makes blind, impiety depraves, pride puffs up, discord exasperates, anger hurries headlong.

17. Yet let not the excessive and headlong faithlessness of many move or disturb us, but rather strengthen our faith in the truthfulness which has foretold the matter. As some have become such, because these things were predicted beforehand, so let other brethren

beware of matters of a like kind, because these also were predicted beforehand, even as the Lord instructs us, and says, "But take ye heed: behold, I have told you all things." Avoid, I beseech you, brethren, men of this kind, and drive away from your side and from your ears, as if it were the contagion of death, their mischievous conversation; as it is written, "Hedge thine ears about with thorns, and refuse to hear a wicked tongue." And again, "Evil communications corrupt good manners." The Lord teaches and warns us to depart from such. He saith, "They are blind leaders of the blind; and if the blind lead the blind, they shall both fall into the ditch." Such a one is to be turned away from and avoided, whosoever he may be, that is separated from the Church. Such a one is perverted and sins and is condemned of his own self. Does he think that he has Christ, who acts in opposition to Christ's priests, who separates himself from the company of His clergy and people? He bears arms against the Church; he contends against God's appointment. An enemy of the altar, a rebel against Christ's sacrifice, for the faith faithless, for religion profane, a disobedient servant, an impious son, a hostile brother, despising the bishops, and forsaking God's priests, he dares to set up another altar, to make another prayer with unauthorized words, to profane the truth of the Lord's offering by false sacrifices, and not to know that he who strives against the appointment of God, is punished on account of the daring of his temerity by divine visitation.

18. Thus Korah, Dathan, and Abiram, who endeavored to claim to themselves the power of sacrificing in opposition to Moses and Aaron the priest, underwent immediate punishment for their attempts. The earth, breaking its fastenings, gaped open into a deep gulf,

and the cleft of the receding ground swallowed up the men standing and living. Nor did the anger of the indignant God strike only those who had been the movers (of the sedition); but two hundred and fifty sharers and associates of that madness besides, who had been mingled with them in that boldness, the fire that went out from the Lord consumed with a hasty revenge; doubtless to admonish and show that whatever those wicked men had endeavored, in order by human will to overthrow God's appointment, had been done in opposition to God. Thus also Uzziah the king,—when he bare the censer and violently claimed to himself to sacrifice against God's law, and when Azariah the priest withstood him, would not be obedient and yield,—was confounded by the divine indignation, and was polluted upon his forehead by the spot of leprosy: he was marked by an offended Lord in that part of his body where they are signed who deserve well of the Lord. And the sons of Aaron, who placed strange fire upon the altar, which the Lord had not commanded, were at once extinguished in the presence of an avenging Lord.

19. These, doubtless, they imitate and follow, who, despising God's tradition, seek after strange doctrines, and bring in teachings of human appointment, whom the Lord rebukes and reproves in His Gospel, saying, "Ye reject the commandment of God, that ye may keep your own tradition." This is a worse crime than that which the lapsed seem to have fallen into, who nevertheless, standing as penitents for their crime, beseech God with full satisfactions. In this case, the Church is sought after and entreated; in that case, the Church is resisted: here it is possible that there has been necessity; there the will is engaged in the wickedness: on

the one hand, he who has lapsed has only injured himself; on the other, he who has endeavored to cause a heresy or a schism has deceived many by drawing them with him. In the former, it is the loss of one soul; in the latter, the risk of many. Certainly the one both understands that he has sinned, and laments and bewails it; the other, puffed up in his heart, and pleasing himself in his very crimes, separates sons from their Mother, entices sheep from their shepherd, disturbs the sacraments of God; and while the lapsed has sinned but once, he sins daily. Finally, the lapsed, who has subsequently attained to martyrdom, may receive the promises of the kingdom; while the other, if he have been slain without the Church, cannot attain to the rewards of the Church.

20. Nor let anyone marvel, beloved brethren, that even some of the confessors advance to these lengths, and thence also that some others sin thus wickedly, thus grievously. For neither does confession make a man free from the snares of the devil, nor does it defend a man who is still placed in the world, with a perpetual security from temptations, and dangers, and onsets, and attacks of the world; otherwise we should never see in confessors those subsequent frauds, and fornications, and adulteries, which now with groans and sorrow we witness in some. Whosoever that confessor is, he is not greater, or better, or dearer to God than Solomon, who, although so long as he walked in God's ways, retained that grace which he had received from the Lord, yet after he forsook the Lord's way he lost also then Lord's grace. And therefore it is written, "Hold fast that which thou hast, lest another take thy crown." But assuredly the Lord would not threaten that the crown of righteousness might be taken away, were it not that, when righteousness departs, the

crown must also depart.

21. Confession is the beginning of glory, not the full desert of the crown; nor does it perfect our praise, but it initiates our dignity; and since it is written, "He that endures to the end, the same shall be saved," whatever has been before the end is a step by which we ascend to the summit of salvation, not a terminus wherein the full result of the ascent is already gained. He is a confessor; but after confession his peril is greater, because the adversary is more provoked. He is a confessor; for this cause he ought the more to stand on the side of the Lord's Gospel, since he has by the Gospel attained glory from the Lord. For the Lord says, "To whom much is given, of him much shall be required; and to whom more dignity is ascribed, of him more service is exacted." Let no one perish by the example of a confessor; let no one learn injustice, let no one learn arrogance, let no one learn treachery, from the manners of a confessor. He is a confessor, let him be lowly and quiet; let him be in his doings modest with discipline, so that he who is called a confessor of Christ may imitate Christ whom he confesses. For since He says, "Whosoever exalted himself shall be abased, and he who humbles himself shall be exalted;" and since He Himself has been exalted by the Father, because as the Word, and the strength, and the wisdom of God the Father, He humbled Himself upon earth, how can He love arrogance, who even by His own law enjoined upon us humility, and Himself received the highest name from the Father as the reward of His humility? He is a confessor of Christ, but only so if the majesty and dignity of Christ be not afterwards blasphemed by him. Let not the tongue which has confessed Christ be evil speaking; let it not be turbulent, let it not be heard jarring with reproaches and

quarrels, let it not after words of praise, dart forth serpents' venom against the brethren and God's priests. But if one shall have subsequently been blameworthy and obnoxious; if he shall have wasted his confession by evil conversation; if he shall have stained his life by disgraceful foulness; if, finally, forsaking the Church in which he has become a confessor, and severing the concord of unity, he shall have exchanged his first faith for a subsequent unbelief, he may not flatter himself on account of his confession that he is elected to the reward of glory, when from this very fact his deserving of punishment has become the greater.

22. For the Lord chose Judas also among the apostles, and yet afterwards Judas betrayed the Lord. Yet not on that account did the faith and firmness of the apostles fail, because the traitor Judas failed from their fellowship: so also in the case in question the holiness and dignity of confessors is not forthwith diminished, because the faith of some of them is broken. The blessed Apostle Paul in his epistle speaks in this manner: "For what if some of them fall away from the faith, shall their unbelief make the faith of God without effect? God forbid for God is true, though every man be a liar." The greater and better part of the confessors stand firm in the strength of their faith, and in the truth of the law and discipline of the Lord; neither do they depart from the peace of the Church, who remember that they have obtained grace in the Church by the condescension of God; and by this very thing they obtain a higher praise of their faith, that they have separated from the faithlessness of those who have been associated with them in the fellowship of confession, and withdrawn from the contagion of crime. Illuminated by the true light of the Gospel, shone upon with the

Lord's pure and white brightness, they are as praiseworthy in maintaining the peace of Christ, as they have been victorious in their combat with the devil.

23. I indeed desire beloved brethren, and I equally endeavor and exhort, that if it be possible, none of the brethren should perish, and that our rejoicing Mother may enclose in her bosom the one body of a people at agreement. Yet if wholesome counsel cannot recall to the way of salvation certain leaders of schisms and originators of dissensions, who abide in blind and obstinate madness, yet do you others, if either taken in simplicity, or induced by error, or deceived by some craftiness of misleading cunning, loose yourselves from the nets of deceit, free your wandering steps from errors, acknowledge the straightway of the heavenly road. The word of the witnessing apostle is: "We command you," says he, "in the name of our Lord Jesus Christ, that ye withdraw yourselves from all brethren that walk disorderly, and not after the tradition that they have received from us." And again he says, "Let no man deceive you with vain words; for because of these things cometh the wrath of God upon the children of disobedience. Be not ye therefore partakers with them." We must withdraw, nay rather must flee, from those who fall away, lest, while any one is associated with those who walk wickedly and goes on in ways of error and of sin, he himself also, wandering away from the path of the true road, should be found in like guilt. God is one, and Christ is one, and His Church is one, and the faith is one, and the people is joined into a substantial unity of body by the cement of concord. Unity cannot be severed; nor can one body be separated by a division of its structure, nor torn into pieces, with its entrails wrenched asunder by

laceration. Whatever has proceeded from the womb cannot live and breathe in its detached condition but loses the substance of health.

24. The Holy Spirit warns us, and says, "What man is he that desires to live, and would fain see good days? Refrain thy tongue from evil, and thy lips that they speak no guile. Eschew evil, and do good; seek peace, and ensue it." The son of peace ought to seek peace and ensue it. He who knows and loves the bond of charity, ought to refrain his tongue from the evil of dissension. Among His divine commands and salutary teachings, the Lord, when He was now very near to His passion, added this one, saying, "Peace I leave with you, my peace I give unto you." He gave this to us as a heritage; He promised all the gifts and rewards of which He spoke through the preservation of peace. If we are fellow heirs with Christ, let us abide in the peace of Christ; if we are sons of God, we ought to be peacemakers. "Blessed," says He, "are the peacemakers; for they shall be called the sons of God." It behooves the sons of God to be peacemakers, gentle in heart, simple in speech, agreeing in affection, faithfully linked to one another in the bonds of unanimity.

25. This unanimity formerly prevailed among the apostles; and thus the new assembly of believers, keeping the Lord's commandments, maintained its charity. Divine Scripture proves this, when it says, "But the multitude of them which believed were of one heart and of one soul." And again: "These all continued with one mind in prayer with the women, and Mary the mother of Jesus, and with His brethren." And thus they prayed with effectual prayers; thus they were able with confidence to obtain whatever they asked from the Lord's mercy.

26. But in us unanimity is diminished in

proportion as liberality of working is decayed. Then they used to give for sale houses and estates; and that they might lay up for themselves treasures in heaven, presented to the apostles the price of them, to be distributed for the use of the poor. But now we do not even give the tenths from our patrimony; and while our Lord bids us sell, we rather buy and increase our store. Thus has the vigor of faith dwindled away among us; thus has the strength of believers grown weak. And therefore the Lord, looking to our days, says in His Gospel, "When the Son of man cometh, think you that He shall find faith on the earth?" We see that what He foretold has come to pass. There is no faith in the fear of God, in the law of righteousness, in love, in labor; none considers the fear of futurity, and none takes to heart the day of the Lord, and the wrath of God, and the punishments to come upon unbelievers, and the eternal torments decreed for the faithless. That which our conscience would fear if it believed, it fears not because it does not at all believe. But if it believed, it would also take heed; and if it took heed, it would escape.

27. Let us, beloved brethren, arouse ourselves as much as we can; and breaking the slumber of our ancient listlessness, let us be watchful to observe and to do the Lord's precepts. Let us be such as He Himself has bidden us to be, saying, "Let your loins be girt, and your lamps burning; and ye yourselves like unto men that wait for their Lord, when He shall come from the wedding, that when He comes and knocks, they may open to Him. Blessed are those servants whom their Lord, when He cometh, shall find watching." We ought to be girt about, lest, when the day of setting forth comes, it should find us burdened and entangled. Let our light shine in good

works, and glow in such wise as to lead us from the night of this world to the daylight of eternal brightness. Let us always with solicitude and caution wait for the sudden coming of the Lord, that when He shall knock, our faith may be on the watch, and receive from the Lord the reward of our vigilance. If these commands be observed, if these warnings and precepts be kept, we cannot be overtaken in slumber by the deceit of the devil; but we shall reign with Christ in His kingdom as servants that watch.

Treatise II.
On the Dress of Virgins.
Argument.—Cyprian Celebrates the Praises of Discipline and Proves Its Usefulness from Scripture. Then, Describing the Glory, Honor, and Merits of Virginity, and of Those Who Had Vowed and Dedicated Their Virginity to Christ, He Teaches that Continence Not Only Consists in Fleshly Purity, But Also in Seemliness of Dress and Ornament, and that Even Wealth Did Not Excuse Superfluous Care for Dress on the Part of Those Who Had Already Renounced the World. Rather, Since the Apostle Prescribes Even to Married Women a Dress to Be Regulated by Fitting Limits, Moderation Ought Even More to Be Observed by a Virgin. Therefore, Even If She Be Wealthy, She Should Consider Certainly How to Use Wealth, But for Good Purposes, for Those Things Which God Has Commanded, to Wit, for Being Spent on the Poor. Moreover, Also, He Forbids Virgins Those Things Which Had Negligently Come into Use, as Being Present at Weddings, as Well as Going to Promiscuous Bathing-Places. Finally, in a Brief Epilogue, Declaring What Benefit the Virtue of Continency Affords, and What

Evil It is Without, He Concludes the Book.

1. Discipline, the safeguard of hope, the bond of faith, the guide of the way of salvation, the stimulus and nourishment of good dispositions, the teacher of virtue, causes us to abide always in Christ, and to live continually for God, and to attain to the heavenly promises and to the divine rewards. To follow her is wholesome, and to turn away from her and neglect her is deadly. The Holy Spirit says in the Psalms, "Keep discipline, lest perchance the Lord be angry, and ye perish from the right way, when His wrath is quickly kindled against you." And again: "But unto the ungodly saith God, "Why do you preach my laws, and take my covenant into your mouth? Whereas you hate discipline, and hast cast my words behind thee." And again we read: "He that casted away discipline is miserable." And from Solomon we have received the mandates of wisdom, warning us: "My son, despise not thou the discipline of the Lord, nor faint when thou art rebuked of Him: for whom the Lord loves He corrects." But if God rebukes whom He loves, and rebukes him for the very purpose of amending him, brethren also, and especially priests, do not hate, but love those whom they rebuke, that they may mend them; since God also before predicted by Jeremiah, and pointed to our times, when he said, "And I will give you shepherds according to my heart: and they shall feed you with the food of discipline."

2. But if in Holy Scripture discipline is frequently and everywhere prescribed, and the whole foundation of religion and of faith proceeds from obedience and fear; what is more fitting for us urgently to desire, what more to wish for and to hold fast, than to stand with roots strongly fixed, and with our houses based with solid mass

upon the rock unshaken by the storms and whirlwinds of the world, so that we may come by the divine precepts to the rewards of God? considering as well as knowing that our members, when purged from all the filth of the old contagion by the sanctification of the laver of life, are God's temples, and must not be violated nor polluted, since he who does violence to them is himself injured. We are the worshippers and priests of those temples; let us obey Him whose we have already begun to be. Paul tells us in his epistles, in which he has formed us to a course of living by divine teaching, "Ye are not your own, for ye are bought with a great price; glorify and bear God in your body." Let us glorify and bear God in a pure and chaste body, and with a more complete obedience; and since we have been redeemed by the blood of Christ, let us obey and give furtherance to the empire of our Redeemer by all the obedience of service, that nothing impure or profane may be brought into the temple of God, lest He should be offended, and forsake the temple which He inhabits. The words of the Lord giving health and teaching, as well curing as warning, are: "Behold, thou art made whole: sin no more, lest a worse thing come unto thee." He gives the course of life, He gives the law of innocency after He has conferred health, nor suffers the man afterwards to wander with free and unchecked reins, but more severely threatens him who is again enslaved by those same things of which he had been healed, because it is doubtless a smaller fault to have sinned before, while as yet you had not known God's discipline; but there is no further pardon for sinning after you have begun to know God. And, indeed, let as well men as women, as well boys as girls; let each sex and every age observe this, and take care in this respect, according to the religion and faith which they owe to God, that what is received holy and pure from the condescension of the Lord be preserved with a no less anxious fear.

3. My address is now to virgins, whose glory, as it is more eminent, excites the greater interest. This is the flower of the ecclesiastical seed, the grace and ornament of spiritual endowment, a joyous disposition, the wholesome and uncorrupted work of praise and honor, God's image answering to the holiness of the Lord, the more illustrious portion of Christ's flock. The glorious fruitfulness of Mother Church rejoices by their means, and in them abundantly flourishes; and in proportion as a copious virginity is added to her number, so much the more it increases the joy of the Mother. To these I speak, these I exhort with affection rather than with power; not that I would claim—last and least, and very conscious of my lowliness as I am—any right to censure, but because, being unceasingly careful even to solicitude, I fear more from the onset of Satan.

4. For that is not an empty carefulness nor a vain fear, which takes counsel for the way of salvation, which guards the commandments of the Lord and of life; so that they who have dedicated themselves to Christ, and who depart from carnal concupiscence, and have vowed themselves to God as well in the flesh as in the spirit, may consummate their work, destined as it is to a great reward, and may not study any longer to be adorned or to please anybody but their Lord, from whom also they expect the reward of virginity; as He Himself says: "All men cannot receive this word, but they to whom it is given. For there are some eunuchs, which were so born from their mother's womb; and there are some eunuchs, which were made eunuchs of men; and there are eunuchs which have

made themselves eunuchs for the kingdom of heaven's sake." Again, also by this word of the angel the gift of continency is set forth, and virginity is preached: "These are they which have not defiled themselves with women, for they have remained virgins; these are they which follow the Lamb whithersoever He goes." For not only thus does the Lord promise the grace of continency to men and pass over women; but since the woman is a portion of the man, and is taken and formed from him, God in Scripture almost always speaks to the Protoplast, the first formed, because they are two in one flesh, and in the male is at the same time signified the woman also.

5. But if continency follows Christ, and virginity is destined for the kingdom of God, what have they to do with earthly dress, and with ornaments, wherewith while they are striving to please men they offend God? Not considering that it is declared, "They who please men are put to confusion, because God hath despised them;" and that Paul also has gloriously and sublimely uttered, "If I yet pleased men, I should not be the servant of Christ." But continence and modesty consist not alone in purity of the flesh, but also in seemliness, as well as in modesty of dress and adornment; so that, according to the apostle, she who is unmarried may be holy both in body and in spirit. Paul instructs and teaches us, saying, "He that is unmarried cares for the things of the Lord, how he may please God: but he who has contracted marriage cares for the things which are of this world, how he may please his wife. So both the virgin and the unmarried woman consider those things which are the Lord's, that they may be holy both in body and spirit." A virgin ought not only to be so, but also to be perceived and believed to be so: no one on seeing a virgin should be in any doubt as to

whether she is one. Perfectness should show itself equal in all things; nor should the dress of the body discredit the good of the mind. Why should she walk out adorned? Why with dressed hair, as if she either had or sought for a husband? Rather let her dread to please if she is a virgin; and let her not invite her own risk, if she is keeping herself for better and divine things. They who have not a husband whom they profess that they please, should persevere, sound and pure not only in body, but also in spirit. For it is not right that a virgin should have her hair braided for the appearance of her beauty, or boast of her flesh and of its beauty, when she has no struggle greater than that against her flesh, and no contest more obstinate than that of conquering and subduing the body.

    6. Paul proclaims in a loud and lofty voice, "But God forbid that I should glory, save in the cross of our Lord Jesus Christ, by whom the world is crucified unto me, and I unto the world." And yet a virgin in the Church glories concerning her fleshly appearance and the beauty of her body! Paul adds, and says, "For they that are Christ's have crucified their flesh, with its faults and lusts." And she who professes to have renounced the lusts and vices of the flesh, is found in the midst of those very things which she has renounced! Virgin, you art taken, you art exposed, you boast one thing and affect another. You sprinkle yourself with the stains of carnal concupiscence, although you are a candidate of purity and modesty. "Cry," says the Lord to Isaiah, "All flesh is grass, and all the glory of it as the flower of the grass: the grass withered, and the flower fades; but the word of the Lord endures forever." It is becoming for no Christian, and especially it is not becoming for a virgin, to regard any glory and honor of the flesh, but only to desire the

word of God, to embrace benefits which shall endure forever. Or, if she must glory in the flesh, then assuredly let her glory when she is tortured in confession of the name; when a woman is found to be stronger than the tortures; when she suffers fire, or the cross, or the sword, or the wild beasts, that she may be crowned. These are the precious jewels of the flesh; these are the better ornaments of the body.

7. But there are some rich women, and wealthy in the fertility of means, who prefer their own wealth, and contend that they ought to use these blessings. Let them know first of all that she is rich who is rich in God; that she is wealthy who is wealthy in Christ; that those are blessings which are spiritual, divine, heavenly, which lead us to God, which abide with us in perpetual possession with God. But whatever things are earthly, and have been received in this world, and will remain here with the world, ought so to be contemned even as the world itself is contemned, whose pomps and delights we have already renounced when by a blessed passage we came to God. John stimulates and exhorts us, witnessing with a spiritual and heavenly voice. "Love not the world," says he, "neither the things that are in the world. If any man love the world, the love of the Father is not in him. For all that is in the world, is lust of the flesh, and the lust of the eyes, and the pride of life, which is not from the Father, but is of the lust of the world. And the world passes away, and the lust thereof: but he that doeth the will of God abides forever, even as God also abides forever." Therefore eternal and divine things are to be followed, and all things must be done after the will of God, that we may follow the divine footsteps and teachings of our Lord, who warned us, and said, "I came down from heaven, not to do

my own will, but the will of Him that sent me." But if the servant is not greater than his lord, and he that is freed owes obedience to his deliverer, we who desire to be Christians ought to imitate what Christ said and did. It is written, and it is read and heard, and is celebrated for our example by the Church's mouth, "He that saith he abides in Christ, ought himself also so to walk even as He walked." Therefore we must walk with equal steps; we must strive with emulous walk. Then the following of truth answers to the faith of our name, and a reward is given to the believer, if what is believed is also done.

8. You call yourself wealthy and rich; but Paul meets your riches, and with his own voice prescribes for the moderating of your dress and ornament within a just limit. "Let women," said he, "adorn themselves with shamefacedness and sobriety, not with broidered hair, nor gold, nor pearls, nor costly array, but as becometh women professing chastity, with a good conversation." Also Peter consents to these same precepts, and says, "Let there be in the woman not the outward adorning of array, or gold, or apparel, but the adorning of the heart." But if these also warn us that the women who are accustomed to make an excuse for their dress by reference to their husband, should be restrained and limited by religious observance to the Church's discipline, how much more is it right that the virgin should keep that observance, who has no excuse for adorning herself, nor can the deceitfulness of her fault be laid upon another, but she herself remains in its guilt!

9. You say that you are wealthy and rich. But not everything that can be done ought also to be done; nor ought the broad desires that arise out of the pride of the world to be extended beyond the honor and modesty of

virginity; since it is written, "All things are lawful, but all things are not expedient: all things are lawful, but all things edify not." For the rest, if you dress your hair sumptuously, and walk so as to draw attention in public, and attract the eyes of youth upon you, and draw the sighs of young men after you, nourish the lust of concupiscence, and inflame the fuel of sighs, so that, although you yourself perish not, yet you cause others to perish, and offer yourself, as it were, a sword or poison to the spectators; you cannot be excused on the pretense that you are chaste and modest in mind. Your shameful dress and immodest ornament accuse you; nor can you be counted now among Christ's maidens and virgins, since you live in such a manner as to make yourselves objects of desire.

10. You say that you are wealthy and rich; but it becomes not a virgin to boast of her riches, since Holy Scripture says, "What hath pride profited us? or what benefit hath the vaunting of riches conferred upon us? And all these things have passed away like a shadow." And the apostle again warns us, and says, "And they that buy, as though they bought not; and they that possess, as though they possessed not; and they that use this world, as though they used it not. For the fashion of this world passes away." Peter also, to whom the Lord commends His sheep to be fed and guarded, on whom He placed and founded the Church, says indeed that he has no silver and gold, but says that he is rich in the grace of Christ—that he is wealthy in his faith and virtue—wherewith he performed many great works with miracle, wherewith he abounded in spiritual blessings to the grace of glory. These riches, this wealth, she cannot possess, who had rather be rich to this world than to Christ.

11. You say that you are wealthy and rich, and you think that you should use those things which God has willed you to possess. Use them, certainly, but for the things of salvation; use them, but for good purposes; use them, but for those things which God has commanded, and which the Lord has set forth. Let the poor feel that you are wealthy; let the needy feel that you are rich. Lend your estate to God; give food to Christ. Move Him by the prayers of many to grant you to carry out the glory of virginity, and to succeed in coming to the Lord's rewards. There entrust your treasures, where no thief digs through, where no insidious plunderer breaks in. Prepare for yourself possessions; but let them rather be heavenly ones, where neither rust wears out, nor hail bruises, nor sun burns, nor rain spoils your fruits constant and perennial, and free from all contact of worldly injury. For in this very matter you are sinning against God, if you think that riches were given you by Him for this purpose, to enjoy them thoroughly, without a view to salvation. For God gave man also a voice; and yet love-songs and indecent things are not on that account to be sung. And God willed iron to be for the culture of the earth, but not on that account must murders be committed. Or because God ordained incense, and wine, and fire, are we thence to sacrifice to idols? Or because the flocks of cattle abound in your fields, ought you to immolate victims and offerings to the gods? Otherwise a large estate is a temptation, unless the wealth minister to good uses; so that every man, in proportion to his wealth, ought by his patrimony rather to redeem his transgressions than to increase them.

12. The characteristics of ornaments, and of garments, and the allurements of beauty, are not fitting for

any but prostitutes and immodest women; and the dress of none is more precious than of those whose modesty is lowly. Thus in the Holy Scriptures, by which the Lord wished us to be both instructed and admonished, the harlot city is described more beautifully arrayed and adorned, and with her ornaments; and the rather on account of those very ornaments about to perish. "And there came," it is said, "one of the seven angels, which had the seven phials, and talked with me, saying, Come hither, I will show thee the judgment of the great whore, that sits upon many waters, with whom the kings of the earth have committed fornication. And he carried me away in spirit; and I saw a woman sit upon a beast, and that woman was arrayed in a purple and scarlet mantle, and was adorned with gold, and precious stones, and pearls, having a golden cup in her hand, full of curses, and filthiness, and fornication of the whole earth." Let chaste and modest virgins avoid the dress of the unchaste, the manners of the immodest, the ensigns of brothels, the ornaments of harlots.

13. Moreover Isaiah, full of the Holy Spirit, cries out and chides the daughters of Sion, corrupted with gold, and silver, and raiment, and rebukes them, affluent as they were in pernicious wealth, and departing from God for the sake of the world's delights. "The daughters of Sion," says he, "are haughty, and walk with stretched-out neck and beckoning of the eyes, trailing their gowns as they go, and mincing with their feet. And God will humble the princely daughters of Sion, and the Lord will unveil their dress; and the Lord will take away the glory of their apparel, and their ornaments, and their hair, and their curls, and their round tires like the moon, and their crisping-pins, and their bracelets, and their clusters of

pearls, and their armlets and rings, and earrings, and silks woven with gold and hyacinth. And instead of a sweet smell there shall be dust; and thou shalt be girt with a rope instead of with a girdle; and for a golden ornament of thy head thou shalt have baldness." This God blames, this He marks out: hence He declares that virgins are corrupted; hence, that they have departed from the true and divine worship. Lifted up, they have fallen; with their heads adorned, they merited dishonor and disgrace. Having put on silk and purple, they cannot put on Christ; adorned with gold, and pearls, and necklaces, they have lost the ornaments of the heart and spirit. Who would not execrate and avoid that which has been the destruction of another? Who would desire and take up that which has served as the sword and weapon for the death of another? If he who had drunk should die by draining the cup, you would know that what he had drunk was poison; if, on taking food, he who had taken it were to perish, you would know that what, when taken could kill, was deadly; nor would you eat or drink of that whence you had before seen that others had perished. Now what ignorance of truth is it, what madness of mind, to wish for that which both has hurt and always will hurt and to think that you yourself will not perish by those means whereby you know that others have perished!

14. For God neither made the sheep scarlet or purple, nor taught the juices of herbs and shell-fish to dye and color wool, nor arranged necklaces with stones set in gold, and with pearls distributed in a woven series or numerous cluster, wherewith you would hide the neck which He made; that what God formed in man may be covered, and that may be seen upon it which the devil has invented in addition. Has God willed that wounds should

be made in the ears, wherewith infancy, as yet innocent, and unconscious of worldly evil, may be put to pain, that subsequently from the scars and holes of the ears precious beads may hang, heavy, if not by their weight, still by the amount of their cost? All which things sinning and apostate angels put forth by their arts, when, lowered to the contagious of earth, they forsook their heavenly vigor. They taught them also to paint the eyes with blackness drawn round them in a circle, and to stain the cheeks with a deceitful red, and to change the hair with false colors, and to drive out all truth, both of face and head, by the assault of their own corruption.

15. And indeed in that very matter, for the sake of the fear which faith suggests to me, for the sake of the love which brotherhood requires, I think that not virgins only and widows, but married women also, and all of the sex alike, should be admonished, that the work of God and His fashioning and formation ought in no manner to be adulterated, either with the application of yellow color, or with black dust or rouge, or with any kind of medicament which can corrupt the native lineaments. God says, "Let us make man in our image and likeness;" and does anyone dare to alter and to change what God has made? They are laying hands on God when they try to reform that which He formed, and to transfigure it, not knowing that everything which comes into being is God's work, everything that is changed is the devil's. If any artist, in painting, were to delineate in envious coloring the countenance and likeness and bodily appearance of anyone; and the likeness being now painted and completed, another person were to lay hands on it, as if, when it was already formed and already painted, he, being more skilled, could amend it, a serious wrong and a just

cause of indignation would seem natural to the former artist. And do you think yourself likely with impunity to commit a boldness of such wicked temerity, an offence to God the artificer? For although you may not be immodest among men, and are not unchaste with your seducing dyes, yet when those things which belong to God are corrupted and violated, you are engaged in a worse adultery. That you think yourself to be adorned, that you think your hair to be dressed, is an assault upon the divine work, is a prevarication of the truth.

16. The voice of the warning apostle is, "Purge out the old leaven, that ye may be a new lump, as ye are unleavened; for even Christ our Passover is sacrificed. Therefore let us keep the feast, not with old leaven, neither with the leaven of malice and wickedness, but with the unleavened bread of sincerity and truth." But are sincerity and truth preserved, when what is sincere is polluted by adulterous colors, and what is true is changed into a lie by the deceitful dyes of medicaments? Your Lord says, "You cannot make one hair white or black;" and you, in order to overcome the word of your Lord, will be more mighty than He, and stain your hair with a daring endeavor and with profane contempt. With evil presage of the future, you make a beginning to yourself already of flame-colored hair; and sin (oh, wickedness!) with your head—that is, with the nobler part of your body! And although it is written of the Lord, "His head and His hair were white like wool or snow," you curse that whiteness and hate that hoariness which is like to the Lord's head.

17. Are you not afraid, I entreat you, being such as you are, that when the day of resurrection comes, your Maker may not recognize you again, and may turn you away when you come to His rewards and promises, and

may exclude you, rebuking you with the vigor of a Censor and Judge, and say: "This is not my work, nor is this our image. You have polluted your skin with a false medicament, you have changed your hair with an adulterous color, your face is violently taken possession of by a lie, your figure is corrupted, your countenance is another's. You cannot see God, since your eyes are not those which God made, but those which the devil has spoiled. You have followed him, you have imitated the red and painted eyes of the serpent. As you are adorned in the fashion of your enemy, with him also you shall burn by and by." Are not these, I beg, matters to be reflected on by God's servants? Are they not always to be dreaded day and night? Let married women see to it, in what respect they are flattering themselves concerning the solace of their husbands with the desire of pleasing them, and while they put them forward indeed as their excuse, they make them partners in the association of guilty consent. Virgins, assuredly, to whom this address is intended to appeal, who have adorned themselves with arts of this kind, I should think ought not to be counted among virgins, but, like infected sheep and diseased cattle, to be driven from the holy and pure flock of virginity, lest by living together they should pollute the rest with their contagion; lest they ruin others even as they have perished themselves.

18. And since we are seeking the advantage of continency, let us also avoid everything that is pernicious and hostile to it. And I will not pass over those things, which while by negligence they come into use, have made for themselves a usurped license, contrary to modest and sober manners. Some are not ashamed to be present at marriage parties, and in that freedom of lascivious

discourse to mingle in unchaste conversation, to hear what is not becoming, to say what is not lawful, to expose themselves, to be present in the midst of disgraceful words and drunken banquets, by which the ardor of lust is kindled, and the bride is animated to bear, and the bridegroom to dare lewdness. What place is there at weddings for her whose mind is not towards marriage? Or what can there be pleasant or joyous in those engagements for her, where both desires and wishes are different from her own? What is learnt there—what is seen? How greatly a virgin falls short of her resolution, when she who had come there modest goes away immodest! Although she may remain a virgin in body and mind, yet in eyes, in ears, in tongue, she has diminished the virtues that she possessed.

19. But what of those who frequent promiscuous baths; who prostitute to eyes that are curious to lust, bodies that are dedicated to chastity and modesty? They who disgracefully behold naked men, and are seen naked by men, do they not themselves afford enticement to vice, do they not solicit and invite the desires of those present to their own corruption and wrong? "Let everyone," say you, "look to the disposition with which he comes thither: my care is only that of refreshing and washing my poor body." That kind of defense does not clear you, nor does it excuse the crime of lasciviousness and wantonness. Such a washing defiles; it does not purify nor cleanse the limbs but stains them. You behold no one immodestly, but you yourself are gazed upon immodestly. You do not pollute your eyes with disgraceful delight, but in delighting others you yourself are polluted. You make a show of the bathing-place; the places where you assemble are fouler than a theatre. There all modesty is put off

together with the clothing of garments, the honor and modesty of the body is laid aside; virginity is exposed, to be pointed at and to be handled. And now, then, consider whether when you are clothed you are modest among men, when the boldness of nakedness has conduced to immodesty.

20. For this reason, therefore, the Church frequently mourns over her virgins; hence she groans at their scandalous and detestable stories; hence the flower of her virgins is extinguished, the honor and modesty of continency are injured, and all its glory and dignity are profaned. Thus the hostile besieger insinuates himself by his arts; thus by snares that deceive, by secret ways, the devil creeps in. Thus, while virgins wish to be more carefully adorned, and to wander with more liberty, they cease to be virgins, corrupted by a furtive dishonor; widows before they are married, adulterous, not to their husband, but to Christ. In proportion as they had been as virgins destined to great rewards, so will they experience great punishments for the loss of their virginity.

21. Therefore hear me, O virgins, as a parent; hear, I beseech you, one who fears while he warns; hear one who is faithfully consulting for your advantage and your profit. Be such as God the Creator made you; be such as the hand of your Father ordained you. Let your countenance remain in you incorrupt, your neck unadorned, your figure simple; let not wounds be made in your ears, nor let the precious chain of bracelets and necklaces circle your arms or your neck; let your feet be free from golden bands, your hair stained with no dye, your eyes worthy of beholding God. Let your baths be performed with women, among whom your bathing is modest. Let the shameless feasts and lascivious banquets

of marriages be avoided, the contagion of which is perilous. Overcome dress, since you are a virgin; overcome gold, since you overcome the flesh and the world. It is not consistent to be unable to be conquered by the greater, and to be found no match for the less. Straight and narrow is the way which leadeth to life; hard and difficult is the track which tends to glory. By this pathway the martyrs progress, the virgins pass, the just of all kinds advance. Avoid the broad and roomy ways. There are deadly snares and death-bringing pleasures; there the devil flatters, that he may deceive; smiles, that he may do mischief; entices, that he may slay. The first fruit for the martyrs is a hundred-fold; the second is yours, sixty-fold. As with the martyrs there is no thought of the flesh and of the world, no small, and trifling, and delicate encounter; so also in you, whose reward is second in grace, let there be the strength in endurance next to theirs. The ascent to great things is not easy. What toil we suffer, what labor, when we endeavor to ascend the hills and the tops of mountains! What, then, that we may ascend to heaven? If you look to the reward of the promise, your labor is less. Immortality is given to the persevering; eternal life is set before them; the Lord promises a kingdom.

22. Hold fast, O virgins! hold fast what you have begun to be; hold fast what you shall be. A great reward awaits you, a great recompense of virtue, the immense advantage of chastity. Do you wish to know what ill the virtue of continence avoids, what good it possesses? "I will multiply," says God to the woman, "thy sorrows and thy groanings; and in sorrow shalt thou bring forth children; and thy desire shall be to thy husband, and he shall rule over you." You are free from this sentence. You do not fear the sorrows and the groans of women. You

have no fear of childbearing; nor is your husband lord over you; but your Lord and Head is Christ, after the likeness and in the place of the man; with that of men your lot and your condition is equal. It is the word of the Lord which says, "The children of this world beget and are begotten; but they who are counted worthy of that world, and of the resurrection from the dead, neither marry nor are given in marriage: neither shall they die any more: for they are equal to the angels of God, being the children of the resurrection." That which we shall be, you have already begun to be. You possess already in this world the glory of the resurrection. You pass through the world without the contagion of the world; in that you continue chaste and virgins, you are equal to the angels of God. Only let your virginity remain and endure substantial and uninjured; and as it began bravely, let it persevere continuously, and not seek the ornaments of necklaces nor garments, but of conduct. Let it look towards God and heaven, and not lower to the lust of the flesh and of the world, the eyes uplifted to things above, or set them upon earthly things.

23. The first decree commanded to increase and to multiply; the second enjoined continency. While the world is still rough and void, we are propagated by the fruitful begetting of numbers, and we increase to the enlargement of the human race. Now, when the world is filled and the earth supplied, they who can receive continency, living after the manner of eunuchs, are made eunuchs unto the kingdom. Nor does the Lord command this, but He exhorts it; nor does He impose the yoke of necessity, since the free choice of the will is left. But when He says that in His Father's house are many mansions, He points out the dwellings of the better

habitation. Those better habitations you are seeking; cutting away the desires of the flesh, you obtain the reward of a greater grace in the heavenly home. All indeed who attain to the divine gift and inheritance by the sanctification of baptism, therein put off the old man by the grace of the saving laver, and, renewed by the Holy Spirit from the filth of the old contagion, are purged by a second nativity. But the greater holiness and truth of that repeated birth belongs to you, who have no longer any desires of the flesh and of the body. Only the things which belong to virtue and the Spirit have remained in you to glory. It is the apostle's word whom the Lord called His chosen vessel, whom God sent to proclaim the heavenly command: "The first man," says he, "is from the earth, of earth; the second man is from heaven. Such as is the earthy, such are they also who are earthy; and such as is the heavenly, such also are the heavenly. As we have borne the image of him who is earthy, let us also bear the image of Him who is heavenly." Virginity bears this image, integrity bears it, holiness bears it, and truth. Disciplines which are mindful of God bear it, retaining righteousness with religion, steadfast in faith, humble in fear, brave to all suffering, meek to sustain wrong, easy to show mercy, of one mind and one heart in fraternal peace.

24. Every one of which things, O good virgins, you ought to observe, to love, to fulfil, who, giving yourselves to God and Christ, are advancing in both the higher and better part to the Lord, to whom you have dedicated yourselves. You that are advanced in years, suggest a teaching to the younger. You that are younger, give a stimulus to your coevals. Stir one another up with mutual exhortations; provoke to glory by rival proofs of virtue. Endure bravely, go on spiritually, attain happily.

Only remember us at that time, when virginity shall begin to be rewarded in you.

Treatise III.
On the Lapsed.
Argument.—Having Enlarged Upon the Unlooked-for Peace of the Church, and the Constancy of the Confessors and Those Who Had Stood Fast in the Faith; And Then with Extreme Grief Having Pointed to the Downfall of the Lapsed, and Unfolded the Causes of the Bygone Persecution, Namely, the Neglect of Discipline, and the Sins of the Faithful; Our Author Severely Reproaches the Lapsed, That, at the Very First Words of the Enemy Threatening Them, They Had Sacrificed to Idols, and Had Not Rather Withdrawn, According to Christ's Counsel. Lastly, He Warns His Readers to Avoid the Novatians, Confuting Their Heresy with Many Scriptures.

1. Behold, beloved brethren, peace is restored to the Church; and although it lately seemed to incredulous people difficult, and to traitors impossible, our security is by divine aid and retribution re-established. Our minds return to gladness; and the season of affliction and the cloud being dispersed, tranquility and serenity have shone forth once more. Praises must be given to God, and His benefits and gifts must be celebrated with giving of thanks, although even in the time of persecution our voice has not ceased to give thanks. For not even an enemy has so much power as to prevent us, who love the Lord with our whole heart, and life, and strength, from declaring His blessings and praises always and everywhere with glory. The day earnestly desired, by the prayers of all has come; and after the dreadful and loathsome darkness of a long

night, the world has shone forth irradiated by the light of the Lord.

2. We look with glad countenances upon confessors illustrious with the heraldry of a good name, and glorious with the praises of virtue and of faith; clinging to them with holy kisses, we embrace them long desired with insatiable eagerness. The white-robed cohort of Christ's soldiers is here, who in the fierce conflict have broken the ferocious turbulence of an urgent persecution, having been prepared for the suffering of the dungeon, armed for the endurance of death. Bravely you have resisted the world: you have afforded a glorious spectacle in the sight of God; you have been an example to your brethren that shall follow you. That religious voice has named the name of Christ, in whom it has once confessed that it believed; those illustrious hands, which had only been accustomed to divine works, have resisted the sacrilegious sacrifices; those lips, sanctified by heavenly food after the body and blood of the Lord, have rejected the profane contacts and the leavings of the idols. Your head has remained free from the impious and wicked veil with which the captive heads of those who sacrificed were there veiled; your brow, pure with the sign of God, could not bear the crown of the devil, but reserved itself for the Lord's crown. How joyously does your Mother Church receive you in her bosom, as you return from the battle! How blissfully, how gladly, does she open her gates, that in united bands you may enter, bearing the trophies from a prostrate enemy! With the triumphing men come women also, who, while contending with the world, have also overcome their sex; and virgins also come with the double glory of their warfare, and boys transcending their years with their virtues. Moreover, also, the rest of the

multitude of those who stand fast follow your glory, and accompany your footsteps with the insignia of praise, very near to, and almost joined with, your own. In them also is the same sincerity of heart, the same soundness of a tenacious faith. Resting on the unshaken roots of the heavenly precepts, and strengthened by the evangelical traditions, the prescribed banishment, the destined tortures, the loss of property, the bodily punishments, have not terrified them. The days for proving their faith were limited beforehand; but he who remembers that he has renounced the world knows no day of worldly appointment, neither does he who hopes for eternity from God calculate the seasons of earth anymore.

3. Let none, my beloved brethren, let none depreciate this glory; let none by malignant dispraise detract from the uncorrupted steadfastness of those who have stood. When the day appointed for denying was gone by, everyone who had not professed within that time not to be a Christian, confessed that he was a Christian. It is the first title to victory to confess the Lord under the violence of the hands of the Gentiles. It is the second step to glory to be withdrawn by a cautious retirement, and to be reserved for the Lord. The former is a public, the latter is a private confession. The former overcomes the judge of this world; the latter, content with God as its judge, keeps a pure conscience in integrity of heart. In the former case there is a readier fortitude; in the latter, solicitude is more secure. The former, as his hour approached, was already found mature; the latter perhaps was delayed, who, leaving his estate, withdrew for a while, because he would not deny, but would certainly confess if he too had been apprehended.

4. One cause of grief saddens these heavenly

crowns of martyrs, these glorious spiritual confessions, these very great and illustrious virtues of the brethren who stand; which is, that the hostile violence has torn away a part of our own bowels and thrown it away in the destructiveness of its own cruelty. What shall I do in this matter, beloved brethren? Wavering in the various tide of feeling, what or how shall I speak? I need tears rather than words to express the sorrow with which the wound of our body should be bewailed, with which the manifold loss of a people once numerous should be lamented. For whose heart is so hard or cruel, who is so unmindful of brotherly love, as, among the varied ruins of his friends, and the mournful relics disfigured with all degradation, to be able to stand and to keep dry eyes, and not in the breaking out of his grief to express his groanings rather with tears than with words? I grieve, brethren, I grieve with you; nor does my own integrity and my personal soundness beguile me to the soothing of my griefs, since it is the shepherd that is chiefly wounded in the wound of his flock. I join my breast with each one, and I share in the grievous burden of sorrow and mourning. I wail with the wailing, I weep with the weeping, I regard myself as prostrated with those that are prostrate. My limbs are at the same time stricken with those darts of the raging enemy; their cruel swords have pierced through my bowels; my mind could not remain untouched and free from the inroad of persecution among my downfallen brethren; sympathy has cast me down also.

5. Yet, beloved brethren, the cause of truth is to be had in view; nor ought the gloomy darkness of the terrible persecution so to have blinded the mind and feeling, that there should remain no light and illumination whence the divine precepts may be beheld. If the cause of disaster is

recognized, there is at once found a remedy for the wound. The Lord has desired His family to be proved; and because a long peace had corrupted the discipline that had been divinely delivered to us, the heavenly rebuke has aroused our faith, which was giving way, and I had almost said slumbering; and although we deserved more for our sins, yet the most merciful Lord has so moderated all things, that all which has happened has rather seemed a trial than a persecution.

6. Each one was desirous of increasing his estate; and forgetful of what believers had either done before in the times of the apostles, or always ought to do, they, with the insatiable ardor of covetousness, devoted themselves to the increase of their property. Among the priests there was no devotedness of religion; among the ministers there was no sound faith: in their works there was no mercy; in their manners there was no discipline. In men, their beards were defaced; in women, their complexion was dyed: the eyes were falsified from what God's hand had made them; their hair was stained with a falsehood. Crafty frauds were used to deceive the hearts of the simple, subtle meanings for circumventing the brethren. They united in the bond of marriage with unbelievers; they prostituted the members of Christ to the Gentiles. They would swear not only rashly, but even more, would swear falsely; would despise those set over them with haughty swelling, would speak evil of one another with envenomed tongue, would quarrel with one another with obstinate hatred. Not a few bishops who ought to furnish both exhortation and example to others, despising their divine charge, became agents in secular business, forsook their throne, deserted their people, wandered about over foreign provinces, hunted the markets for gainful

merchandise, while brethren were starving in the Church. They sought to possess money in hoards, they seized estates by crafty deceits, they increased their gains by multiplying usuries. What do not such as we deserve to suffer for sins of this kind, when even already the divine rebuke has forewarned us, and said, "If they shall forsake my law, and walk not in my judgments; if they shall profane my statutes, and shall not observe my precepts, I will visit their offences with a rod, and their sins with scourges?"

7. These things were declared to us, and predicted. But we, forgetful of the law and obedience required of us, have so acted by our sins, that while we despise the Lord's commandments, we have come by severer remedies to the correction of our sin and probation of our faith. Nor indeed have we at last been converted to the fear of the Lord, so as to undergo patiently and courageously this our correction and divine proof. Immediately at the first words of the threatening foe, the greatest number of the brethren betrayed their faith, and were cast down, not by the onset of persecution, but cast themselves down by voluntary lapse. What unheard-of thing, I beg of you, what new thing had happened, that, as if on the occurrence of things unknown and unexpected, the obligation to Christ should be dissolved with headlong rashness? Have not prophets aforetime, and subsequently apostles, told of these things? Have not they, full of the Holy Spirit, predicted the afflictions of the righteous, and always the injuries of the heathens? Does not the sacred Scripture, which ever arms our faith and strengthens with a voice from heaven the servants of God, say, "Thou shalt worship the Lord thy God, and Him only shalt thou serve?" Does it not again show the anger of the divine

indignation, and warn of the fear of punishment beforehand, when it says, "They worshipped them whom their fingers have made; and the mean man bowed down, and the great man humbled himself, and I will forgive them not?" And again, God speaks, and says, "He that sacrifices unto any gods, save unto the Lord only, shall be destroyed." In the Gospel also subsequently, the Lord, who instructs by His words and fulfils by His deeds, teaching what should be done, and doing whatever He had taught, did He not before admonishing us of whatever is now done and shall be done? Did He not before ordain both for those who deny Him eternal punishments, and for those that confess Him saving rewards?

8. From some—ah, misery!—all these things have fallen away, and have passed from memory. They indeed did not wait to be apprehended ere they ascended, or to be interrogated ere they denied. Many were conquered before the battle, prostrated before the attack. Nor did they even leave it to be said for them, that they seemed to sacrifice to idols unwillingly. They ran to the marketplace of their own accord; freely they hastened to death, as if they had formerly wished it, as if they would embrace an opportunity now given which they had always desired. How many were put off by the magistrates at that time, when evening was coming on; how many even asked that their destruction might not be delayed! What violence can such a one plead as an excuse? How can he purge his crime, when it was he himself who rather used force to bring about his own ruin? When they came voluntarily to the Capitol,—when they freely approached to the obedience of the terrible wickedness,—did not their tread falter? Did not their sight darken, their heart tremble, their arms fall helplessly down? Did not their senses fail, their

tongue cleave to their mouth, their speech grow weak? Could the servant of God stand there, and speak and renounce Christ, when he had already renounced the devil and the world? Was not that altar, whither he drew near to perish, to him a funeral pile? Ought he not to shudder at and flee from the devil's altar, which he had seen to smoke, and to be redolent of a foul fetor, as if it were the funeral and sepulcher of his life? Why bring with you, O wretched man, a sacrifice? why immolate a victim? You yourself have come to the altar an offering; you yourself have come a victim: there you have immolated your salvation, your hope; there you have burnt up your faith in those deadly fires.

9. But to many their own destruction was not sufficient. With mutual exhortations, people were urged to their ruin; death was pledged by turns in the deadly cup. And that nothing might be wanting to aggravate the crime, infants also, in the arms of their parents, either carried or conducted, lost, while yet little ones, what in the very first beginning of their nativity they had gained. Will not they, when the day of judgment comes, say, "We have done nothing; nor have we forsaken the Lord's bread and cup to hasten freely to a profane contact; the faithlessness of others has ruined us. We have found our parents our murderers; they have denied to us the Church as a Mother; they have denied God as a Father: so that, while we were little, and unforeseeing, and unconscious of such a crime, we were associated by others to the partnership of wickedness, and we were snared by the deceit of others?"

10. Nor is there, alas, any just and weighty reason which excuses such a crime. One's country was to be left, and loss of one's estate was to be suffered. Yet to whom

that is born and dies is there not a necessity at some time to leave his country, and to suffer the loss of his estate? But let not Christ be forsaken, so that the loss of salvation and of an eternal home should be feared. Behold, the Holy Spirit cries by the prophet, "Depart ye, depart ye, go ye out from thence, touch not the unclean thing; go ye out from the midst of her, and be ye separate, that bear the vessels of the Lord." Yet those who are the vessels of the Lord and the temple of God do not go out from the midst, nor depart, that they may not be compelled to touch the unclean thing, and to be polluted and corrupted with deadly food. Elsewhere also a voice is heard from heaven, forewarning what is becoming for the servants of God to do, saying, "Come out of her, my people, that ye be not partakers of her sins, and that ye receive not of her plagues." He who goes out and departs does not become a partaker of the guilt; but he will be wounded with the plagues who is found a companion in the crime. And therefore the Lord commanded us in the persecution to depart and to flee; and both taught that this should be done, and Himself did it. For as the crown is given of the condescension of God and cannot be received unless the hour comes for accepting it, whosoever abiding in Christ departs for a while does not deny his faith, but waits for the time; but he who has fallen, after refusing to depart, remained to deny it.

11. The truth, brethren, must not be disguised; nor must the matter and cause of our wound be concealed. A blind love of one's own property has deceived many; nor could they be prepared for, or at ease in, departing when their wealth fettered them like a chain. Those were the chains to them that remained—those were the bonds by which both virtue was retarded, and faith burdened, and

the spirit bound, and the soul hindered; so that they who were involved in earthly things might become a booty and food for the serpent, which, according to God's sentence, feeds upon earth. And therefore the Lord the teacher of good things, forewarning for the future time, says, "If thou wilt be perfect, go, sell all that thou hast, and give to the poor, and thou shalt have treasure in heaven: and come and follow me." If rich men did this, they would not perish by their riches; if they laid up treasure in heaven, they would not now have a domestic enemy and assailant. Heart and mind and feeling would be in heaven, if the treasure were in heaven; nor could he be overcome by the world who had nothing in the world whereby he could be overcome. He would follow the Lord loosed and free, as did the apostles, and many in the times of the apostles, and many who forsook both their means and their relatives, and clave to Christ with undivided ties.

12. But how can they follow Christ, who are held back by the chain of their wealth? Or how can they seek heaven, and climb to sublime and lofty heights, who are weighed down by earthly desires? They think that they possess, when they are rather possessed; as slaves of their profit, and not lords with respect to their own money, but rather the bond-slaves of their money. These times and these men are indicated by the apostle, when he says, "But they that will be rich, fall into temptation, and a snare, and into many foolish and hurtful lusts, which drown men in destruction and in perdition. For the root of all evil is the love of money, which, while some have coveted, they have erred from the faith, and pierced themselves through with many sorrows." But with what rewards does the Lord invite us to contempt of worldly wealth? With what compensations does He atone for the

small and trifling losses of this present time? "There is no man," saith He, "that leaves house, or land, or parents, or brethren, or wife, or children, for the kingdom of God's sake, but he shall receive seven-fold even in this time, but in the world to come life everlasting." If we know these things, and have found them out from the truth of the Lord who promises, not only is not loss of this kind to be feared, but even to be desired; as the Lord Himself again announces and warns us, "Blessed are ye when men shall persecute you, and when they shall separate you from their company, and shall cast you out, and shall speak of your name as evil, for the Son of man's sake! Rejoice ye in that day, and leap for joy; for, behold, your reward is great in heaven."

13. But (say they) subsequently tortures had come, and severe sufferings were threatening those who resisted. He may complain of tortures who has been overcome by tortures; he may offer the excuse of suffering who has been vanquished in suffering. Such a one may ask, and say, "I wished indeed to strive bravely, and, remembering my oath, I took up the arms of devotion and faith; but as I was struggling in the encounter, varied tortures and long-continued sufferings overcame me. My mind stood firm, and my faith was strong, and my soul struggled long, unshaken with the torturing pains; but when, with the renewed barbarity of the most cruel judge, wearied out as I was, the scourges were now tearing me, the clubs bruised me, the rack strained me, the claw dug into me, the fire roasted me; my flesh deserted me in the struggle, the weakness of my bodily frame gave way,—not my mind, but my body, yielded in the suffering." Such a plea may readily avail to forgiveness; an apology of that kind may excite compassion. Thus at one time the Lord

forgave Castus and Æmilius; thus, overcome in the first encounter, they were made victors in the second battle. So that they who had formerly given way to the fires became stronger than the fires, and in that in which they had been vanquished they were conquerors. They entreated not for pity of their tears, but of their wounds; nor with a lamentable voice alone, but with laceration and suffering of body. Blood flowed instead of weeping; and instead of tears, gore poured forth from their half-scorched entrails.

14. But now, what wounds can those who are overcome show? what gashes of gaping entrails, what tortures of the limbs, in cases where it was not faith that fell in the encounter, but faithlessness that anticipated the struggle? Nor does the necessity of the crime excuse the person compelled, where the crime is committed of free will. Nor do I say this in such a way as that I would burden the cases of the brethren, but that I may rather instigate the brethren to a prayer of atonement. For, as it is written, "They who call you happy cause you to err, and destroy the paths of your feet," he who soothes the sinner with flattering blandishments furnishes the stimulus to sin; nor does he repress but nourishes wrong-doing. But he who, with braver counsel, rebukes at the same time that he instructs a brother, urges him onward to salvation. "As many as I love," saith the Lord, "I rebuke and chasten." And thus also it behooves the Lord's priest not to mislead by deceiving concessions, but to provide with salutary remedies. He is an unskillful physician who handles the swelling edges of wounds with a tender hand, and, by retaining the poison shut up in the deep recesses of the body, increases it. The wound must be opened, and cut, and healed by the stronger remedy of cutting out the corrupting parts. The sick man may cry out, may

vociferate, and may complain, in impatience of the pain; but he will afterwards give thanks when he has felt that he is cured.

15. Moreover, beloved brethren, a new kind of devastation has appeared; and, as if the storm of persecution had raged too little, there has been added to the heap, under the title of mercy, a deceiving mischief and a fair-seeming calamity. Contrary to the vigor of the Gospel, contrary to the law of the Lord and God, by the temerity of some, communion is relaxed to heedless persons,—a vain and false peace, dangerous to those who grant it, and likely to avail nothing to those who receive it. They do not seek for the patience necessary to health nor the true medicine derived from atonement. Penitence is driven forth from their breasts, and the memory of their very grave and extreme sin is taken away. The wounds of the dying are covered over, and the deadly blow that is planted in the deep and secret entrails is concealed by a dissimulated suffering. Returning from the altars of the devil, they draw near to the holy place of the Lord, with hands filthy and reeking with smell, still almost breathing of the plague-bearing idol-meats; and even with jaws still exhaling their crime, and reeking with the fatal contact, they intrude on the body of the Lord, although the sacred Scripture stands in their way, and cries, saying, "Every one that is clean shall eat of the flesh; and whatever soul eats of the flesh of the saving sacrifice, which is the Lord's, having his uncleanness upon him, that soul shall be cut off from his people." Also, the apostle testifies, and says, "Ye cannot drink the cup of the Lord and the cup of devils; ye cannot be partakers of the Lord's table and of the table of devils." He threatens, moreover, the stubborn and froward, and denounces them, saying,

"Whosoever eats the bread or drinks the cup of the Lord unworthily, is guilty of the body and blood of the Lord."

16. All these warnings being scorned and contemned,—before their sin is expiated, before confession has been made of their crime, before their conscience has been purged by sacrifice and by the hand of the priest, before the offence of an angry and threatening Lord has been appeased, violence is done to His body and blood; and they sin now against their Lord more with their hand and mouth than when they denied their Lord. They think that that is peace which some with deceiving words are blazoning forth: that is not peace, but war; and he is not joined to the Church who is separated from the Gospel. Why do they call an injury a kindness? Why do they call impiety by the name of piety? Why do they hinder those who ought to weep continually and to entreat their Lord, from the sorrowing of repentance, and pretend to receive them to communion? This is the same kind of thing to the lapsed as hail to the harvests; as the stormy star to the trees; as the destruction of pestilence to the herds; as the raging tempest to shipping. They take away the consolation of eternal hope; they overturn the tree from the roots; they creep on to a deadly contagion with their pestilent words; they dash the ship on the rocks, so that it may not reach to the harbor. Such a facility does not grant peace but takes it away; nor does it give communion, but it hinders from salvation. This is another persecution, and another temptation, by which the crafty enemy still further assaults the lapsed; attacking them by a secret corruption, that their lamentation may be hushed, that their grief may be silent, that the memory of their sin may pass away, that the groaning of their heart may be repressed, that the weeping of their eyes may be

quenched; nor long and full penitence deprecate the Lord so grievously offended, although it is written, "Remember from whence thou art fallen, and repent."

17. Let no one cheat himself, let no one deceive himself. The Lord alone can have mercy. He alone can bestow pardon for sins which have been committed against Himself, who bare our sins, who sorrowed for us, whom God delivered up for our sins. Man cannot be greater than God, nor can a servant remit or forego by his indulgence what has been committed by a greater crime against the Lord, lest to the person lapsed this be moreover added to his sin, if he be ignorant that it is declared, "Cursed is the man that puts his hope in man." The Lord must be besought. The Lord must be appeased by our atonement, who has said, that him that denies Him He will deny, who alone has received all judgment from His Father. We believe, indeed, that the merits of martyrs and the works of the righteous are of great avail with the Judge; but that will be when the day of judgment shall come; when, after the conclusion of this life and the world, His people shall stand before the tribunal of Christ.

18. But if anyone, by an overhurried haste, rashly thinks that he can give remission of sins to all, or dares to rescind the Lord's precepts, not only does it in no respect advantage the lapsed, but it does them harm. Not to have observed His judgment is to have provoked His wrath, and to think that the mercy of God must not first of all be entreated, and, despising the Lord, to presume on His power. Under the altar of God the souls of the slain martyrs cry with a loud voice, saying, "How long, O Lord, holy and true, do You not judge and avenge our blood upon those who dwell on the earth?" And they are bidden to rest, and still to keep patience. And does anyone

think that, in opposition to the Judge, a man can become of avail for the general remission and pardon of sins, or that he can shield others before he himself is vindicated? The martyrs order something to be done; but only if this thing be just and lawful, if it can be done without opposing the Lord Himself by God's priest, if the consent of the obeying party be easy and yielding, if the moderation of the asking party be religious. The martyrs order something to be done; but if what they order be not written in the law of the Lord, we must first know that they have obtained what they ask from God, and then do what they command. For that may not always appear to be immediately conceded by the divine majesty, which has been promised by man's undertaking.

19. For Moses also besought for the sins of the people; and yet, when he had sought pardon for these sinners, he did not receive it. "I pray Thee," said he, "O Lord, this people have sinned a great sin, and have made them gods of gold. Yet now, if Thou wilt forgive their sin, forgive it; but if not, blot me out of the book which Thou hast written. And the Lord said unto Moses, Whosoever hath sinned against me, him will I blot out of my book." He, the friend of God; he who had often spoken face to face with the Lord, could not obtain what he asked, nor could appease the wrath of an indignant God by his entreaty. God praises Jeremiah, and announces, saying, "Before I formed you in the belly, I knew you; and before you came out of the womb I sanctified you, and I ordained you a prophet unto the nations." And to the same man He saith, when he often entreated and prayed for the sins of the people, "Pray not thou for this people, neither lift up cry nor prayer for them; for I will not hear them in the time wherein they call on me, in the time of their

affliction." But who was more righteous than Noah, who, when the earth was filled with sins, was alone found righteous on the earth? Who more glorious than Daniel? Who stronger for suffering martyrdom in firmness of faith, more happy in God's condescension, who so many times, both when he was in conflict conquered, and, when he had conquered, lived on? Was any more ready in good works than Job, braver in temptations, more patient in sufferings, more submissive in his fear, more true in his faith? And yet God said that He would not grant to them if they were to seek. When the prophet Ezekiel entreated for the sin of the people, "Whatsoever land," said He, "shall sin against me by trespassing grievously, I will stretch out mine hand upon it, and will break the staff of bread thereof, and will send famine upon it, and will cut off man and beast from it. Though these three men, Noah, Daniel, and Job, were in it, they should deliver neither sons nor daughters; but they only should be delivered themselves." Thus, not everything that is asked is in the pre-judgment of the asker, but in the free will of the giver; neither can human judgment claim to itself or usurp anything, unless the divine pleasure approve.

20. In the Gospel the Lord speaks, and says, "Whosoever shall confess me before men, him will I also confess before my Father which is in heaven: but he that denies me, him will I also deny." If He does not deny him that denies, neither does He confess him that confesses; the Gospel cannot be sound in one part and waver in another. Either both must stand firm, or both must lose the force of truth. If they who deny shall not be guilty of a crime, neither shall they who confess receive the reward of a virtue. Again, if faith which has conquered be crowned, it is of necessity that faithlessness which is

conquered should be punished. Thus the martyrs can either do nothing if the Gospel may be broken; or if the Gospel cannot be broken, they can do nothing against the Gospel, since they become martyrs on account of the Gospel. Let no one, beloved brethren, let no one decry the dignity of martyrs, let no one degrade their glories and their crowns. The strength of their uncorrupted faith abides sound; nor can he either say or do anything against Christ, whose hope, and faith, and virtue, and glory, are all in Christ: those cannot be the authority for the bishops doing anything against God's command, who themselves have done God's command. Is anyone greater than God, or more merciful than God's goodness, that he should either wish that undone which God has suffered to be done, or, as if God had too little power to protect His Church, should think that we could be preserved by his help?

21. Unless, perchance, these things have been done without God's knowledge, or all these things have happened without His permission; although Holy Scripture teaches the indocile, and admonishes the unmindful, where it speaks, saying, "Who gave Jacob for a spoil, and Israel to those who made a booty of him? Did not the Lord against whom they sinned, and would not walk in His ways, neither were obedient unto His law? And He has poured upon them the fury of His anger." And elsewhere it testifies and says, "Is the Lord's hand shortened, that it cannot save; or His ear heavy, that it cannot hear? But your iniquities separate between you and your God; and because of your sins He hath hid His face from you, that He may not have mercy." Let us rather consider our offences, revolving our doings and the secrets of our mind; let us weigh the deserts of our

conscience; let it come back upon our heart that we have not walked in the Lord's ways, and have cast away God's law, and have never been willing to keep His precepts and saving counsels.

22. What good can you think of him, what fear can you suppose to have been with him, or what faith, whom neither fear could correct nor persecution itself could reform? His high and rigid neck, even when it has fallen, is unbent; his swelling and haughty soul is not broken, even when it is conquered. Prostrate, he threatens those who stand; and wounded, the sound. And because he may not at once receive the body of the Lord in his polluted hands, the sacrilegious one is angry with the priests. And—oh your excessive madness, O frantic one—you are angry with him who endeavors to avert the anger of God from you; you threaten him who beseeches the divine mercy on your behalf, who feels your wound which you yourself do not feel, who sheds tears for you, which perhaps you never shed yourself. You are still aggravating and enhancing your crime; and while you yourself are implacable against the ministers and priests of God, do you think that the Lord can be appeased concerning you?

23. Receive rather and admit what we say. Why do your deaf ears not hear the salutary precepts with which we warn you? Why do your blind eyes not see the way of repentance which we point out? Why does your stricken and alienated mind not perceive the lively remedies which we both learn and teach from the heavenly Scriptures? Or if some unbelievers have little faith in future events, let them be terrified with present ones. Lo, what punishments do we behold of those who have denied! what sad deaths of theirs do we bewail! Not even here can they be without punishment, although the

day of punishment has not yet arrived. Some are punished in the meantime, that others may be corrected. The torments of a few are the examples of all.

24. One of those who of his own will ascended the Capitol to make denial, after he had denied Christ, became dumb. The punishment began from that point whence the crime also began; so that now he could not ask, since he had no words for entreating mercy. Another, who was in the baths, (for this was wanting to her crime and to her misfortunes, that she even went at once to the baths, when she had lost the grace of the laver of life); there, unclean as she was, was seized by an unclean spirit, and tore with her teeth the tongue with which she had either impiously eaten or spoken. After the wicked food had been taken, the madness of the mouth was armed to its own destruction. She herself was her own executioner, nor did she long continue to live afterwards: tortured with pangs of the belly and bowels, she expired.

25. Learn what occurred when I myself was present and a witness. Some parents who by chance were escaping, being little careful on account of their terror, left a little daughter under the care of a wet nurse. The nurse gave up the forsaken child to the magistrates. They gave it, in the presence of an idol whither the people flocked (because it was not yet able to eat flesh on account of its years), bread mingled with wine, which however itself was the remainder of what had been used in the immolation of those that had perished. Subsequently the mother recovered her child. But the girl was no longer able to speak, or to indicate the crime that had been committed, than she had before been able to understand or to prevent it. Therefore it happened unawares in their ignorance that when we were

sacrificing, the mother brought it in with her. Moreover, the girl mingled with the saints, became impatient of our prayer and supplications, and was at one moment shaken with weeping, and at another tossed about like a wave of the sea by the violent excitement of her mind; as if by the compulsion of a torturer the soul of that still tender child confessed a consciousness of the fact with such signs as it could. When, however, the solemnities were finished, and the deacon began to offer the cup to those present, and when, as the rest received it, its turn approached, the little child, by the instinct of the divine majesty, turned away its face, compressed its mouth with resisting lips, and refused the cup. Still the deacon persisted, and, although against her efforts, forced on her some of the sacrament of the cup. Then there followed sobbing and vomiting. In a profane body and mouth the Eucharist could not remain; the draught sanctified in the blood of the Lord burst forth from the polluted stomach. So great is the Lord's power, so great is His majesty. The secrets of darkness were disclosed under His light, and not even hidden crimes deceived God's priest.

26. This much about an infant, which was not yet of an age to speak of the crime committed by others in respect of herself. But the woman who in advanced life and of more mature age secretly crept in among us when we were sacrificing, received not food, but a sword for herself; and as if taking some deadly poison into her jaws and body, began presently to be tortured, and to become stiffened with frenzy; and suffering the misery no longer of persecution, but of her crime, shivering and trembling, she fell down. The crime of her dissimulated conscience was not long unpunished or concealed. She who had deceived man, felt that God was taking vengeance. And

another woman, when she tried with unworthy hands to open her box, in which was the holy (body) of the Lord, was deterred by fire rising from it from daring to touch it. And when one, who himself was defiled, dared with the rest to receive secretly a part of the sacrifice celebrated by the priest; he could not eat nor handle the holy of the Lord, but found in his hands when opened that he had a cinder. Thus by the experience of one it was shown that the Lord withdraws when He is denied; nor does that which is received benefit the undeserving for salvation, since saving grace is changed by the departure of the sanctity into a cinder. How many there are daily who do not repent nor make confession of the consciousness of their crime, who are filled with unclean spirits! How many are shaken even to unsoundness of mind and idiocy by the raging of madness! Nor is there any need to go through the deaths of individuals, since through the manifold lapses occurring in the world the punishment of their sins is as varied as the multitude of sinners is abundant. Let each one considers not what another has suffered, but what he himself deserves to suffer; nor think that he has escaped if his punishment delay for a time, since he ought to fear it the more that the wrath of God the judge has reserved it for Himself.

27. Nor let those persons flatter themselves that they need repent the less, who, although they have not polluted their hands with abominable sacrifices yet have defiled their conscience with certificates. That profession of one who denies, is the testimony of a Christian disowning what he had been. He says that he has done what another has actually committed; and although it is written, "Ye cannot serve two masters," he has served an earthly master in that he has obeyed his edict; he has been

more obedient to human authority than to God. It matters not whether he has published what he has done with less either of disgrace or of guilt among men. Be that as it may, he will not be able to escape and avoid God his judge, seeing that the Holy Spirit says in the Psalms, "Thine eyes did see my substance, that it was imperfect, and in Thy book shall all men be written." And again: "Man sees the outward appearance, but God sees the heart." The Lord Himself also forewarns and prepares us, saying, "And all the churches shall know that I am He which searches the reins and the heart." He looks into the hidden and secret things, and considers those things which are concealed; nor can anyone evade the eyes of the Lord, who says, "I am a God at hand, and not a God afar off. If a man be hidden in secret places, shall not I therefore see him? Do not I fill heaven and earth?" He sees the heart and mind of every person; and He will judge not alone of our deeds, but even of our words and thoughts. He looks into the minds, and the wills, and conceptions of all men, in the very lurking-places of the heart that is still closed up.

28. Moreover, how much are they both greater in faith and better in their fear, who, although bound by no crime of sacrifice to idols or of certificate, yet, since they have even thought of such things, with grief and simplicity confess this very thing to God's priests, and make the conscientious avowal, put off from them the load of their minds, and seek out the salutary medicine even for slight and moderate wounds, knowing that it is written, "God is not mocked." God cannot be mocked, nor deceived, nor deluded by any deceptive cunning. Yea, he sins the more, who, thinking that God is like man, believes that he evades the penalty of his crime if he has

not openly admitted his crime. Christ says in His precepts, "Whosoever shall be ashamed of me, of him shall the Son of man be ashamed." And does he think that he is a Christian, who is either ashamed or afraid to be a Christian? How can he be one with Christ, who either blushes or fears to belong to Christ? He will certainly have sinned less, by not seeing the idols, and not profaning the sanctity of the faith under the eyes of a people standing round and insulting, and not polluting his hands by the deadly sacrifices, nor defiling his lips with the wicked food. This is advantageous to this extent, that the fault is less, not that the conscience is guiltless. He can more easily attain to pardon of his crime, yet he is not free from crime; and let him not cease to carry out his repentance, and to entreat the Lord's mercy, lest what seems to be less in the quality of his fault, should be increased by his neglect of atonement.

29. I entreat you, beloved brethren, that each one should confess his own sin, while he who has sinned is still in this world, while his confession may be received, while the satisfaction and remission made by the priests are pleasing to the Lord. Let us turn to the Lord with our whole heart and expressing our repentance for our sin with true grief, let us entreat God's mercy. Let our soul lie low before Him. Let our mourning atone to Him. Let all our hope lean upon Him. He Himself tells us in what manner we ought to ask. "Turn ye," He says, "to me with all your heart, and at the same time with fasting, and with weeping, and with mourning; and rend your hearts, and not your garments." Let us return to the Lord with our whole heart. Let us appease His wrath and indignation with fasting, with weeping, with mourning, as He Himself admonishes us.

30. Do we believe that a man is lamenting with his whole heart, that he is entreating the Lord with fasting, and with weeping, and with mourning, who from the first day of his sin daily frequents the bathing-places with women; who, feeding at rich banquets, and puffed out with fuller dainties, belches forth on the next day his indigestions, and does not dispense of his meat and drink so as to aid the necessity of the poor? How does he who walks with joyous and glad step mourn for his death? And although it is written, "Ye shall not mar the figure of your beard," he plucks out his beard, and dresses his hair; and does he now study to please anyone who displeases God? Or does she groan and lament who has time to put on the clothing of precious apparel, and not to consider the robe of Christ which she has lost; to receive valuable ornaments and richly wrought necklaces, and not to bewail the loss of divine and heavenly ornament? Although you clothe yourself in foreign garments and silken robes, you are naked; although you adorns yourself to excess both in pearls, and gems, and gold, yet without the adornment of Christ thou art unsightly. And you who stain your hair, now at least cease in the midst of sorrows; and you who paint the edges of your eyes with a line drawn around them of black powder, now at least wash your eyes with tears. If you had lost any dear one of your friends by the death incident to mortality, you would groan grievously, and weep with disordered countenance, with changed dress, with neglected hair, with clouded face, with dejected appearance, you would show the signs of grief. Miserable creature, you have lost your soul; spiritually dead here, you are continuing to live to yourself, and although yourself walking about, you have begun to carry your own death with you. And do you not

bitterly moan; do you not continually groan; do you not hide yourself, either for shame of your sin or for continuance of your lamentation? Behold, these are still worse wounds of sinning; behold, these are greater crimes—to have sinned, and not to make atonement—to have committed crimes, and not to bewail your crimes.

31. Ananias, Azarias, and Misael, the illustrious and noble youths, even amid the flames and the ardors of a raging furnace, did not desist from making public confession to God. Although possessed of a good conscience and having often deserved well of the Lord by obedience of faith and fear, yet they did not cease from maintaining their humility, and from making atonement to the Lord, even amid the glorious martyrdoms of their virtues. The sacred Scripture speaks, saying, "Azarias stood up and prayed, and, opening his mouth, made confession before God together with his companions in the midst of the fire." Daniel also, after the manifold grace of his faith and innocency, after the condescension of the Lord often repeated in respect of his virtues and praises, strives by fasting still further to deserve well of God, wraps himself in sackcloth and ashes, sorrowfully making confession, and saying, "O Lord God, great, and strong, and dreadful, keeping Thy covenant and mercy for them that love Thee and keep Thy commandments, we have sinned, we have committed iniquity, and have done wickedly: we have transgressed, and departed from Thy precepts, and from Thy judgments; neither have we hearkened to the words of Thy servants the prophets, which they spoke in Thy name to our kings, and to all the nations, and to all the earth. O Lord, righteousness belongs unto Thee, but unto us confusion."

32. These things were done by men, meek, simple,

innocent, in deserving well of the majesty of God; and now those who have denied the Lord refuse to make atonement to the Lord, and to entreat Him. I beg you, brethren, acquiesce in wholesome remedies, obey better counsels, associate your tears with our tears, join your groans with ours; we beseech you in order that we may beseech God for you: we turn our very prayers to you first; our prayers with which we pray God for you that He would pity you. Repent abundantly, prove the sorrow of a grieving and lamenting mind.

33. Neither let that imprudent error or vain stupor of some move you, who, although they are involved in so grave a crime, are struck with blindness of mind, so that they neither understand nor lament their sins. This is the greater visitation of an angry God; as it is written, "And God gave them the spirit of deadness." And again: "They received not the love of the truth, that they might be saved. And for this cause God shall send them the working of error, that they should believe a lie; that they all might be damned who believed not the truth but had pleasure in unrighteousness." Unrighteously pleasing themselves, and mad with the alienation of a hardened mind, they despise the Lord's precepts, neglect the medicine for their wound, and will not repent. Thoughtless before their sin was acknowledged, after their sin they are obstinate; neither steadfast before, nor suppliant afterwards: when they ought to have stood fast, they fell; when they ought to fall and prostrate themselves to God, they think they stand fast. They have taken peace for themselves of their own accord when nobody granted it; seduced by false promises, and linked with apostates and unbelievers, they take hold of error instead of truth: they regard a communion as valid with those who are not

communicants; they believe men against God, although they have not believed God against men.

34. Flee from such men as much as you can; avoid with a wholesome caution those who adhere to their mischievous contact. Their word doth eat as doth a cancer; their conversation advances like a contagion; their noxious and envenomed persuasion kills worse than persecution itself. In such a case there remains only penitence which can make atonement. But they who take away repentance for a crime, close the way of atonement. Thus it happens that, while by the rashness of some a false safety is either promised or trusted, the hope of true safety is taken away.

35. But you, beloved brethren, whose fear is ready towards God, and whose mind, although it is placed in the midst of lapse, is mindful of its misery, do you in repentance and grief look into your sins; acknowledge the very grave sin of your conscience; open the eyes of your heart to the understanding of your sin, neither despairing of the Lord's mercy nor yet at once claiming His pardon. God, in proportion as with the affection of a Father He is always indulgent and good, in the same proportion is to be dreaded with the majesty of a judge. Even as we have sinned greatly, so let us greatly lament. To a deep wound let there not be wanting a long and careful treatment; let not the repentance be less than the sin. Think you that the Lord can be quickly appeased, whom with faithless words you have denied, to whom you have rather preferred your worldly estate, whose temple you have violated with a sacrilegious contact? Think you that He will easily have mercy upon you whom you have declared not to be your God? You must pray more eagerly and entreat; you must spend the day in grief; wear out nights in watching and

weeping; occupy all your time in wailful lamentations; lying stretched on the ground, you must cling close to the ashes, be surrounded with sackcloth and filth; after losing the raiment of Christ, you must be willing now to have no clothing; after the devil's meat, you must prefer fasting; be earnest in righteous works, whereby sins may be purged; frequently apply yourself to almsgiving, whereby souls are freed from death. What the adversary took from you, let Christ receive; nor ought your estate now either to be held or loved, by which you have been both deceived and conquered. Wealth must be avoided as an enemy; must be fled from as a robber; must be dreaded by its possessors as a sword and as poison. To this end only so much as remains should be of service, that by it the crime and the fault may be redeemed. Let good works be done without delay, and largely; let all your estate be laid out for the healing of your wound; let us lend of our wealth and our means to the Lord, who shall judge concerning us. Thus faith flourished in the time of the apostles; thus the first people of believers kept Christ's commands: they were prompt, they were liberal, they gave their all to be distributed by the apostles; and yet they were not redeeming sins of such a character as these.

36. If a man make prayer with his whole heart, if he groan with the true lamentations and tears of repentance, if he incline the Lord to pardon of his sin by righteous and continual works, he who expressed His mercy in these words may pity such men: "When you turn and lament, then shall you be saved, and shall know where you have been." And again: "I have no pleasure in the death of him that dies, says the Lord, but that he should return and live." And Joel the prophet declares the mercy of the Lord in the Lord's own admonition, when he

says: "Turn you to the Lord your God, for He is merciful and gracious, and patient, and of great mercy, and repented Him with respect to the evil that He hath inflicted." He can show mercy; He can turn back His judgment. He can mercifully pardon the repenting, the laboring, the beseeching sinner. He can regard as effectual whatever, in behalf of such as these, either martyrs have besought or priests have done. Or if anyone move Him still more by his own atonement, if he appease His anger, if he appease the wrath of an indignant God by righteous entreaty, He gives arms again whereby the vanquished may be armed; He restores and confirms the strength whereby the refreshed faith may be invigorated. The soldier will seek his contest anew; he will repeat the fight, he will provoke the enemy, and indeed by his very suffering he is made braver for the battle. He who has thus made atonement to God; he who by repentance for his deed, who by shame for his sin, has conceived more both of virtue and of faith from the very grief of his fall, heard and aided by the Lord, shall make the Church which he had lately saddened glad, and shall now deserve of the Lord not only pardon, but a crown.

Treatise IV.
On the Lord's Prayer.
Argument.—The Treatise of Cyprian on the Lord's Prayer Comprises Three Portions, in Which Division He Imitates Tertullian in His Book on Prayer. In the First Portion, He Points Out that the Lord's Prayer is the Most Excellent of All Prayers, Profoundly Spiritual, and Most Effectual for Obtaining Our Petitions. In the Second Part, He Undertakes an Explanation of the Lord's Prayer; And, Still Treading in the Footsteps of Tertullian,

He Goes Through Its Seven Chief Clauses. Finally, in the Third Part, He Considers the Conditions of Prayer, and Tells Us What Prayer Ought to Be.—

    1. The evangelical precepts, beloved brethren, are nothing else than divine teachings,—foundations on which hope is to be built, supports to strengthen faith, nourishments for cheering the heart, rudders for guiding our way, guards for obtaining salvation,—which, while they instruct the docile minds of believers on the earth, lead them to heavenly kingdoms. God, moreover, willed many things to be said and to be heard by means of the prophets His servants; but how much greater are those which the Son speaks, which the Word of God who was in the prophets testifies with His own voice; not now bidding to prepare the way for His coming, but Himself coming and opening and showing to us the way, so that we who have before been wandering in the darkness of death, without forethought and blind, being enlightened by the light of grace, might keep the way of life, with the Lord for our ruler and guide!

    2. He, among the rest of His salutary admonitions and divine precepts wherewith He counsels His people for their salvation, Himself also gave a form of praying—Himself advised and instructed us what we should pray for. He who made us to live, taught us also to pray, with that same benignity, to wit, wherewith He has condescended to give and confer all things else; in order that while we speak to the Father in that prayer and supplication which the Son has taught us, we may be the more easily heard. Already He had foretold that the hour was coming "when the true worshippers should worship the Father in spirit and in truth;" and He thus fulfilled what He before promised, so that we who by His

sanctification have received the Spirit and truth, may also by His teaching worship truly and spiritually. For what can be a more spiritual prayer than that which was given to us by Christ, by whom also the Holy Spirit was given to us? What praying to the Father can be more truthful than that which was delivered to us by the Son who is the Truth, out of His own mouth? So that to pray otherwise than He taught is not ignorance alone, but also sin; since He Himself has established, and said, "Ye reject the commandments of God, that ye may keep your own traditions."

3. Let us therefore, brethren beloved, pray as God our Teacher has taught us. It is a loving and friendly prayer to beseech God with His own word, to come up to His ears in the prayer of Christ. Let the Father acknowledge the words of His Son when we make our prayer and let Him also who dwells within in our breast Himself dwell in our voice. And since we have Him as an Advocate with the Father for our sins, let us, when as sinners we petition on behalf of our sins, put forward the words of our Advocate. For since He says, that "whatsoever we shall ask of the Father in His name, He will give us," how much more effectually do we obtain what we ask in Christ's name, if we ask for it in His own prayer!

4. But let our speech and petition when we pray be under discipline, observing quietness and modesty. Let us consider that we are standing in God's sight. We must please the divine eyes both with the habit of body and with the measure of voice. For as it is characteristic of a shameless man to be noisy with his cries, so, on the other hand, it is fitting to the modest man to pray with moderated petitions. Moreover, in His teaching the Lord

has bidden us to pray in secret—in hidden and remote places, in our very bed-chambers—which is best suited to faith, that we may know that God is everywhere present, and hears and sees all, and in the plenitude of His majesty penetrates even into hidden and secret places, as it is written, "I am a God at hand, and not a God afar off. If a man shall hide himself in secret places, shall I not then see him? Do not I fill heaven and earth?" And again: "The eyes of the Lord are in every place, beholding the evil and the good." And when we meet together with the brethren in one place, and celebrate divine sacrifices with God's priest, we ought to be mindful of modesty and discipline—not to throw abroad our prayers indiscriminately, with unsubdued voices, nor to cast to God with tumultuous wordiness a petition that ought to be commended to God by modesty; for God is the hearer, not of the voice, but of the heart. Nor need He be clamorously reminded, since He sees men's thoughts, as the Lord proves to us when He says, "Why think ye evil in your hearts?" And in another place: "And all the churches shall know that I am He that searches the hearts and reins."

5. And this Hannah in the first book of Kings, who was a type of the Church, maintains and observes, in that she prayed to God not with clamorous petition, but silently and modestly, within the very recesses of her heart. She spoke with hidden prayer, but with manifest faith. She spoke not with her voice, but with her heart, because she knew that thus God hears; and she effectually obtained what she sought, because she asked it with belief. Divine Scripture asserts this, when it says, "She spoke in her heart, and her lips moved, and her voice was not heard; and God did hear her." We read also in the Psalms, "Speak in your hearts, and in your beds, and be

ye pierced." The Holy Spirit, moreover, suggests these same things by Jeremiah, and teaches, saying, "But in the heart ought God to be adored by thee."

6. And let not the worshipper, beloved brethren, be ignorant in what manner the publican prayed with the Pharisee in the temple. Not with eyes lifted up boldly to heaven, nor with hands proudly raised; but beating his breast, and testifying to the sins shut up within, he implored the help of divine mercy. And while the Pharisee was pleased with himself, this man who thus asked, the rather deserved to be sanctified, since he placed the hope of salvation not in the confidence of his innocence, because there is none who is innocent; but confessing his sinfulness he humbly prayed, and He who pardons the humble heard the petitioner. And these things the Lord records in His Gospel, saying, "Two men went up into the temple to pray; the one a Pharisee, and the other a publican. The Pharisee stood, and prayed thus with himself: God, I thank Thee that I am not as other men are, unjust, extortioners, adulterers, even as this publican. I fast twice a week, I give tithes of all that I possess. But the publican stood afar off and would not so much as lift up his eyes unto heaven, but smote upon his breast, saying, God, be merciful to me a sinner. I say unto you, this man went down to his house justified rather than the Pharisee: for everyone that exalted himself shall be abased; and whosoever humbles himself shall be exalted."

7. These things, beloved brethren, when we have learnt from the sacred reading, and have gathered in what way we ought to approach to prayer, let us know also from the Lord's teaching what we should pray. "Thus," says He, "pray ye:—

"Our Father, which art in heaven, Hallowed be

Thy name. Thy kingdom come. Thy will be done, as in heaven so in earth. Give us this day our daily bread. And forgive us our debts, as we forgive our debtors. And suffer us not to be led into temptation; but deliver us from evil. Amen."

8. Before all things, the Teacher of peace and the Master of unity would not have prayer to be made singly and individually, as for one who prays to pray for himself alone. For we say not "My Father, which art in heaven," nor "Give me this day my daily bread;" nor does each one ask that only his own debt should be forgiven him; nor does he request for himself alone that he may not be led into temptation, and delivered from evil. Our prayer is public and common; and when we pray, we pray not for one, but for the whole people, because we the whole people are one. The God of peace and the Teacher of concord, who taught unity, willed that one should thus pray for all, even as He Himself bore us all in one. This law of prayer the three children observed when they were shut up in the fiery furnace, speaking together in prayer, and being of one heart in the agreement of the spirit; and this the faith of the sacred Scripture assures us, and in telling us how such as these prayed, gives an example which we ought to follow in our prayers, in order that we may be such as they were: "Then these three," it says, "as if from one mouth sang an hymn, and blessed the Lord." They spoke as if from one mouth, although Christ had not yet taught them how to pray. And therefore, as they prayed, their speech was availing and effectual, because a peaceful, and sincere, and spiritual prayer deserved well of the Lord. Thus also we find that the apostles, with the disciples, prayed after the Lord's ascension: "They all," says the Scripture, "continued with one accord in prayer,

with the women, and Mary who was the mother of Jesus, and with His brethren." They continued with one accord in prayer, declaring both by the urgency and by the agreement of their praying, that God, "who makes men to dwell of one mind in a house," only admits into the divine and eternal home those among whom prayer is unanimous.

9. But what matters of deep moment are contained in the Lord's prayer! How many and how great, briefly collected in the words, but spiritually abundant in virtue! so that there is absolutely nothing passed over that is not comprehended in these our prayers and petitions, as in a compendium of heavenly doctrine. "After this manner," says He, "pray ye: Our Father, which art in heaven." The new man, born again and restored to his God by His grace, says "Father," in the first place because he has now begun to be a son. "He came," He says, "to His own, and His own received Him not. But as many as received Him, to them gave He power to become the sons of God, even to them that believe in His name." The man, therefore, who has believed in His name, and has become God's son, ought from this point to begin both to give thanks and to profess himself God's son, by declaring that God is his Father in heaven; and also to bear witness, among the very first words of his new birth, that he has renounced an earthly and carnal father, and that he has begun to know as well as to have as a father Him only who is in heaven, as it is written: "They who say unto their father and their mother, I have not known thee, and who have not acknowledged their own children; these have observed Thy precepts and have kept Thy covenant." Also the Lord in His Gospel has bidden us to call "no man our father upon earth, because there is to us one Father, who is in

heaven." And to the disciple who had made mention of his dead father, He replied, "Let the dead bury their dead;" for he had said that his father was dead, while the Father of believers is living.

10. Nor ought we, beloved brethren, only to observe and understand that we should call Him Father who is in heaven; but we add to it, and say our Father, that is, the Father of those who believe—of those who, being sanctified by Him, and restored by the nativity of spiritual grace, have begun to be sons of God. A word this, moreover, which rebukes and condemns the Jews, who not only unbelievingly despised Christ, who had been announced to them by the prophets, and sent first to them, but also cruelly put Him to death; and these cannot now call God their Father, since the Lord confounds and confutes them, saying, "Ye are born of your father the devil, and the lusts of your father ye will do. For he was a murderer from the beginning, and abode not in the truth, because there is no truth in him." And by Isaiah the prophet God cries in wrath, "I have begotten and brought up children; but they have despised me. The ox knows his owner, and the ass his master's crib; but Israel hath not known me, and my people hath not understood me. Ah sinful nation, a people laden with sins, a wicked seed, corrupt children! Ye have forsaken the Lord; ye have provoked the Holy One of Israel to anger." In repudiation of these, we Christians, when we pray, say Our Father; because He has begun to be ours, and has ceased to be the Father of the Jews, who have forsaken Him. Nor can a sinful people be a son; but the name of sons is attributed to those to whom remission of sins is granted, and to them immortality is promised anew, in the words of our Lord Himself: "Whosoever committeth sin is the servant of

sin. And the servant abides not in the house for ever, but the son abides ever."

11. But how great is the Lord's indulgence! how great His condescension and plenteousness of goodness towards us, seeing that He has wished us to pray in the sight of God in such a way as to call God Father, and to call ourselves sons of God, even as Christ is the Son of God,—a name which none of us would dare to venture on in prayer, unless He Himself had allowed us thus to pray! We ought then, beloved brethren, to remember and to know, that when we call God Father, we ought to act as God's children; so that in the measure in which we find pleasure in considering God as a Father, He might also be able to find pleasure in us. Let us converse as temples of God, that it may be plain that God dwells in us. Let not our doings be degenerate from the Spirit; so that we who have begun to be heavenly and spiritual, may consider and do nothing but spiritual and heavenly things; since the Lord God Himself has said, "Them that honor me I will honor; and he that despises me shall be despised." The blessed apostle also has laid down in his epistle: "Ye are not your own; for ye are bought with a great price. Glorify and bear about God in your body."

12. After this we say, "Hallowed be Thy name;" not that we wish for God that He may be hallowed by our prayers, but that we beseech of Him that His name may be hallowed in us. But by whom is God sanctified, since He Himself sanctifies? Well, because He says, "Be ye holy, even as I am holy," we ask and entreat, that we who were sanctified in baptism may continue in that which we have begun to be. And this we daily pray for; for we have need of daily sanctification, that we who daily fall away may wash out our sins by continual sanctification. And what

the sanctification is which is conferred upon us by the condescension of God, the apostle declares, when he says, "neither fornicators, nor idolaters, nor adulterers, nor effeminate, nor abusers of themselves with mankind, nor thieves, nor deceivers, nor drunkards, nor revilers, nor extortioners, shall inherit the kingdom of God. And such indeed were you; but ye are washed; but ye are justified; but ye are sanctified in the name of our Lord Jesus Christ, and by the Spirit of our God." He says that we are sanctified in the name of our Lord Jesus Christ, and by the Spirit of our God. We pray that this sanctification may abide in us and because our Lord and Judge warns the man that was healed and quickened by Him, to sin no more lest a worse thing happen unto him, we make this supplication in our constant prayers, we ask this day and night, that the sanctification and quickening which is received from the grace of God may be preserved by His protection.

13. There follows in the prayer, Thy kingdom come. We ask that the kingdom of God may be set forth to us, even as we also ask that His name may be sanctified in us. For when does God not reign, or when does that begin with Him which both always has been, and never ceases to be? We pray that our kingdom, which has been promised us by God, may come, which was acquired by the blood and passion of Christ; that we who first are His subjects in the world, may hereafter reign with Christ when He reigns, as He Himself promises and says, "Come, ye blessed of my Father, receive the kingdom which has been prepared for you from the beginning of the world." Christ Himself, dearest brethren, however, may be the kingdom of God, whom we day by day desire to come, whose advent we crave to be quickly manifested

to us. For since He is Himself the Resurrection, since in Him we rise again, so also the kingdom of God may be understood to be Himself, since in Him we shall reign. But we do well in seeking the kingdom of God, that is, the heavenly kingdom, because there is also an earthly kingdom. But he who has already renounced the world, is moreover greater than its honors and its kingdom. And therefore he who dedicates himself to God and Christ, desires not earthly, but heavenly kingdoms. But there is need of continual prayer and supplication, that we fall not away from the heavenly kingdom, as the Jews, to whom this promise had first been given, fell away; even as the Lord sets forth and proves: "Many," says He, "shall come from the east and from the west, and shall recline with Abraham, and Isaac, and Jacob in the kingdom of heaven. But the children of the kingdom shall be cast out into outer darkness: there shall be weeping and gnashing of teeth." He shows that the Jews were previously children of the kingdom, so long as they continued also to be children of God; but after the name of Father ceased to be recognized among them, the kingdom also ceased; and therefore we Christians, who in our prayer begin to call God our Father, pray also that God's kingdom may come to us.

14. We add, also, and say, "Thy will be done, as in heaven so in earth;" not that God should do what He wills, but that we may be able to do what God wills. For who resists God, that He may not do what He wills? But since we are hindered by the devil from obeying with our thought and deed God's will in all things, we pray and ask that God's will may be done in us; and that it may be done in us we have need of God's good will, that is, of His help and protection, since no one is strong in his own

strength, but he is safe by the grace and mercy of God. And further, the Lord, setting forth the infirmity of the humanity which He bore, says, "Father, if it be possible, let this cup pass from me;" and affording an example to His disciples that they should do not their own will, but God's, He went on to say, "Nevertheless not as I will, but as Thou wilt." And in another place He says, "I came down from heaven not to do my own will, but the will of Him that sent me." Now if the Son was obedient to do His Father's will, how much more should the servant be obedient to do his Master's will! as in his epistle John also exhorts and instructs us to do the will of God, saying, "Love not the world, neither the things that are in the world. If any man love the world, the love of the Father is not in him. For all that is in the world is the lust of the flesh, and the lust of the eyes, and the ambition of life, which is not of the Father, but of the lust of the world. And the world shall pass away, and the lust thereof: but he that doeth the will of God abides forever, even as God also abides forever." We who desire to abide forever should do the will of God, who is everlasting.

15. Now that is the will of God which Christ both did and taught. Humility in conversation; steadfastness in faith; modesty in words; justice in deeds; mercifulness in works; discipline in morals; to be unable to do a wrong, and to be able to bear a wrong when done; to keep peace with the brethren; to love God with all one's heart; to love Him in that He is a Father; to fear Him in that He is God; to prefer nothing whatever to Christ, because He did not prefer anything to us; to adhere inseparably to His love; to stand by His cross bravely and faithfully; when there is any contest on behalf of His name and honor, to exhibit in discourse that constancy wherewith we make confession;

in torture, that confidence wherewith we do battle; in death, that patience whereby we are crowned;—this is to desire to be fellow heirs with Christ; this is to do the commandment of God; this is to fulfil the will of the Father.

16. Moreover, we ask that the will of God may be done both in heaven and in earth, each of which things pertains to the fulfilment of our safety and salvation. For since we possess the body from the earth and the spirit from heaven, we ourselves are earth and heaven; and in both—that is, both in body and spirit—we pray that God's will may be done. For between the flesh and spirit there is a struggle; and there is a daily strife as they disagree one with the other, so that we cannot do those very things that we would, in that the spirit seeks heavenly and divine things, while the flesh lusts after earthly and temporal things; and therefore we ask that, by the help and assistance of God, agreement may be made between these two natures, so that while the will of God is done both in the spirit and in the flesh, the soul which is new-born by Him may be preserved. This is what the Apostle Paul openly and manifestly declares by his words: "The flesh," says he, "lusted against the spirit, and the spirit against the flesh: for these are contrary the one to the other; so that ye cannot do the things that ye would. Now the works of the flesh are manifest, which are these; adulteries, fornications, uncleanness, lasciviousness, idolatry, witchcraft, murders, hatred, variance, emulations, wraths, strife, seditions, dissensions, heresies, envying, drunkenness, reveling, and such like: of the which I tell you before, as I have also told you in times past, that they which do such things shall not inherit the kingdom of God. But the fruit of the spirit is love, joy, peace,

magnanimity, goodness, faith, gentleness, continence, chastity." And therefore we make it our prayer in daily, yea, in continual supplications, that the will of God concerning us should be done both in heaven and in earth; because this is the will of God, that earthly things should give place to heavenly, and that spiritual and divine things should prevail.

17. And it may be thus understood, beloved brethren, that since the Lord commands and admonishes us even to love our enemies, and to pray even for those who persecute us, we should ask, moreover, for those who are still earth, and have not yet begun to be heavenly, that even in respect of these God's will should be done, which Christ accomplished in preserving and renewing humanity. For since the disciples are not now called by Him earth, but the salt of the earth, and the apostle designates the first man as being from the dust of the earth, but the second from heaven, we reasonably, who ought to be like God our Father, who makes His sun to rise upon the good and bad, and sends rain upon the just and the unjust, so pray and ask by the admonition of Christ as to make our prayer for the salvation of all men; that as in heaven—that is, in us by our faith—the will of God has been done, so that we might be of heaven; so also in earth—that is, in those who believe not—God's will may be done, that they who as yet are by their first birth of earth, may, being born of water and of the Spirit, begin to be of heaven.

18. As the prayer goes forward, we ask and say, "Give us this day our daily bread." And this may be understood both spiritually and literally, because either way of understanding it is rich in divine usefulness to our salvation. For Christ is the bread of life; and this bread

does not belong to all men, but it is ours. And according as we say, "Our Father," because He is the Father of those who understand and believe; so also we call it "our bread," because Christ is the bread of those who are in union with His body. And we ask that this bread should be given to us daily, that we who are in Christ, and daily receive the Eucharist for the food of salvation, may not, by the interposition of some heinous sin, by being prevented, as withheld and not communicating, from partaking of the heavenly bread, be separated from Christ's body, as He Himself predicts, and warns, "I am the bread of life which came down from heaven. If any man eats of my bread, he shall live forever: and the bread which I will give is my flesh, for the life of the world." When, therefore, He says, that whoever shall eat of His bread shall live forever; as it is manifest that those who partake of His body and receive the Eucharist by the right of communion are living, so, on the other hand, we must fear and pray lest anyone who, being withheld from communion, is separate from Christ's body should remain at a distance from salvation; as He Himself threatens, and says, "Unless ye eat the flesh of the Son of man, and drink His blood, ye shall have no life in you." And therefore we ask that our bread—that is, Christ—may be given to us daily, that we who abide and live in Christ may not depart from His sanctification and body.

19. But it may also be thus understood that we who have renounced the world, and have cast away its riches and pomps in the faith of spiritual grace, should only ask for ourselves food and support, since the Lord instructs us, and says, "Whosoever forsakes not all that he hath, cannot be my disciple." But he who has begun to be Christ's disciple, renouncing all things according to the

word of his Master, ought to ask for his daily food, and not to extend the desires of his petition to a long period, as the Lord again prescribes, and says, "Take no thought for the morrow, for the morrow itself shall take thought for itself. Sufficient for the day is the evil thereof." With reason, then, does Christ's disciple ask food for himself for the day, since he is prohibited from thinking of the morrow; because it becomes a contradiction and a repugnant thing for us to seek to live long in this world, since we ask that the kingdom of God should come quickly. Thus also the blessed apostle admonishes us, giving substance and strength to the steadfastness of our hope and faith: "We brought nothing," says he, "into this world, nor indeed can we carry anything out. Having therefore food and raiment, let us be herewith content. But they that will be rich fall into temptation and a snare, and into many and hurtful lusts, which drown men in perdition and destruction. For the love of money is the root of all evil; which while some coveted after, they have made shipwreck from the faith, and have pierced themselves through with many sorrows."

20. He teaches us that riches are not only to be contemned, but that they are also full of peril; that in them is the root of seducing evils, that deceive the blindness of the human mind by a hidden deception. Whence also God rebukes the rich fool, who thinks of his earthly wealth, and boasts himself in the abundance of his overflowing harvests, saying, "Thou fool, this night thy soul shall be required of thee; then whose shall those things be which thou hast provided?" The fool who was to die that very night was rejoicing in his stores, and he to whom life already was failing, was thinking of the abundance of his food. But, on the other hand, the Lord tells us that he

becomes perfect and complete who sells all his goods, and distributes them for the use of the poor, and so lays up for himself treasure in heaven. He says that that man is able to follow Him, and to imitate the glory of the Lord's passion, who, free from hindrance, and with his loins girded, is involved in no entanglements of worldly estate, but, at large and free himself, accompanies his possessions, which before have been sent to God. For which result, that every one of us may be able to prepare himself, let him thus learn to pray, and know, from the character of the prayer, what he ought to be.

21. For daily bread cannot be wanting to the righteous man, since it is written, "The Lord will not slay the soul of the righteous by hunger;" and again "I have been young and now am old, yet have I not seen the righteous forsaken, nor his seed begging their bread." And the Lord moreover promises and says, "Take no thought, saying, 'What shall we eat, or what shall we drink, or wherewithal shall we be clothed?' For after all these things do the nations seek. And your Father knows that ye have need of all these things. Seek ye first the kingdom of God and His righteousness, and all these things shall be added unto you." To those who seek God's kingdom and righteousness, He promises that all things shall be added. For since all things are God's, nothing will be wanting to him who possesses God, if God Himself be not wanting to him. Thus a meal was divinely provided for Daniel: when he was shut up by the king's command in the den of lions, and in the midst of wild beasts who were hungry, and yet spared him, the man of God was fed. Thus Elijah in his flight was nourished both by ravens ministering to him in his solitude, and by birds bringing him food in his persecution. And—oh detestable cruelty of the malice of

man!—the wild beasts spare, the birds feed, while men lay snares, and rage!

22. After this we also entreat for our sins, saying, "And forgive us our debts, as we also forgive our debtors." After the supply of food, pardon of sin is also asked for, that he who is fed by God may live in God, and that not only the present and temporal life may be provided for, but the eternal also, to which we may come if our sins are forgiven; and these the Lord calls debts, as He says in His Gospel, "I forgave thee all that debt, because thou desires me." And how necessarily, how providently and salutarily, are we admonished that we are sinners, since we are compelled to entreat for our sins, and while pardon is asked for from God, the soul recalls its own consciousness of sin! Lest anyone should flatter himself that he is innocent, and by exalting himself should more deeply perish, he is instructed and taught that he sins daily, in that he is bidden to entreat daily for his sins. Thus, moreover, John also in his epistle warns us, and says, "If we say that we have no sin, we deceive ourselves, and the truth is not in us; but if we confess our sins, the Lord is faithful and just to forgive us our sins." In his epistle he has combined both, that we should entreat for our sins, and that we should obtain pardon when we ask. Therefore he said that the Lord was faithful to forgive sins, keeping the faith of His promise; because He who taught us to pray for our debts and sins, has promised that His fatherly mercy and pardon shall follow.

23. He has clearly joined herewith and added the law and has bound us by a certain condition and engagement, that we should ask that our debts be forgiven us in such a manner as we ourselves forgive our debtors, knowing that that which we seek for our sins cannot be

obtained unless we ourselves have acted in a similar way in respect of our debtors. Therefore also He says in another place, "With what measure ye mete, it shall be measured to you again." And the servant who, after having had all his debt forgiven him by his master, would not forgive his fellow servant, is cast back into prison; because he would not forgive his fellow servant, he lost the indulgence that had been shown to himself by his lord. And these things Christ still more urgently sets forth in His precepts with yet greater power of His rebuke. "When ye stand praying," says He, "forgive if ye have aught against any, that your Father which is in heaven may forgive you your trespasses. But if ye do not forgive, neither will your Father which is in heaven forgive you your trespasses." There remains no ground of excuse in the day of judgment when you will be judged according to your own sentence; and whatever you have done, that you also will suffer. For God commands us to be peacemakers, and in agreement, and of one mind in His house; and such as He makes us by a second birth, such He wishes us when new-born to continue, that we who have begun to be sons of God may abide in God's peace, and that, having one spirit, we should also have one heart and one mind. Thus God does not receive the sacrifice of a person who is in disagreement, but commands him to go back from the altar and first be reconciled to his brother, that so God also may be appeased by the prayers of a peacemaker. Our peace and brotherly agreement is the greater sacrifice to God,—and a people united in one in the unity of the Father, and of the Son, and of the Holy Spirit.

24. For even in the sacrifices which Abel and Cain first offered, God looked not at their gifts, but at their

hearts, so that he was acceptable in his gift who was acceptable in his heart. Abel, peaceable and righteous in sacrificing in innocence to God, taught others also, when they bring their gift to the altar, thus to come with the fear of God, with a simple heart, with the law of righteousness, with the peace of concord. With reason did he, who was such in respect of God's sacrifice, become subsequently himself a sacrifice to God; so that he who first set forth martyrdom, and initiated the Lord's passion by the glory of his blood, had both the Lord's righteousness and His peace. Finally, such are crowned by the Lord, such will be avenged with the Lord in the day of judgment; but the quarrelsome and disunited, and he who has not peace with his brethren, in accordance with what the blessed apostle and the Holy Scripture testifies, even if he have been slain for the name of Christ, shall not be able to escape the crime of fraternal dissension, because, as it is written, "He who hated his brother is a murderer," and no murderer attains to the kingdom of heaven, nor does he live with God. He cannot be with Christ, who had rather be an imitator of Judas than of Christ. How great is the sin which cannot even be washed away by a baptism of blood—how heinous the crime which cannot be expiated by martyrdom!

25. Moreover, the Lord of necessity admonishes us to say in prayer, "And suffer us not to be led into temptation." In which words it is shown that the adversary can do nothing against us except God shall have previously permitted it; so that all our fear, and devotion, and obedience may be turned towards God, since in our temptations nothing is permitted to evil unless power is given from Him. This is proved by divine Scripture, which says, "Nebuchadnezzar king of Babylon came to

Jerusalem, and besieged it; and the Lord delivered it into his hand." But power is given to evil against us according to our sins, as it is written, "Who gave Jacob for a spoil, and Israel to those who make a prey of Him? Did not the Lord, against whom they sinned, and would not walk in His ways, nor hear His law? and He has brought upon them the anger of His wrath." And again, when Solomon sinned, and departed from the Lord's commandments and ways, it is recorded, "And the Lord stirred up Satan against Solomon himself."

26. Now power is given against us in two modes: either for punishment when we sin, or for glory when we are proved, as we see was done with respect to Job; as God Himself sets forth, saying, "Behold, all that he hath I give unto thy hands; but be careful not to touch himself." And the Lord in His Gospel says, in the time of His passion, "Thou could have no power against me unless it were given thee from above." But when we ask that we may not come into temptation, we are reminded of our infirmity and weakness in that we thus ask, lest any should insolently vaunt himself, lest any should proudly and arrogantly assume anything to himself, lest any should take to himself the glory either of confession or of suffering as his own, when the Lord Himself, teaching humility, said, "Watch and pray, that ye enter not into temptation; the spirit indeed is willing, but the flesh is weak;" so that while a humble and submissive confession comes first, and all is attributed to God, whatever is sought for suppliantly with fear and honor of God, may be granted by His own loving-kindness.

27. After all these things, in the conclusion of the prayer comes a brief clause, which shortly and comprehensively sums up all our petitions and our

prayers. For we conclude by saying, "But deliver us from evil," comprehending all adverse things which the enemy attempts against us in this world, from which there may be a faithful and sure protection if God deliver us, if He afford His help to us who pray for and implore it. And when we say, Deliver us from evil, there remains nothing further which ought to be asked. When we have once asked for God's protection against evil, and have obtained it, then against everything which the devil and the world work against us we stand secure and safe. For what fear is there in this life, to the man whose guardian in this life is God?

28. What wonder is it, beloved brethren, if such is the prayer which God taught, seeing that He condensed in His teaching all our prayer in one saving sentence? This had already been before foretold by Isaiah the prophet, when, being filled with the Holy Spirit, he spoke of the majesty and loving-kindness of God, "consummating and shortening His word," He says, "in righteousness, because a shortened word will the Lord make in the whole earth." For when the Word of God, our Lord Jesus Christ, came unto all, and gathering alike the learned and unlearned, published to every sex and every age the precepts of salvation, He made a large compendium of His precepts, that the memory of the scholars might not be burdened in the celestial learning, but might quickly learn what was necessary to a simple faith. Thus, when He taught what is life eternal, He embraced the sacrament of life in a large and divine brevity, saying, "And this is life eternal, that they might know Thee, the only and true God, and Jesus Christ, whom Thou hast sent." Also, when He would gather from the law and the prophets the first and greatest commandments, He said, "Hear, O Israel; the Lord thy

God is one God: and thou shalt love the Lord thy God with all thy heart, and with all thy mind, and with all thy strength. This is the first commandment. And the second is like unto it, Thou shalt love thy neighbor as thyself." "On these two commandments hang all the law and the prophets." And again: "Whatsoever good things ye would that men should do unto you, do ye even so to them. For this is the law and the prophets."

29. Nor was it only in words, but in deeds also, that the Lord taught us to pray, Himself praying frequently and beseeching, and thus showing us, by the testimony of His example, what it behooved us to do, as it is written, "But Himself departed into a solitary place, and there prayed." And again: "He went out into a mountain to pray and continued all night in prayer to God." But if He prayed who was without sin, how much more ought sinners to pray; and if He prayed continually, watching through the whole night in uninterrupted petitions, how much more ought we to watch nightly in constantly repeated prayer!

30. But the Lord prayed and besought not for Himself—for why should He who was guiltless pray on His own behalf?—but for our sins, as He Himself declared, when He said to Peter, "Behold, Satan hath desired that he might sift you as wheat. But I have prayed for thee, that thy faith fail not." And subsequently He beseeches the Father for all, saying, "Neither pray I for these alone, but for them also which shall believe on me through their word; that they all may be one; as Thou, Father, art in me, and I in Thee, that they also may be one in us." The Lord's loving-kindness, no less than His mercy, is great in respect of our salvation, in that, not content to redeem us with His blood, He in addition also

prayed for us. Behold now what was the desire of His petition, that like as the Father and Son are one, so also we should abide in absolute unity; so that from this it may be understood how greatly he sins who divides unity and peace, since for this same thing even the Lord besought, desirous doubtless that His people should thus be saved and live in peace, since He knew that discord cannot come into the kingdom of God.

31. Moreover, when we stand praying, beloved brethren, we ought to be watchful and earnest with our whole heart, intent on our prayers. Let all carnal and worldly thoughts pass away, nor let the soul at that time think on anything but the object only of its prayer. For this reason also the priest, by way of preface before his prayer, prepares the minds of the brethren by saying, "Lift up your hearts," that so upon the people's response, "We lift them up unto the Lord," he may be reminded that he himself ought to think of nothing but the Lord. Let the breast be closed against the adversary, and be open to God alone; nor let it suffer God's enemy to approach to it at the time of prayer. For frequently he steals upon us, and penetrates within, and by crafty deceit calls away our prayers from God, that we may have one thing in our heart and another in our voice, when not the sound of the voice, but the soul and mind, ought to be praying to the Lord with a simple intention. But what carelessness it is, to be distracted and carried away by foolish and profane thoughts when you are praying to the Lord, as if there were anything which you should rather be thinking of than that you are speaking with God! How can you ask to be heard of God, when you yourself do not hear yourself? Do you wish that God should remember you when you ask, if you yourself do not remember yourself? This is

absolutely to take no precaution against the enemy; this is, when you pray to God, to offend the majesty of God by the carelessness of your prayer; this is to be watchful with your eyes, and to be asleep with your heart, while the Christian, even though he is asleep with his eyes, ought to be awake with his heart, as it is written in the person of the Church speaking in the Song of Songs, "I sleep, yet my heart wakes." Wherefore the apostle anxiously and carefully warns us, saying, "Continue in prayer, and watch in the same;" teaching, that is, and showing that those are able to obtain from God what they ask, whom God sees to be watchful in their prayer.

32. Moreover, those who pray should not come to God with fruitless or naked prayers. Petition is ineffectual when it is a barren entreaty that beseeches God. For as every tree that bringeth not forth fruit is cut down and cast into the fire; assuredly also, words that do not bear fruit cannot deserve anything of God, because they are fruitful in no result. And thus Holy Scripture instructs us, saying, "Prayer is good with fasting and almsgiving." For He who will give us in the day of judgment a reward for our labors and alms, is even in this life a merciful hearer of one who comes to Him in prayer associated with good works. Thus, for instance, Cornelius the centurion, when he prayed, had a claim to be heard. For he was in the habit of doing many alms-deeds towards the people, and of ever praying to God. To this man, when he prayed about the ninth hour, appeared an angel bearing testimony to his labors, and saying, "Cornelius, thy prayers and thine alms are gone up in remembrance before God."

33. Those prayers quickly ascend to God which the merits of our labors urge upon God. Thus also Raphael the angel was a witness to the constant prayer

and the constant good works of Tobias, saying, "It is honorable to reveal and confess the works of God. For when you did pray, and Sarah, I did bring the remembrance of your prayers before the holiness of God. And when you did bury the dead in simplicity, and because thou didst not delay to rise up and to leave thy dinner, but didst go out and cover the dead, I was sent to prove thee; and again God has sent me to heal thee, and Sarah thy daughter-in-law. For I am Raphael, one of the seven holy angels which stand and go in and out before the glory of God." By Isaiah also the Lord reminds us, and teaches similar things, saying, "Loosen every knot of iniquity, release the oppressions of contracts which have no power, let the troubled go into peace, and break every unjust engagement. Break thy bread to the hungry, and bring the poor that are without shelter into thy house. When thou sees the naked, clothe him; and despise not those of the same family and race as thyself. Then shall thy light break forth in season, and thy raiment shall spring forth speedily; and righteousness shall go before thee, and the glory of God shall surround thee. Then shalt thou call, and God shall hear thee; and while thou shalt yet speak, He shall say, Here I am." He promises that He will be at hand, and says that He will hear and protect those who, loosening the knots of unrighteousness from their heart, and giving alms among the members of God's household according to His commands, even in hearing what God commands to be done, do themselves also deserve to be heard by God. The blessed Apostle Paul, when aided in the necessity of affliction by his brethren, said that good works which are performed are sacrifices to God. "I am full," saith he, "having received of Epaphroditus the things which were sent from you, an odor of a sweet smell, a sacrifice acceptable, well pleasing to God." For when one has pity on the poor, he lends to God; and he who gives to the least gives to God—sacrifices spiritually to God an odor of a sweet smell.

34. And in discharging the duties of prayer, we find that the three children with Daniel, being strong in faith and victorious in captivity, observed the third, sixth, and ninth hour, as it were, for a sacrament of the Trinity, which in the last times had to be manifested. For both the first hour in its progress to the third shows forth the consummated number of the Trinity, and also the fourth proceeding to the sixth declares another Trinity; and when from the seventh the ninth is completed, the perfect Trinity is numbered every three hours, which spaces of hours the worshippers of God in time past having spiritually decided on, made use of for determined and lawful times for prayer. And subsequently the thing was manifested, that these things were of old Sacraments, in that anciently righteous men prayed in this manner. For upon the disciples at the third hour the Holy Spirit descended, who fulfilled the grace of the Lord's promise. Moreover, at the sixth hour, Peter, going up unto the house☐top, was instructed as well by the sign as by the word of God admonishing him to receive all to the grace of salvation, whereas he was previously doubtful of the receiving of the Gentiles to baptism. And from the sixth hour to the ninth, the Lord, being crucified, washed away our sins by His blood; and that He might redeem and quicken us, He then accomplished His victory by His passion.

35. But for us, beloved brethren, besides the hours of prayer observed of old, both the times and the

St. Cyprian

sacraments have now increased in number. For we must also pray in the morning, that the Lord's resurrection may be celebrated by morning prayer. And this formerly the Holy Spirit pointed out in the Psalms, saying, "My King, and my God, because unto Thee will I cry; O Lord, in the morning shalt Thou hear my voice; in the morning will I stand before Thee, and will look up to Thee." And again, the Lord speaks by the mouth of the prophet: "Early in the morning shall they watch for me, saying, Let us go, and return unto the Lord our God." Also at the sunsetting and at the decline of day, of necessity we must pray again. For since Christ is the true sun and the true day, as the worldly sun and worldly day depart, when we pray and ask that light may return to us again, we pray for the advent of Christ, which shall give us the grace of everlasting light. Moreover, the Holy Spirit in the Psalms manifests that Christ is called the day. "The stone," says He, "which the builders rejected, is become the head of the corner. This is the Lord's doing; and it is marvelous in our eyes. This is the day which the Lord hath made; let us walk and rejoice in it." Also the prophet Malachi testifies that He is called the Sun, when he says, "But to you that fear the name of the Lord shall the Sun of righteousness arise, and there is healing in His wings." But if in the Holy Scriptures the true sun and the true day is Christ, there is no hour excepted for Christians wherein God ought not frequently and always to be worshipped; so that we who are in Christ—that is, in the true Sun and the true Day—should be instant throughout the entire day in petitions, and should pray; and when, by the law of the world, the revolving night, recurring in its alternate changes, succeeds, there can be no harm arising from the darkness of night to those who pray, because the children of light have the day even in the night. For when is he without light who has light in his heart? or when has not he the sun and the day, whose Sun and Day is Christ?

36. Let not us, then, who are in Christ—that is, always in the light—cease from praying even during night. Thus the widow Anna, without intermission praying and watching, persevered in deserving well of God, as it is written in the Gospel: "She departed not," it says, "from the temple, serving with fasting and prayers night and day." Let the Gentiles look to this, who are not yet enlightened, or the Jews who have remained in darkness by having forsaken the light. Let us, beloved brethren, who are always in the light of the Lord, who remember and hold fast what by grace received we have begun to be, reckon night for day; let us believe that we always walk in the light, and let us not be hindered by the darkness which we have escaped. Let there be no failure of prayers in the hours of night—no idle and reckless waste of the occasions of prayer. New-created and newborn of the Spirit by the mercy of God, let us imitate what we shall one day be. Since in the kingdom we shall possess day alone, without intervention of night, let us so watch in the night as if in the daylight. Since we are to pray and give thanks to God for ever, let us not cease in this life also to pray and give thanks.

Treatise V.
An Address to Demetrianus.
Argument.—Cyprian, in Reply to Demetrianus the Proconsul of Africa, Who Contended that the Wars, and Famine, and Pestilence with Which the World Was Then

Plagued Must Be Imputed to the Christians Because They Did Not Worship the Gods; Fairly Urges (Having Argued that All Things are Gradually Deteriorating with the Old Age of the World) that It Was Rather the Heathens Themselves Who Were the Cause of Such Mischiefs, Because They Did Not Worship God, And, Moreover, Were Distressing the Christians with Unjust Persecutions.

1. I had frequently, Demetrianus, treated with contempt your railing and noisy clamor with sacrilegious mouth and impious words against the one and true God, thinking it more modest and better, silently to scorn the ignorance of a mistaken man, than by speaking to provoke the fury of a senseless one. Neither did I do this without the authority of the divine teaching, since it is written, "Speak not in the ears of a fool, lest when he hear thee he should despise the wisdom of thy words;" and again, "Answer not a fool according to his folly, lest thou also be like unto him." And we are, moreover, bidden to keep what is holy within our own knowledge, and not expose it to be trodden down by swine and dogs, since the Lord speaks, saying, "Give not that which is holy unto the dogs, neither cast ye your pearls before swine, lest they trample them under their feet, and turn again and rend you." For when you used often to come to me with the desire of contradicting rather than with the wish to learn, and preferred impudently to insist on your own views, which you shouted with noisy words, to patiently listening to mine, it seemed to me foolish to contend with you; since it would be an easier and slighter thing to restrain the angry waves of a turbulent sea with shouts, than to check your madness by arguments. Assuredly it would be both a vain and ineffectual labor to offer light to a blind man, discourse to a deaf one, or wisdom to a

brute; since neither can a brute apprehend, nor can a blind man admit the light, nor can a deaf man hear.

2. In consideration of this, I have frequently held my tongue, and overcome an impatient man with patience; since I could neither teach an unteachable man, nor check an impious one with religion, nor restrain a frantic man with gentleness. But yet, when you say that very many are complaining that to us it is ascribed that wars arise more frequently, that plague, that famines rage, and that long droughts are suspending the showers and rains, it is not fitting that I should be silent any longer, lest my silence should begin to be attributed to mistrust rather than to modesty; and while I am treating the false charges with contempt, I may seem to be acknowledging the crime. I reply, therefore, as well to you, Demetrianus, as to others whom perhaps you have stirred up, and many of whom, by sowing hatred against us with malicious words, you have made your own partisans, from the budding forth of your own root and origin, who, however, I believe, will admit the reasonableness of my discourse; for he who is moved to evil by the deception of a lie, will much more easily be moved to good by the cogency of truth.

3. You have said that all these things are caused by us, and that to us ought to be attributed the misfortunes wherewith the world is now shaken and distressed, because your gods are not worshipped by us. And in this behalf, since you are ignorant of divine knowledge, and a stranger to the truth, you must in the first place know this, that the world has now grown old, and does not abide in that strength in which it formerly stood; nor has it that vigor and force which it formerly possessed. This, even were we silent, and if we alleged no proofs from the

sacred Scriptures and from the divine declarations, the world itself is now announcing, and, bearing witness to its decline by the testimony of its failing estate.3408 In the winter there is not such an abundance of showers for nourishing the seeds; in the summer the sun has not so much heat for cherishing the harvest; nor in the spring season are the corn-fields so joyous; nor are the autumnal seasons so fruitful in their leafy products. The layers of marble are dug out in less quantity from the disemboweled and wearied mountains; the diminished quantities of gold and silver suggest the early exhaustion of the metals, and the impoverished veins are straitened and decreased day by day; the husbandman is failing in the fields, the sailor at sea, the soldier in the camp, innocence in the market, justice in the tribunal, concord in friendships, skillfulness in the arts, discipline in morals. Think you that the substantial character of a thing that is growing old remains so robust as that wherewith it might previously flourish in its youth while still new and vigorous? Whatever is tending downwards to decay, with its end nearly approaching, must of necessity be weakened. Thus, the sun at his setting darts his rays with a less bright and fiery splendor; thus, in her declining course, the moon wanes with exhausted horns; and the tree, which before had been green and fertile, as its branches dry up, becomes by and by misshapen in a barren old age; and the fountain which once gushed forth liberally from its overflowing veins, as old age causes it to fail, scarcely trickles with a sparing moisture. This is the sentence passed on the world, this is God's law; that everything that has had a beginning should perish, and things that have grown should become old, and that strong things should become weak, and great things become small, and that, when they have become weakened and diminished, they should come to an end.

4. You impute it to the Christians that everything is decaying as the world grows old. What if old men should charge it on the Christians that they grow less strong in their old age; that they no longer, as formerly, have the same facilities, in the hearing of their ears, in the swiftness of their feet, in the keenness of their eyes, in the vigor of their strength, in the freshness of their organic powers, in the fulness of their limbs, and that although once the life of men endured beyond the age of eight and nine hundred years, it can now scarcely attain to its hundredth year? We see grey hair in boys—the hair fails before it begins to grow; and life does not cease in old age, but it begins with old age. Thus, even at its very commencement, birth hastens to its close; thus, whatever is now born degenerates with the old age of the world itself; so that no one ought to wonder that everything begins to fail in the world, when the whole world itself is already in process of failing, and in its end.

5. Moreover, that wars continue frequently to prevail, that death and famine accumulate anxiety, that health is shattered by raging diseases, that the human race is wasted by the desolation of pestilence, know that this was foretold; that evils should be multiplied in the last times, and that misfortunes should be varied; and that as the day of judgment is now drawing nigh, the censure of an indignant God should be more and more aroused for the scourging of the human race. For these things happen not, as your false complaining and ignorant inexperience of the truth asserts and repeats, because your gods are not worshipped by us, but because God is not worshipped by you. For since He is Lord and Ruler of the world, and all

things are carried on by His will and direction, nor can anything be done save what He Himself has done or allowed to be done, certainly when those things occur which show the anger of an offended God, they happen not on account of us by whom God is worshipped, but they are called down by your sins and deserving, by whom God is neither in any way sought nor feared, because your vain superstitions are not forsaken, nor the true religion known in such wise that He who is the one God over all might alone be worshipped and petitioned.

6. In fine, listen to Himself speaking; Himself with a divine voice at once instructing and warning us: "Thou shalt worship the Lord thy God," says He, "and Him only shalt thou serve." And again, "Thou shalt have none other gods but me." And again, "Go not after other gods, to serve them; and worship them not, and provoke not me to anger with the works of your hands to destroy you." Moreover, the prophet, filled with the Holy Spirit, attests and denounces the anger of God, saying, "Thus saith the Lord Almighty: Because of mine house that is waste, and ye run every man to his own house, therefore the heavens shall be stayed from dew, and the earth shall withhold her fruits: and I will bring a sword upon the earth, and upon the corn, and upon the wine, and upon the oil, and upon men, and upon cattle, and upon all the labors of their hands." Moreover, another prophet repeats, and says, "And I will cause it to rain upon one city, and upon another city I will cause it not to rain. One piece shall be rained upon, and the piece whereon I send no rain shall be withered. And two and three cities shall be gathered into one city to drink water, and shall not be satisfied; and ye are not converted unto me, saith the Lord."

7. Behold, the Lord is angry and wrathful, and

threatens, because you turn not unto Him. And you wonder or complain in this your obstinacy and contempt, if the rain comes down with unusual scarcity; and the earth falls into neglect with dusty corruption; if the barren glebe hardly brings forth a few jejune and pallid blades of grass; if the destroying hail weakens the vines; if the overwhelming whirlwind roots out the olive; if drought stanches the fountain; a pestilent breeze corrupts the air; the weakness of disease wastes away man; although all these things come as the consequence of the sins that provoke them, and God is more deeply indignant when such and so great evils avail nothing! For that these things occur either for the discipline of the obstinate or for the punishment of the evil, the same God declares in the Holy Scriptures, saying, "In vain have I smitten your children; they have not received correction." And the prophet devoted and dedicated to God answers to these words in the same strain, and says, "Thou hast stricken them, but they have not grieved; Thou hast scourged them, but they have refused to receive correction." Lo, stripes are inflicted from God, and there is no fear of God. Lo, blows and scourging from above are not wanting, and there is no trembling, no fear. What if even no such rebuke as that interfered in human affairs? How much greater still would be the audacity in men, if it were secure in the impunity of their crimes!

8. You complain that the fountains are now less plentiful to you, and the breezes less salubrious, and the frequent showers and the fertile earth afford you less ready assistance; that the elements no longer subserve your uses and your pleasures as of old. But do you serve God, by whom all things are ordained to your service; do you wait upon Him by whose good pleasure all things

wait upon you? From your slave you yourself require service; and though a man, you compel your fellow-man to submit, and to be obedient to you; and although you share the same lot in respect of being born, the same condition in respect of dying; although you have like bodily substance and a common order of souls, and although you come into this world of ours and depart from it after a time with equal rights, and by the same law; yet, unless you are served by him according to your pleasure, unless you are obeyed by him in conformity to your will, you, as an imperious and excessive exactor of his service, flog and scourge him: you afflict and torture him with hunger, with thirst and nakedness, and even frequently with the sword and with imprisonment. And wretch that you are, do you not acknowledge the Lord your God while you yourself are thus exercising lordship?

9. And therefore with reason in these plagues that occur, there are not wanting God's stripes and scourges; and since they are of no avail in this matter, and do not convert individuals to God by such terror of destructions, there remains after all the eternal dungeon, and the continual fire, and the everlasting punishment; nor shall the groaning of the suppliants be heard there, because here the terror of the angry God was not heard, crying by His prophet, and saying, "Hear the word of the Lord, ye children of Israel: for the judgment of the Lord is against the inhabitants of the earth; because there is neither mercy, nor truth, nor knowledge of God upon the earth. But cursing, and lying, and killing, and stealing, and committing adultery, is broken out over the land, they mingle blood with blood. Therefore shall the land mourn, with everyone that dwelleth therein, with the beasts of the field, with things that creep on the earth, and with the

fowls of heaven; and the fishes of the sea shall languish, so that no man shall judge, no man shall rebuke." God says He is wrathful and angry, because there is no acknowledgment of God in the earth, and God is neither known nor feared. The sins of lying, of lust, of fraud, of cruelty, of impiety, of anger, God rebukes and finds fault with, and no one is converted to innocence. Lo, those things are happening which were before foretold by the words of God; nor is anyone admonished by the belief of things present to take thought for what is to come. Amongst those very misfortunes wherein the soul, closely bound and shut up, can scarcely breathe, there is still found opportunity for men to be evil, and in such great dangers to judge not so much of themselves as of others. You are indignant that God is angry, as if by an evil life you were deserving any good, as if all things of that kind which happen were not infinitely less and of smaller account than your sins.

10. You who judge others, be for once also a judge of yourself; look into the hiding places of your own conscience; nay, since now there is not even any shame in your sin, and you are wicked, as if it were rather the very wickedness itself that pleased you, do you, who are seen clearly and nakedly by all other men, yourself also look upon yourself. For either you are swollen with pride, or greedy with avarice, or cruel with anger, or prodigal with gambling, or flushed with intemperance, or envious with jealousy, or unchaste with lust, or violent with cruelty; and do you wonder that God's anger increases in punishing the human race, when the sin that is punished is daily increasing? You complain that the enemy rises up, as if, though an enemy were wanting, there could be peace for you even among the very togas of peace. You

complain that the enemy rises up, as if, even although external arms and dangers from barbarians were repressed, the weapons of domestic assault from the calumnies and wrongs of powerful citizens, would not be more ferocious and more harshly wielded within. You complain of barrenness and famine, as if drought made a greater famine than rapacity, as if the fierceness of want did not increase more terribly from grasping at the increase of the year's produce, and the accumulation of their price. You complain that the heaven is shut up from showers, although in the same way the barns are shut up on earth. You complain that now less is produced, as if what had already been produced were given to the indigent. You reproach plague and disease, while by plague itself and disease the crimes of individuals are either detected or increased, while mercy is not manifested to the weak, and avarice and rapine are waiting open-mouthed for the dead. The same men are timid in the duties of affection, but rash in quest of implores gains; shunning the deaths of the dying, and craving the spoils of the dead, so that it may appear as if the wretched are probably forsaken in their sickness for this cause, that they may not, by being cured, escape: for he who enters so eagerly upon the estate of the dying, probably desired the sick man to perish.

    11. So great a terror of destruction cannot give the teaching of innocence; and in the midst of a people dying with constant havoc, nobody considers that he himself is mortal. Everywhere there is scattering, there is seizure, there is taking possession; no dissimulation about spoiling, and no delay. As if it were all lawful, as if it were all becoming, as if he who does not rob were suffering loss and wasting his own property, thus

everyone hastens to the rapine. Among thieves there is at any rate some modesty in their crimes. They love pathless ravines and deserted solitudes; and they do wrong in such a way, that still the crime of the wrong doers is veiled by darkness and night. Avarice, however, rages openly, and, safe by its very boldness, exposes the weapons of its headlong craving in the light of the marketplace. Thence cheats, thence poisoners, thence assassins in the midst of the city, are as eager for wickedness as they are wicked with impunity. The crime is committed by the guilty, and the guiltless who can avenge it is not found. There is no fear from accuser or judge: the wicked obtain impunity, while modest men are silent; accomplices are afraid, and those who are to judge are for sale. And therefore by the mouth of the prophet the truth of the matter is put forth with the divine spirit and instinct: it is shown in a certain and obvious way that God can prevent adverse things, but that the evil deserts of sinners prevent His bringing aid. "Is the Lord's hand," says he, "not strong to save you; or has He made heavy His ear, that He cannot hear you? But your sins separate between you and God; and because of your sins He hath hid His face from you, that He may not have mercy." Therefore let your sins and offences be reckoned up; let the wounds of your conscience be considered; and let each one cease complaining about God, or about us, if he should perceive that himself deserves what he suffers.

12. Look what that very matter is of which is chiefly our discourse—that you molest us, although innocent; that, in contempt of God, you attack and oppress God's servants. It is little, in your account, that your life is stained with a variety of gross vices, with the iniquity of deadly crimes, with the summary of all bloody

rapines; that true religion is overturned by false superstitions; that God is neither sought at all, nor feared at all; but over and above this, you weary God's servants, and those who are dedicated to His majesty and His name, with unjust persecutions. It is not enough that you yourself do not worship God, but, over and above, you persecute those who do worship, with a sacrilegious hostility. You neither worship God, nor do you at all permit Him to be worshipped; and while others who venerate not only those foolish idols and images made by man's hands, but even portents and monsters besides, are pleasing to you, it is only the worshipper of God who is displeasing to you. The ashes of victims and the piles of cattle everywhere smoke in your temples, and God's altars are either nowhere or are hidden. Crocodiles, and apes, and stones, and serpents are worshipped by you; and God alone in the earth is not worshipped, or if worshipped, not with impunity. You deprive the innocent, the just, the dear to God, of their home; you spoil them of their estate, you load them with chains, you shut them up in prison, you punish them with the sword, with the wild beasts, with the flames. Nor, indeed, are you content with a brief endurance of our sufferings, and with a simple and swift exhaustion of pains. You set on foot tedious tortures, by tearing our bodies; you multiply numerous punishments, by lacerating our vitals; nor can your brutality and fierceness be content with ordinary tortures; your ingenious cruelty devises new sufferings.

13. What is this insatiable madness for bloodshedding, what this interminable lust of cruelty? Rather make your election of one of two alternatives. To be a Christian is either a crime, or it is not. If it be a crime, why do you not put the man that confesses it to death? If

it be not a crime, why do you persecute an innocent man? For I ought to be put to torture if I denied it. If in fear of your punishment I should conceal, by a deceitful falsehood, what I had previously been, and the fact that I had not worshipped your gods, then I might deserve to be tormented, then I ought to be compelled to confession of my crime by the power of suffering, as in other examinations the guilty, who deny that they are guilty of the crime of which they are accused, are tortured in order that the confession of the reality of the crime, which the tell-tale voice refuses to make, may be wrung out by the bodily suffering. But now, when of my own free will I confess, and cry out, and with words frequent and repeated to the same effect bear witness that I am a Christian, why do you apply tortures to one who avows it, and who destroys your gods, not in hidden and secret places, but openly, and publicly, and in the very market-place, in the hearing of your magistrates and governors; so that, although it was a slight thing which you blamed in me before, that which you ought rather to hate and punish has increased, that by declaring myself a Christian in a frequented place, and with the people standing around, I am confounding both you and your gods by an open and public announcement?

14. Why do you turn your attention to the weakness of our body? why do you strive with the feebleness of this earthly flesh? Contend rather with the strength of the mind, break down the power of the soul, destroy our faith, conquer if you can by discussion, overcome by reason; or, if your gods have any deity and power, let them themselves rise to their own vindication, let them defend themselves by their own majesty. But what can they advantage their worshippers, if they cannot

avenge themselves on those who worship them not? For if he who avenges is of more account than he who is avenged, then you are greater than your gods. And if you are greater than those whom you worship, you ought not to worship them, but rather to be worshipped and feared by them as their lord. Your championship defends them when injured, just as your protection guards them when shut up from perishing. You should be ashamed to worship those whom you yourself defend; you should be ashamed to hope for protection from those whom you yourself protect.

    15. Oh, would you but hear and see them when they are adjured by us, and tortured with spiritual scourges, and are ejected from the possessed bodies with tortures of words, when howling and groaning at the voice of man and the power of God, feeling the stripes and blows, they confess the judgment to come! Come and acknowledge that what we say is true; and since you say that you thus worship gods, believe even those whom you worship. Or if you will even believe yourself, he—i.e., the demon—who has now possessed your breast, who has now darkened your mind with the night of ignorance, shall speak concerning yourself in your hearing. You will see that we are entreated by those whom you entreat, that we are feared by those whom you fear, whom you adore. You will see that under our hands they stand bound, and tremble as captives, whom you look up to and venerate as lords: assuredly even thus you might be confounded in those errors of yours, when you see and hear your gods, at once upon our interrogation betraying what they are, and even in your presence unable to conceal those deceits and trickeries of theirs.

    16. What, then, is that sluggishness of mind; yea,

what blind and stupid madness of fools, to be unwilling to come out of darkness into light, and to be unwilling, when bound in the toils of eternal death, to receive the hope of immortality, and not to fear God when He threatens and says, "He that sacrifices unto any gods, but unto the Lord only, shall be rooted out?" And again: "They worshipped them whom their fingers made; and the mean man hath bowed down, and the great man hath humbled himself, and I will not forgive them." Why do you humble and bend yourself to false gods? Why do you bow your body captive before foolish images and creations of earth? God made you upright; and while other animals are down looking, and are depressed in posture bending towards the earth, yours is a lofty attitude; and your countenance is raised upwards to heaven, and to God. Look thither, lift your eyes thitherward, seek God in the highest, that you may be free from things below; lift your heart to a dependence on high and heavenly things. Why do you prostrate yourself into the ruin of death with the serpent whom you worship? Why do you fall into the destruction of the devil, by his means and in his company? Keep the lofty estate in which you were born. Continue such as you were made by God. To the posture of your countenance and of your body, conform your soul. That you may be able to know God, first know yourself. Forsake the idols which human error has invented. Be turned to God, whom if you implore He will aid you. Believe in Christ, whom3428 the Father has sent to quicken and restore us. Cease to hurt the servants of God and of Christ with your persecutions, since when they are injured the divine vengeance defends them.

17. For this reason it is that none of us, when he is apprehended, makes resistance, nor avenges himself

against your unrighteous violence, although our people are numerous and plentiful. Our certainty of a vengeance to follow makes us patient. The innocent give place to the guilty; the harmless acquiesce in punishments and tortures, sure and confident that whatsoever we suffer will not remain unavenged, and that in proportion to the greatness of the injustice of our persecution so will be the justice and the severity of the vengeance exacted for those persecutions. Nor does the wickedness of the impious ever rise up against the name we bear, without immediate vengeance from above attending it. To say nothing of the memories of ancient times, and not to recur with wordy commemoration to frequently repeated vengeance on behalf of God's worshippers, the instance of a recent matter is sufficient to prove that our defense, so speedily, and in its speed so powerfully, followed of late in the ruins of things, in the destruction of wealth, in the waste of soldiers, and the diminution of forts. Nor let anyone think that this occurred by chance, or think that it was fortuitous, since long ago Scripture has laid down, and said, "Vengeance is mine; I will repay, saith the Lord." And again the Holy Spirit forewarns, and says, "Say not thou, I will avenge myself of mine enemy, but wait on the Lord, that He may be thy help." Whence it is plain and manifest, that not by our means, but for our sakes, all those things are happening which come down from the anger of God.

18. Nor let anybody think that Christians are not avenged by those things that are happening, for the reason that they also themselves seem to be affected by their visitation. A man feels the punishment of worldly adversity, when all his joy and glory are in the world. He grieves and groans if it is ill with him in this life, with

whom it cannot be well after this life, all the fruit of whose life is received here, all whose consolation is ended here, whose fading and brief life here reckons some sweetness and pleasure, but when it has departed hence, there remains for him only punishment added to sorrow. But they have no suffering from the assault of present evils who have confidence in future good things. In fact, we are never prostrated by adversity, nor are we broken down, nor do we grieve or murmur in any external misfortune or weakness of body: living by the Spirit rather than by the flesh, we overcome bodily weakness by mental strength. By those very things which torment and weary us, we know and trust that we are proved and strengthened.

19. Do you think that we suffer adversity equally with yourselves, when you see that the same adverse things are not borne equally by us and by you? Among you there is always a clamorous and complaining impatience; with us there is a strong and religious patience, always quiet and always grateful to God. Nor does it claim for itself anything joyous or prosperous in this world, but, meek and gentle and stable against all the gusts of this tossing world, it waits for the time of the divine promise; for as long as this body endures, it must needs have a common lot with others, and its bodily condition must be common. Nor is it given to any of the human race to be separated one from another, except by withdrawal from this present life. In the meantime, we are all, good and evil, contained in one household. Whatever happens within the house, we suffer with equal fate, until, when the end of the temporal life shall be attained, we shall be distributed among the homes either of eternal death or immortality. Thus, therefore, we are not on the

same level, and equal with you, because, placed in this present world and in this flesh, we incur equally with you the annoyances of the world and of the flesh; for since in the sense of pain is all punishment, it is manifest that he is not a sharer of your punishment who, you see, does not suffer pain equally with yourselves.

20. There flourishes with us the strength of hope and the firmness of faith. Among these very ruins of a decaying world our soul is lifted up, and our courage unshaken: our patience is never anything but joyous; and the mind is always secure of its God, even as the Holy Spirit speaks through the prophet, and exhorts us, strengthening with a heavenly word the firmness of our hope and faith. "The fig-tree," says He, "shall not bear fruit, and there shall be no blossom in the vines. The labor of the olive shall fail, and the fields shall yield no meat. The flock shall be cut off from the fold, and there shall be no herd in the stalls. But I will rejoice in the Lord, and I will joy in the God of my salvation." He says that the man of God and the worshipper of God, depending on the truth of his hope, and founded on the steadfastness of his faith, is not moved by the attacks of this world and this life. Although the vine should fail, and the olive deceive, and the field parched with grass dying with drought should wither, what is this to Christians? what to God's servants whom paradise is inviting, whom all the grace and all the abundance of the kingdom of heaven is waiting for? They always exult in the Lord, and rejoice and are glad in their God; and the evils and adversities of the world they bravely suffer, because they are looking forward to gifts and prosperities to come: for we who have put off our earthly birth, and are now created and regenerated by the Spirit, and no longer live to the world but to God, shall

not receive God's gifts and promises until we arrive at the presence of God. And yet we always ask for the repulse of enemies, and for obtaining showers, and either for the removal or the moderating of adversity; and we pour forth our prayers, and, propitiating and appeasing God, we entreat constantly and urgently, day and night, for your peace and salvation.

21. Let no one, however, flatter himself, because there is for the present to us and to the profane, to God's worshippers and to God's opponents, by reason of the equality of the flesh and body, a common condition of worldly troubles, in such a way as to think from this, that all those things which happen are not drawn down by you; since by the announcement of God Himself, and by prophetic testimony, it has previously been foretold that upon the unjust should come the wrath of God, and that persecutions which humanly would hurt us should not be wanting; but, moreover, that vengeance, which should defend with heavenly defense those who were hurt, should attend them.

22. And how great, too, are those things which in the meantime are happening in that respect on our behalf! Something is given for an example, that the anger of an avenging God may be known. But the day of judgment is still future which the Holy Scripture denounces, saying, "Howl ye, for the day of the Lord is at hand, and destruction from God shall come; for, lo, the day of the Lord cometh, cruel with wrath and anger, to lay the earth desolate, and to destroy the sinners out of it." And again: "Behold, the day of the Lord cometh, burning as an oven; and all the aliens and all that do wickedly shall be as stubble, and the day that cometh shall burn them up, saith the Lord." The Lord prophesies that the aliens shall be

burnt up and consumed; that is, aliens from the divine race, and the profane, those who are not spiritually new-born, nor made children of God. For that those only can escape who have been new-born and signed with the sign of Christ, God says in another place, when, sending forth His angels to the destruction of the world and the death of the human race, He threatens more terribly in the last time, saying, "Go ye, and smite, and let not your eye spare. Have no pity upon old or young, and slay the virgins and the little ones and the women, that they may be utterly destroyed. But touch not any man upon whom is written the mark." Moreover, what this mark is, and in what part of the body it is placed, God sets forth in another place, saying, "Go through the midst of Jerusalem, and set a mark upon the foreheads of the men that sigh and that cry for all the abominations that be done in the midst thereof." And that the sign pertains to the passion and blood of Christ, and that whoever is found in this sign is kept safe and unharmed, is also proved by God's testimony, saying, "And the blood shall be to you for a token upon the houses in which ye shall be; and I will see the blood, and will protect you, and the plague of diminution shall not be upon you when I smite the land of Egypt." What previously preceded by a figure in the slain lamb is fulfilled in Christ, the truth which followed afterwards. As, then, when Egypt was smitten, the Jewish people could not escape except by the blood and the sign of the lamb; so also, when the world shall begin to be desolated and smitten, whoever is found in the blood and the sign of Christ alone shall escape.

23. Look, therefore, while there is time, to the true and eternal salvation; and since now the end of the world is at hand, turn your minds to God, in the fear of God; nor

let that powerless and vain dominion in the world over the just and meek delight you, since in the field, even among the cultivated and fruitful corn, the tares and the darnel have dominion. Nor say ye that ill fortunes happen because your gods are not worshipped by us; but know that this is the judgment of God's anger, that He who is not acknowledged on account of His benefits may at least be acknowledged through His judgments. Seek the Lord even late; for long ago, God, forewarning by His prophet, exhorts and says, "Seek ye the Lord, and your soul shall live." Know God even late; for Christ at His coming admonishes and teaches this, saying, "This is life eternal, that they might know Thee, the only true God, and Jesus Christ, whom Thou hast sent." Believe Him who deceives not at all. Believe Him who foretold that all these things should come to pass. Believe Him who will give to all that believe the reward of eternal life. Believe Him who will call down on them that believe not, eternal punishments in the fires of Gehenna.

24. What will then be the glory of faith? what the punishment of faithlessness? When the day of judgment shall come, what joy of believers, what sorrow of unbelievers; that they should have been unwilling to believe here, and now that they should be unable to return that they might believe! An ever-burning Gehenna will burn up the condemned, and a punishment devouring with living flames; nor will there be any source whence at any time they may have either respite or end to their torments. Souls with their bodies will be reserved in infinite tortures for suffering. Thus the man will be for ever seen by us who here gazed upon us for a season; and the short joy of those cruel eyes in the persecutions that they made for us will be compensated by a perpetual

spectacle, according to the truth of Holy Scripture, which says, "Their worm shall not die, and their fire shall not be quenched; and they shall be for a vision to all flesh." And again: "Then shall the righteous men stand in great constancy before the face of those who have afflicted them, and have taken away their labors. When they see it, they shall be troubled with horrible fear, and shall be amazed at the suddenness of their unexpected salvation; and they, repenting and groaning for anguish of spirit, shall say within themselves, These are they whom we had some time in derision, and a proverb of reproach; we fools counted their life madness, and their end to be without honor. How are they numbered among the children of God, and their lot is among the saints! Therefore have we erred from the way of truth, and the light of righteousness hath not shined upon us, and the sun rose not on us. We wearied ourselves in the way of wickedness and destruction; we have gone through deserts where there lay no way; but we have not known the way of the Lord. What hath pride profited us, or what good hath the boasting of riches done us? All those things are passed away like a shadow." The pain of punishment will then be without the fruit of penitence; weeping will be useless, and prayer ineffectual. Too late they will believe in eternal punishment who would not believe in eternal life.

25. Provide, therefore, while you may, for your safety and your life. We offer you the wholesome help of our mind and advice. And because we may not hate, and we please God more by rendering no return for wrong, we exhort you while you have the power, while there yet remains to you something of life, to make satisfaction to God, and to emerge from the abyss of darkling

superstition into the bright light of true religion. We do not envy your comforts, nor do we conceal the divine benefits. We repay kindness for your hatred; and for the torments and penalties which are inflicted on us, we point out to you the ways of salvation. Believe and live, and do ye who persecute us in time rejoice with us for eternity. When you have once departed thither, there is no longer any place for repentance, and no possibility of making satisfaction. Here life is either lost or saved; here eternal safety is provided for by the worship of God and the fruits of faith. Nor let anyone be restrained either by his sins or by his years from coming to obtain salvation. To him who still remains in this world no repentance is too late. The approach to God's mercy is open, and the access is easy to those who seek and apprehend the truth. Do you entreat for your sins, although it be in the very end of life, and at the setting of the sun of time; and implore God, who is the one and true God, in confession and faith of acknowledgment of Him, and pardon is granted to the man who confesses, and saving mercy is given from the divine goodness to the believer, and a passage is opened to immortality even in death itself. This grace Christ bestows; this gift of His mercy He confers upon us, by overcoming death in the trophy of the cross, by redeeming the believer with the price of His blood, by reconciling man to God the Father, by quickening our mortal nature with a heavenly regeneration. If it be possible, let us all follow Him; let us be registered in His sacrament and sign. He opens to us the way of life; He brings us back to paradise; He leads us on to the kingdom of heaven. Made by Him the children of God, with Him we shall ever live; with Him we shall always rejoice, restored by His own blood. We Christians shall be glorious together with

Christ, blessed of God the Father, always rejoicing with perpetual pleasures in the sight of God, and ever giving thanks to God. For none can be other than always glad and grateful, who, having been once subject to death, has been made secure in the possession of immortality.

Treatise VI.

On the Vanity of Idols: Showing that the Idols are Not Gods, and that God is One, and that Through Christ Salvation is Given to Believers.

Argument.—This Heading Embraces the Three Leading Divisions of This Treatise. The Writer First of All Shows that They in Whose Honor Temples Were Founded, Statues Modelled, Victims Sacrificed, and Festal Days Celebrated, Were Kings and Men and Not Gods; And Therefore that Their Worship Could Be of No Avail Either to Strangers or to Romans, and that the Power of the Roman Empire Was to Attributed to Fate Rather Than to Them, Inasmuch as It Had Arisen by a Certain Good Fortune, and Was Ashamed of Its Own Origin.

1. That those are no gods whom the common people worship, is known from this. They were formerly kings, who on account of their royal memory subsequently began to be adored by their people even in death. Thence temples were founded to them; thence images were sculptured to retain the countenances of the deceased by the likeness; and men sacrificed victims, and celebrated festal days, by way of giving them honor. Thence to posterity those rites became sacred, which at first had been adopted as a consolation. And now let us see whether this truth is confirmed in individual instances.

2. Melicertes and Leucothea are precipitated into

the sea, and subsequently become sea divinities. The Castors die by turns, that they may live. Æsculapius is struck by lightning, that he may rise into a god. Hercules, that he may put off the man, is burnt up in the fires of Œta. Apollo fed the flocks of Admetus; Neptune founded walls for Laomedon, and received—unfortunate builder—no wages for his work. The cave of Jupiter is to be seen in Crete, and his sepulcher is shown; and it is manifest that Saturn was driven away by him, and that from him Latium received its name, as being his lurking-place. He was the first that taught to print letters; he was the first that taught to stamp money in Italy, and thence the treasury is called the treasury of Saturn. And he also was the cultivator of the rustic life, whence he is painted as an old man carrying a sickle. Janus had received him to hospitality when he was driven away, from whose name the Janiculum is so called, and the month of January is appointed. He himself is portrayed with two faces, because, placed in the middle, he seems to look equally towards the commencing and the closing year. The Mauri, indeed, manifestly worship kings, and do not conceal their name by any disguise.

3. From this the religion of the gods is variously changed among individual nations and provinces, inasmuch as no one god is worshipped by all, but by each one the worship of its own ancestors is kept peculiar. Proving that this is so, Alexander the Great writes in the remarkable volume addressed to his mother, that through fear of his power the doctrine of the gods being men, which was kept secret, had been disclosed to him by a priest, that it was the memory of ancestors and kings that was (really) kept up, and that from this the rites of worship and sacrifice have grown up. But if gods were

born at any time, why are they not born in these days also?—unless, indeed, Jupiter possibly has grown too old, or the faculty of bearing has failed Juno.

4. But why do you think that the gods can avail on behalf of the Romans, when you see that they can do nothing for their own worshipers in opposition to the Roman arms? For we know that the gods of the Romans are indigenous. Romulus was made a god by the perjury of Proculus, and Picus, and Tiberinus, and Pilumnus, and Consus, whom as a god of treachery Romulus would have to be worshipped, just as if he had been a god of counsels, when his perfidy resulted in the rape of the Sabines. Tatius also both invented and worshipped the goddess Cloacina; Hostilius, Fear and Paleness. By and by, I know not by whom, Fever was dedicated, and Acca and Flora the harlots. These are the Roman gods. But Mars is a Thracian, and Jupiter a Cretan, and Juno either Argive or Samian or Carthaginian, and Diana of Taurus, and the mother of the gods of Ida; and there are Egyptian monsters, not deities, who assuredly, if they had had any power, would have preserved their own and their people's kingdoms. Certainly there are also among the Romans the conquered Penates whom the fugitive Æneas introduced thither. There is also Venus the bald,—far more dishonored by the fact of her baldness in Rome than by her having been wounded in Homer.

5. Kingdoms do not rise to supremacy through merit, but are varied by chance. Empire was formerly held by both Assyrians and Medes and Persians; and we know, too, that both Greeks and Egyptians have had dominion. Thus, in the varying vicissitudes of power, the period of empire has also come to the Romans as to the others. But if you recur to its origin, you must needs blush. A people

are collected together from profligates and criminals, and by founding an asylum, impunity for crimes makes the number great; and that their king himself may have a superiority in crime, Romulus becomes a fratricide; and in order to promote marriage, he makes a beginning of that affair of concord by discords. They steal, they commit violence, they deceive in order to increase the population of the state; their marriage consists of the broken covenants of hospitality and cruel wars with their fathers-in-law. The consulship, moreover, is the highest degree in Roman honors, yet we see that the consulship began even as did the kingdom. Brutus puts his sons to death, that the commendation of his dignity may increase by the approval of his wickedness. The Roman kingdom, therefore, did not grow from the sanctities of religion, nor from auspices and auguries, but it keeps its appointed time within a definite limit. Moreover, Regulus observed the auspices, yet was taken prisoner; and Mancinus observed their religious obligation, yet was sent under the yoke. Paulus had chickens that fed, and yet he was slain at Cannæ. Caius Cæsar despised the auguries and auspices that were opposed to his sending ships before the winter to Africa; yet so much more easily he both sailed and conquered.

6. Of all these, however, the principle is the same, which misleads and deceives, and with tricks which darken the truth, leads away a credulous and foolish rabble. They are impure and wandering spirits, who, after having been steeped in earthly vices, have departed from their celestial vigor by the contagion of earth, and do not cease, when ruined themselves, to seek the ruin of others; and when degraded themselves, to infuse into others the error of their own degradation. These demons the poets

also acknowledge, and Socrates declared that he was instructed and ruled at the will of a demon; and thence the Magi have a power either for mischief or for mockery, of whom, however, the chief Hostanes both says that the form of the true God cannot be seen, and declares that true angels stand round about His throne. Wherein Plato also on the same principle concurs, and, maintaining one God, calls the rest angels or demons. Moreover, Hermes Trismegistus speaks of one God, and confesses that He is incomprehensible, and beyond our estimation.

7. These spirits, therefore, are lurking under the statues and consecrated images: these inspire the breasts of their prophets with their afflatus, animate the fibers of the entrails, direct the flights of birds, rule the lots, give efficiency to oracles, are always mixing up falsehood with truth, for they are both deceived and they deceive; they disturb their life, they disquiet their slumbers; their spirits creeping also into their bodies, secretly terrify their minds, distort their limbs, break their health, excite diseases to force them to worship of themselves, so that when glutted with the steam of the altars and the piles of cattle, they may unloose what they had bound, and so appear to have effected a cure. The only remedy from them is when their own mischief ceases; nor have they any other desire than to call men away from God, and to turn them from the understanding of the true religion, to superstition with respect to themselves; and since they themselves are under punishment, (they wish) to seek for themselves companions in punishment whom they may by their misguidance make sharers in their crime. These, however, when adjured by us through the true God, at once yield and confess, and are constrained to go out from the bodies possessed. You may see them at our voice, and

by the operation of the hidden majesty, smitten with stripes, burnt with fire, stretched out with the increase of a growing punishment, howling, groaning, entreating, confessing whence they came and when depart, even in the hearing of those very persons who worship them, and either springing forth at once or vanishing gradually, even as the faith of the sufferer comes in aid, or the grace of the healer effects. Hence they urge the common people to detest our name, so that men begin to hate us before they know us, lest they should either imitate us if known, or not be able to condemn us.

8. Therefore the one Lord of all is God. For that sublimity cannot possibly have any compeer, since it alone possesses all power. Moreover, let us borrow an illustration for the divine government from the earth. When ever did an alliance in royalty either begin with good faith or end without bloodshed? Thus the brotherhood of the Thebans was broken, and discord endured even in death in their disunited ashes. And one kingdom could not contain the Roman twins, although the shelter of one womb had held them. Pompey and Cæsar were kinsmen, and yet they did not maintain the bond of their relationship in their envious power. Neither should you marvel at this in respect of man, since herein all nature consents. The bees have one king, and in the flocks there is one leader, and in the herds one ruler. Much rather is the Ruler of the world one; who commands all things, whatsoever they are, with His word, disposes them by His wisdom, and accomplishes them by His power.

9. He cannot be seen—He is too bright for vision; nor comprehended—He is too pure for our discernment; nor estimated—He is too great for our perception; and therefore we are only worthily estimating Him when we

say that He is inconceivable. But what temple can God have, whose temple is the whole world? And while man dwells far and wide, shall I shut up the power of such great majesty within one small building? He must be dedicated in our mind; in our breast He must be consecrated. Neither must you ask the name of God. God is His name. Among those there is need of names where a multitude is to be distinguished by the appropriate characteristics of appellations. To God who alone is, belongs the whole name of God; therefore He is one, and He in His entirety is everywhere diffused. For even the common people in many things naturally confess God, when their mind and soul are admonished of their author and origin. We frequently hear it said, "O God," and "God sees," and "I commend to God," and "God give you," and "as God will," and "if God should grant;" and this is the very height of sinfulness, to refuse to acknowledge Him whom you cannot but know.

10. But that Christ is, and in what way salvation came to us through Him, after this manner is the plan, after this manner is the means. First of all, favor with God was given to the Jews. Thus they of old were righteous; thus their ancestors were obedient to their religious engagements. Thence with them both the loftiness of their rule flourished, and the greatness of their race advanced. But subsequently becoming neglectful of discipline, proud, and puffed up with confidence in their fathers, they despised the divine precepts, and lost the favor conferred upon them. But how profane became their life, what offence to their violated religion was contracted, even they themselves bear witness, since, although they are silent with their voice, they confess it by their end. Scattered and straggling, they wander about; outcasts

from their own soil and climate, they are thrown upon the hospitality of strangers.

11. Moreover, God had previously foretold that it would happen, that as the ages passed on, and the end of the world was near at hand, God would gather to Himself from every nation, and people, and place, worshippers much better in obedience and stronger in faith, who would draw from the divine gift that mercy which the Jews had received and lost by despising their religious ordinances. Therefore of this mercy and grace the Word and Son of God is sent as the dispenser and master, who by all the prophets of old was announced as the enlightener and teacher of the human race. He is the power of God, He is the reason, He is His wisdom and glory; He enters into a virgin; being the holy Spirit, He is endued with flesh; God is mingled with man. This is our God, this is Christ, who, as the mediator of the two, puts on man that He may lead them to the Father. What man is, Christ was willing to be, that man also may be what Christ is.

12. And the Jews knew that Christ was to come, for He was always being announced to them by the warnings of prophets. But His advent being signified to them as twofold—the one which should discharge the office and example of a man, the other which should avow Him as God—they did not understand the first advent which preceded, as being hidden in His passion, but believe in the one only which will be manifest in power. But that the people of the Jews could not understand this, was the desert of their sins. They were so punished by their blindness of wisdom and intelligence, that they who were unworthy of life, had life before their eyes, and saw it not.

13. Therefore when Christ Jesus, in accordance

with what had been previously foretold by the prophets, drove out from men the demons by His word, and by the command of His voice nerved up the paralytics, cleansed the leprous, enlightened the blind, gave power of movement to the lame, raised the dead again, compelled the elements to obey Him as servants, the winds to serve Him, the seas to obey Him, the lower regions to yield to Him; the Jews, who had believed Him man only from the humility of His flesh and body, regarded Him as a sorcerer for the authority of His power. Their masters and leaders—that is, those whom He subdued both by learning and wisdom—inflamed with wrath and stimulated with indignation, finally seized Him and delivered Him to Pontius Pilate, who was then the procurator of Syria on behalf of the Romans, demanding with violent and obstinate urgency His crucifixion and death.

14. That they would do this He Himself also had foretold; and the testimony of all the prophets had in like manner preceded Him, that it behooved Him to suffer, not that He might feel death, but that He might conquer death, and that, when He should have suffered, He should return again into heaven, to show the power of the divine majesty. Therefore the course of events fulfilled the promise. For when crucified, the office of the executioner being forestalled, He Himself of His own will yielded up His spirit, and on the third day freely rose again from the dead. He appeared to His disciples like as He had been. He gave Himself to the recognition of those that saw Him, associated together with Him; and being evident by the substance of His bodily existence, He delayed for forty days, that they might be instructed by Him in the precepts of life, and might learn what they were to teach. Then in a

cloud spread around Him He was lifted up into heaven, that as a conqueror He might bring to the Father, Man whom He loved, whom He put on, whom He shielded from death; soon to come from heaven for the punishment of the devil and to the judgment of the human race, with the force of an avenger and with the power of a judge; whilst the disciples, scattered over the world, at the bidding of their Master and God gave forth His precepts for salvation, guided men from their wandering in darkness to the way of light, and gave eyes to the blind and ignorant for the acknowledgment of the truth.

15. And that the proof might not be the less substantial, and the confession of Christ might not be a matter of pleasure, they are tried by tortures, by crucifixions, by many kinds of punishments. Pain, which is the test of truth, is brought to bear, that Christ the Son of God, who is trusted in as given to men for their life, might not only be announced by the heralding of the voice, but by the testimony of suffering. Therefore we accompany Him, we follow Him, we have Him as the Guide of our way, the Source of light, the Author of salvation, promising as well the Father as heaven to those who seek and believe. What Christ is, we Christians shall be, if we imitate Christ.

Treatise VII.
On the Mortality.
Argument.—The Deacon Pontius in a Few Words Unfolds the Burthen of This Treatise in His Life of Cyprian. First of All, Having Pointed Out that Afflictions of This Kind Had Been Foretold by Christ, He Tells

Them that the Mortality or Plague Was Not to Be Feared, in that It Leads to Immortality, and that Therefore, that Man is Wanting in Faith Who is Not Eager for a Better World. Nor is It Wonderful that the Evils of This Life are Common to the Christians with the Heathens, Since They Have to Suffer More Than Others in the World, and Thence, After the Example of Job and Tobias, There is Need of Patience Without Murmuring. For Unless the Struggle Preceded, the Victory Could Not Ensue; And How Much Soever Diseases are Common to the Virtuous and Vicious, Yet that Death is Not Common to Them, for that the Righteous are Taken to Consolation, While the Unrighteous are Taken to Punishment.

1. Although in very many of you, dearly beloved brethren, there is a steadfast mind and a firm faith, and a devoted spirit that is not disturbed at the frequency of this present mortality, but, like a strong and stable rock, rather shatters the turbulent onsets of the world and the raging waves of time, while it is not itself shattered, and is not overcome but tried by these temptations; yet because I observe that among the people some, either through weakness of mind, or through decay of faith, or through the sweetness of this worldly life, or through the softness of their sex, or what is of still greater account, through error from the truth, are standing less steadily, and are not exerting the divine and unvanquished vigor of their heart, the matter may not be disguised nor kept in silence, but as far as my feeble powers suffice with my full strength, and with a discourse gathered from the Lord's lessons, the slothfulness of a luxurious disposition must be restrained, and he who has begun to be already a man of God and of Christ, must be found worthy of God and of Christ.

2. For he who wars for God, dearest brethren,

ought to acknowledge himself as one who, placed in the heavenly camp, already hopes for divine things, so that we may have no trembling at the storms and whirlwinds of the world, and no disturbance, since the Lord had foretold that these would come. With the exhortation of His fore-seeing word, instructing, and teaching, and preparing, and strengthening the people of His Church for all endurance of things to come, He predicted and said that wars, and famines, and earthquakes, and pestilences would arise in each place; and lest an unexpected and new dread of mischiefs should shake us, He previously warned us that adversity would increase more and more in the last times. Behold, the very things occur which were spoken; and since those occur which were foretold before, whatever things were promised will also follow; as the Lord Himself promises, saying, "But when ye see all these things come to pass, know ye that the kingdom of God is at hand." The kingdom of God, beloved brethren, is beginning to be at hand; the reward of life, and the rejoicing of eternal salvation, and the perpetual gladness and possession lately lost of paradise, are now coming, with the passing away of the world; already heavenly things are taking the place of earthly, and great things of small, and eternal things of things that fade away. What room is there here for anxiety and solicitude? Who, in the midst of these things, is trembling and sad, except he who is without hope and faith? For it is for him to fear death who is not willing to go to Christ. It is for him to be unwilling to go to Christ who does not believe that he is about to reign with Christ.

3. For it is written that the just live by faith. If you are just, and live by faith, if you truly believe in Christ, why, since you are about to be with Christ, and are secure

of the Lord's promise, do you not embrace the assurance that you are called to Christ, and rejoice that you are freed from the devil? Certainly Simeon, that just man, who was truly just, who kept God's commands with a full faith, when it had been pledged him from heaven that he should not die before he had seen the Christ, and Christ had come an infant into the temple with His mother, acknowledged in spirit that Christ was now born, concerning whom it had before been foretold to him; and when he had seen Him, he knew that he should soon die. Therefore, rejoicing concerning his now approaching death, and secure of his immediate summons, he received the child into his arms, and blessing the Lord, he exclaimed, and said, "Now let Thou Thy servant depart in peace, according to Thy word; for mine eyes have seen Thy salvation;" assuredly proving and bearing witness that the servants of God then had peace, then free, then tranquil repose, when, withdrawn from these whirlwinds of the world, we attain the harbor of our home and eternal security, when having accomplished this death we come to immortality. For that is our peace, that our faithful tranquility, that our steadfast, and abiding, and perpetual security.

4. But for the rest, what else in the world than a battle against the devil is daily carried on, than a struggle against his darts and weapons in constant conflicts? Our warfare is with avarice, with immodesty, with anger, with ambition; our diligent and toilsome wrestle with carnal vices, with enticements of the world. The mind of man besieged, and in every quarter invested with the onsets of the devil, scarcely in each point meets the attack, scarcely resists it. If avarice is prostrated, lust springs up. If lust is overcome, ambition takes its place. If ambition is

despised, anger exasperates, pride puffs up, winebibbing entices, envy breaks concord, jealousy cuts friendship; you are constrained to curse, which the divine law forbids; you are compelled to swear, which is not lawful.

5. So many persecutions the soul suffers daily, with so many risks is the heart wearied, and yet it delights to abide here long among the devil's weapons, although it should rather be our craving and wish to hasten to Christ by the aid of a quicker death; as He Himself instructs us, and says, "Verily, verily, I say unto you, That ye shall weep and lament, but the world shall rejoice; and ye shall be sorrowful, but your sorrow shall be turned into joy." Who would not desire to be without sadness? who would not hasten to attain to joy? But when our sadness shall be turned into joy, the Lord Himself again declares, when He says, "I will see you again, and your heart shall rejoice; and your joy no man shall take from you." Since, therefore, to see Christ is to rejoice, and we cannot have joy unless when we shall see Christ, what blindness of mind or what folly is it to love the world's afflictions, and punishments, and tears, and not rather to hasten to the joy which can never be taken away!

6. But, beloved brethren, this is so, because faith is lacking, because no one believes that the things which God promises are true, although He is true, whose word to believers is eternal and unchangeable. If a grave and praiseworthy man should promise you anything, you would assuredly have faith in the promiser, and would not think that you should be cheated and deceived by him whom you knew to be steadfast in his words and his deeds. Now God is speaking with you; and do you faithlessly waver in your unbelieving mind? God promises to you, on your departure from this world,

immortality and eternity; and do you doubt? This is not to know God at all; this is to offend Christ, the Teacher of believers, with the sin of incredulity; this is for one established in the Church not to have faith in the house of faith.

7. How great is the advantage of going out of the world, Christ Himself, the Teacher of our salvation and of our good works, shows to us, who, when His disciples were saddened that He said that He was soon to depart, spoke to them, and said, "If ye loved me, ye would surely rejoice because I go to the Father;" teaching thereby, and manifesting that when the dear ones whom we love depart from the world, we should rather rejoice than grieve. Remembering which truth, the blessed Apostle Paul in his epistle lays it down, saying, "To me to live is Christ, and to die is gain;" counting it the greatest gain no longer to be held by the snares of this world, no longer to be liable to the sins and vices of the flesh, but taken away from smarting troubles, and freed from the envenomed fangs of the devil, to go at the call of Christ to the joy of eternal salvation.

8. But nevertheless it disturbs some that the power of this Disease attacks our people equally with the heathens, as if the Christian believed for this purpose, that he might have the enjoyment of the world and this life free from the contact of ills; and not as one who undergoes all adverse things here and is reserved for future joy. It disturbs some that this mortality is common to us with others; and yet what is there in this world which is not common to us with others, so long as this flesh of ours still remains, according to the law of our first birth, common to us with them? So long as we are here in the world, we are associated with the human race in

fleshly equality, but are separated in spirit. Therefore until this corruptible shall put on incorruption, and this mortal receive immortality, and the Spirit lead us to God the Father, whatsoever are the disadvantages of the flesh are common to us with the human race. Thus, when the earth is barren with an unproductive harvest, famine makes no distinction; thus, when with the invasion of an enemy any city is taken, captivity at once desolates all; and when the serene clouds withhold the rain, the drought is alike to all; and when the jagged rocks rend the ship, the shipwreck is common without exception to all that sail in her; and the disease of the eyes, and the attack of fevers, and the feebleness of all the limbs is common to us with others, so long as this common flesh of ours is borne by us in the world.

9. Moreover, if the Christian know and keep fast under what condition and what law he has believed, he will be aware that he must suffer more than others in the world, since he must struggle more with the attacks of the devil. Holy Scripture teaches and forewarns, saying, "My son, when thou comes to the service of God, stand in righteousness and fear, and prepare thy soul for temptation." And again: "In pain endure, and in thy humility have patience; for gold and silver is tried in the fire, but acceptable men in the furnace of humiliation."

10. Thus Job, after the loss of his wealth, after the death of his children, grievously afflicted, moreover, with sores and worms, was not overcome, but proved; since in his very struggles and anguish, showing forth the patience of a religious mind, he says, "Naked came I out of my mother's womb, naked also I shall go under the earth: the Lord gave, the Lord hath taken away; as it seemed fit to the Lord, so it hath been done. Blessed be the name of the

Lord." And when his wife also urged him, in his impatience at the acuteness of his pain, to speak something against God with a complaining and envious voice, he answered and said, "You speak as one of the foolish women. If we have received good from the hand of the Lord, why shall we not suffer evil? In all these things which befell him, Job sinned not with his lips in the sight of the Lord." Therefore the Lord God gives him a testimony, saying, "Hast thou considered my servant Job? for there is none like him in all the earth, a man without complaint, a true worshipper of God." And Tobias, after his excellent works, after the many and glorious illustrations of his merciful spirit, having suffered the loss of his sight, fearing and blessing God in his adversity, by his very bodily affliction increased in praise; and even him also his wife tried to pervert, saying, "Where are thy righteousnesses? Behold what thou suffers!" But he, steadfast and firm in respect of the fear of God, and armed by the faith of his religion to all endurance of suffering, yielded not to the temptation of his weak wife in his trouble, but rather deserved better from God by his greater patience; and afterwards Raphael the angel praises him, saying, "It is honorable to show forth and to confess the works of God. For when thou didst pray, and Sara thy daughter-in-law, I did offer the remembrance of your prayer in the presence of the glory of God. And when thou didst bury the dead in singleness of heart, and because thou didst not delay to rise up and leave thy dinner, and went and didst bury the dead, I was sent to make proof of thee. And God again hath sent me to heal thee and Sara thy daughter-in-law. For I am Raphael, one of the seven holy angels, who are present, and go in and out before the glory of God."

11. Righteous men have ever possessed this endurance. The apostles maintained this discipline from the law of the Lord, not to murmur in adversity, but to accept bravely and patiently whatever things happen in the world; since the people of the Jews in this matter always offended, that they constantly murmured against God, as the Lord God bears witness in the book of Numbers, saying, "Let their murmuring cease from me, and they shall not die." We must not murmur in adversity, beloved brethren, but we must bear with patience and courage whatever happens, since it is written, "The sacrifice to God is a broken spirit; a contrite and humbled heart God does not despise;" since also in Deuteronomy the Holy Spirit warns by Moses, and says, "The Lord thy God will vex thee, and will bring hunger upon thee; and it shall be known in thine heart if thou hast well-kept His commandments or no." And again: "The Lord your God proved you, that He may know whether ye love the Lord your God with all your heart, and with all your soul."

12. Thus Abraham pleased God, who, that he might please God, did not shrink even from losing his son, or from doing an act of parricide. You, who cannot endure to lose your son by the law and lot of mortality, what would you do if you were bidden to slay your son? The fear and faith of God ought to make you prepared for everything, although it should be the loss of private estate, although the constant and cruel harassment of your limbs by agonizing disorders, although the deadly and mournful wrench from wife, from children, from departing dear ones; Let not these things be offences to you, but battles: nor let them weaken nor break the Christian's faith, but rather show forth his strength in the struggle, since all the injury inflicted by present troubles is to be despised in the

assurance of future blessings. Unless the battle has preceded, there cannot be a victory: when there shall have been, in the onset of battle, the victory, then also the crown is given to the victors. For the helmsman is recognized in the tempest; in the warfare the soldier is proved. It is a wanton display when there is no danger. Struggle in adversity is the trial of the truth. The tree which is deeply founded in its root is not moved by the onset of winds, and the ship which is compacted of solid timbers is beaten by the waves and is not shattered; and when the threshing-floor brings out the corn, the strong and robust grains despise the winds, while the empty chaff is carried away by the blast that falls upon it.

13. Thus, moreover, the Apostle Paul, after shipwrecks, after scourging, after many and grievous tortures of the flesh and body, says that he is not grieved, but benefited by his adversity, in order that while he is sorely afflicted he might more truly be proved. "There was given to me," he says, "a thorn in the flesh, the messenger of Satan to buffet me, that I should not be lifted up: for which thing I besought the Lord thrice, that it might depart from me; and He said unto me, My grace is sufficient for thee, for strength is made perfect in weakness." When, therefore, weakness and inefficiency and any destruction seize us, then our strength is made perfect; then our faith, if when tried it shall stand fast, is crowned; as it is written, "The furnace tries the vessels of the potter, and the trial of tribulation just men." This, in short, is the difference between us and others who know not God, that in misfortune they complain and murmur, while adversity does not call us away from the truth of virtue and faith, but strengthens us by its suffering.

14. This trial, that now the bowels, relaxed into a

constant flux, discharge the bodily strength; that a fire originated in the marrow ferments into wounds of the fauces; that the intestines are shaken with a continual vomiting; that the eyes are on fire with the injected blood; that in some cases the feet or some parts of the limbs are taken off by the contagion of diseased putrefaction; that from the weakness arising by the maiming and loss of the body, either the gait is enfeebled, or the hearing is obstructed, or the sight darkened;—is profitable as a proof of faith. What a grandeur of spirit it is to struggle with all the powers of an unshaken mind against so many onsets of devastation and death! what sublimity, to stand erect amid the desolation of the human race, and not to lie prostrate with those who have no hope in God; but rather to rejoice, and to embrace the benefit of the occasion; that in thus bravely showing forth our faith, and by suffering endured, going forward to Christ by the narrow way that Christ trod, we may receive the reward of His life and faith according to His own judgment! Assuredly he may fear to die, who, not being regenerated of water and the Spirit, is delivered over to the fires of Gehenna; he may fear to die who is not enrolled in the cross and passion of Christ; he may fear to die, who from this death shall pass over to a second death; he may fear to die, whom on his departure from this world eternal flame shall torment with never-ending punishments; he may fear to die who has this advantage in a lengthened delay, that in the meanwhile his groanings and his anguish are being postponed.

15. Many of our people die in this mortality, that is, many of our people are liberated from this world. This mortality, as it is a plague to Jews and Gentiles, and enemies of Christ, so it is a departure to salvation to

God's servants. The fact that, without any difference made between one and another, the righteous die as well as the unrighteous, is no reason for you to suppose that it is a common death for the good and evil alike. The righteous are called to their place of refreshing, the unrighteous are snatched away to punishment; safety is the more speedily given to the faithful, penalty to the unbelieving. We are thoughtless and ungrateful, beloved brethren, for the divine benefits, and do not acknowledge what is conferred upon us. Lo, virgins depart in peace, safe with their glory, not fearing the threats of the coming Antichrist, and his corruptions and his brothels. Boys escape the peril of their unstable age, and in happiness attain the reward of continence and innocence. Now the delicate matron does not fear the tortures; for she has escaped by a rapid death the fear of persecution, and the hands and the torments of the executioner. By the dread of the mortality and of the time the lukewarm are inflamed, the slack are nerved up, the slothful are stimulated, the deserters are compelled to return, the heathens are constrained to believe, the ancient congregation of the faithful is called to rest, the new and abundant army is gathered to the battle with a braver vigor, to fight without fear of death when the battle shall come, because it comes to the warfare in the time of the mortality.

16. And further, beloved brethren, what is it, what a great thing is it, how pertinent, how necessary, that pestilence and plague which seems horrible and deadly, searches out the righteousness of each one, and examines the minds of the human race, to see whether they who are in health tend the sick; whether relations affectionately love their kindred; whether masters pity their languishing

servants; whether physicians do not forsake the beseeching patients; whether the fierce suppress their violence; whether the rapacious can quench the ever insatiable ardor of their raging avarice even by the fear of death; whether the haughty bend their neck; whether the wicked soften their boldness; whether, when their dear ones perish, the rich, even then bestow anything, and give, when they are to die without heirs. Even although this mortality conferred nothing else, it has done this benefit to Christians and to God's servants, that we begin gladly to desire martyrdom as we learn not to fear death. These are trainings for us, not deaths: they give the mind the glory of fortitude; by contempt of death they prepare for the crown.

17. But perchance someone may object, and say, "It is this, then, that saddens me in the present mortality, that I, who had been prepared for confession, and had devoted myself to the endurance of suffering with my whole heart and with abundant courage, am deprived of martyrdom, in that I am anticipated by death." In the first place, martyrdom is not in your power, but in the condescension of God; neither can you say that you have lost what you do not know whether you would deserve to receive. Then, besides, God the searcher of the reins and heart, and the investigator and knower of secret things, sees you, and praises and approves you; and He who sees that your virtue was ready in you, will give you a reward for your virtue. Had Cain, when he offered his gift to God, already slain his brother? And yet God, foreseeing the fratricide conceived in his mind, anticipated its condemnation. As in that case the evil thought and mischievous intention were foreseen by a foreseeing God, so also in God's servants, among whom confession is

purposed and martyrdom conceived in the mind, the intention dedicated to good is crowned by God the judge. It is one thing for the spirit to be wanting for martyrdom, and another for martyrdom to have been wanting for the spirit. Such as the Lord finds you when He calls you, such also He judges you; since He Himself bears witness, and says, "And all the churches shall know that I am the searcher of the reins and heart." For God does not ask for our blood, but for our faith. For neither Abraham, nor Isaac, nor Jacob were slain; and yet, being honored by the deserts of faith and righteousness, they deserved to be first among the patriarchs, to whose feast is collected every one that is found faithful, and righteous, and praiseworthy.

18. We ought to remember that we should do not our own will, but God's, in accordance with what our Lord has bidden us daily to pray. How preposterous and absurd it is, that while we ask that the will of God should be done, yet when God calls and summons us from this world, we should not at once obey the command of His will! We struggle and resist, and after the manner of froward servants we are dragged to the presence of the Lord with sadness and grief, departing hence under the bondage of necessity, not with the obedience of free will; and we wish to be honored with heavenly rewards by Him to whom we come unwillingly. Why, then, do we pray and ask that the kingdom of heaven may come, if the captivity of earth delights us? Why with frequently repeated prayers do we entreat and beg that the day of His kingdom may hasten, if our greater desires and stronger wishes are to obey the devil here, rather than to reign with Christ?

19. Besides, that the indications of the divine

providence may be more evidently manifest, proving that the Lord, prescient of the future, takes counsel for the true salvation of His people, when one of our colleagues and fellow-priests, wearied out with infirmity, and anxious about the present approach of death, prayed for a respite to himself; there stood by him as he prayed, and when he was now at the point of death, a youth, venerable in honor and majesty, lofty in stature and shining in aspect, and on whom, as he stood by him, the human glance could scarcely look with fleshly eyes, except that he who was about to depart from the world could already behold such a one. And he, not without a certain indignation of mind and voice, rebuked him, and said, You fear to suffer, you do not wish to depart; what shall I do to you? It was the word of one rebuking and warning, one who, when men are anxious about persecution, and indifferent concerning their summons, consents not to their present desire, but consults for the future. Our dying brother and colleague heard what he was to say to others. For he who heard when he was dying, heard for the very purpose that he might tell it; he heard not for himself, but for us. For what could he, who was already on the eve of departure, learn for himself? Yea, doubtless, he learnt it for us who remain, in order that, when we find the priest who sought for delay rebuked, we might acknowledge what is beneficial for all.

20. To myself also, the very least and last, how often has it been revealed, how frequently and manifestly has it been commanded by the condescension of God, that I should diligently bear witness and publicly declare that our brethren who are freed from this world by the Lord's summons are not to be lamented, since we know that they are not lost, but sent before; that, departing from us, they

precede us as travelers, as navigators are accustomed to do; that they should be desired, but not bewailed; that the black garments should not be taken upon us here, when they have already taken upon them white raiment there; that occasion should not be given to the Gentiles for them deservedly and rightly to reprehend us, that we mourn for those, who, we say, are alive with God, as if they were extinct and lost; and that we do not approve with the testimony of the heart and breast the faith which we express with speech and word. We are prevaricators of our hope and faith: what we say appears to be simulated, feigned, counterfeit. There is no advantage in setting forth virtue by our words and destroying the truth by our deeds.

21. Finally, the Apostle Paul reproaches, and rebukes, and blames any who are in sorrow at the departure of their friends. "I would not," says he, "have you ignorant, brethren, concerning them which are asleep, that ye sorrow not, even as others which have no hope. For if we believe that Jesus died and rose again, even so them which are asleep in Jesus will God bring with Him." He says that those have sorrow in the departure of their friends who have no hope. But we who live in hope, and believe in God, and trust that Christ suffered for us and rose again, abiding in Christ, and through Him and in Him rising again, why either are we ourselves unwilling to depart hence from this life, or do we bewail and grieve for our friends when they depart as if they were lost, when Christ Himself, our Lord and God, encourages us and says, "I am the resurrection and the life: he that believes in me, though he die, yet shall live; and whosoever lives and believes in me shall not die eternally?" If we believe in Christ, let us have faith in His words and promises; and since we shall not die eternally, let us come with a glad

security unto Christ, with whom we are both to conquer and to reign forever.

22. That in the meantime we die, we are passing over to immortality by death; nor can eternal life follow, unless it should befall us to depart from this life. That is not an ending, but a transit, and, this journey of time being traversed, a passage to eternity. Who would not hasten to better things? Who would not crave to be changed and renewed into the likeness of Christ, and to arrive more quickly to the dignity of heavenly glory, since Paul the apostle announces and says, "For our conversation is in heaven, from whence also we look for the Lord Jesus Christ; who shall change the body of our humiliation, and conform it to the body of His glory?" Christ the Lord also promises that we shall be such, when, that we may be with Him, and that we may live with Him in eternal mansions, and may rejoice in heavenly kingdoms, He prays the Father for us, saying, "Father, I will that they also whom Thou hast given me be with me where I am, and may see the glory which Thou hast given me before the world was made." He who is to attain to the throne of Christ, to the glory of the heavenly kingdoms, ought not to mourn nor lament, but rather, in accordance with the Lord's promise, in accordance with his faith in the truth, to rejoice in this his departure and translation.

23. Thus, moreover, we find that Enoch also was translated, who pleased God, as in Genesis the Holy Scripture bears witness, and says, "And Enoch pleased God; and afterwards he was not found, because God translated him." To have been pleasing in the sight of God was thus to have merited to be translated from this contagion of the world. And moreover, also, the Holy Spirit teaches by Solomon, that they who please God are

more early taken hence, and are more quickly set free, lest while they are delaying longer in this world they should be polluted with the contagions of the world. "He was taken away," says he, "lest wickedness should change his understanding. For his soul was pleasing to God; wherefore hasted Him to take him away from the midst of wickedness." So also in the Psalms, the soul that is devoted to its God in spiritual faith hastens to the Lord, saying, "How amiable are thy dwellings, O God of hosts! My soul longs, and hastes unto the courts of God."

24. It is for him to wish to remain long in the world whom the world delights, whom this life, flattering and deceiving, invites by the enticements of earthly pleasure. Again, since the world hates the Christian, why do you love that which hates you? and why do you not rather follow Christ, who both redeemed you and loves you? John in his epistle cries and says, exhorting that we should not follow carnal desires and love the world. "Love not the world," says he, "neither the things which are in the world. If any man loves the world, the love of the Father is not in him. For all that is in the world is the lust of the flesh, and the lust of the eyes, and the pride of life, which is not of the Father, but of the lust of the world. And the world shall pass away, and the lust thereof; but he who doeth the will of God abides forever, even as God abides forever." Rather, beloved brethren, with a sound mind, with a firm faith, with a robust virtue, let us be prepared for the whole will of God: laying aside the fear of death, let us think on the immortality which follows. By this let us show ourselves to be what we believe that we do not grieve over the departure of those dear to us, and that when the day of our summons shall arrive, we come without delay and without resistance to

the Lord when He Himself calls us.

25. And this, as it ought always to be done by God's servants, much more ought to be done now—now that the world is collapsing and is oppressed with the tempests of mischievous ills; in order that we who see that terrible things have begun, and know that still more terrible things are imminent, may regard it as the greatest advantage to depart from it as quickly as possible. If in your dwelling the walls were shaking with age, the roofs above you were trembling, and the house, now worn out and wearied, were threatening an immediate destruction to its structure crumbling with age, would you not with all speed depart? If, when you were on a voyage, an angry and raging tempest, by the waves violently aroused, foretold the coming shipwreck, would you not quickly seek the harbor? Lo, the world is changing and passing away, and witnesses to its ruin not now by its age, but by the end of things. And do you not give God thanks, do you not congratulate yourself, that by an earlier departure you are taken away, and delivered from the shipwrecks and disasters that are imminent?

26. We should consider, dearly beloved brethren—we should ever and anon reflect that we have renounced the world, and are in the meantime living here as guests and strangers. Let us greet the day which assigns each of us to his own home, which snatches us hence, and sets us free from the snares of the world, and restores us to paradise and the kingdom. Who that has been placed in foreign lands would not hasten to return to his own country? Who that is hastening to return to his friends would not eagerly desire a prosperous gale, that he might the sooner embrace those dear to him? We regard paradise as our country—we already begin to consider the

patriarchs as our parents: why do we not hasten and run, that we may behold our country, that we may greet our parents? There a great number of our dear ones is awaiting us, and a dense crowd of parents, brothers, children, is longing for us, already assured of their own safety, and still solicitous for our salvation. To attain to their presence and their embrace, what a gladness both for them and for us in common! What a pleasure is there in the heavenly kingdom, without fear of death; and how lofty and perpetual a happiness with eternity of living! There the glorious company of the apostles—there the host of the rejoicing prophets—there the innumerable multitude of martyrs, crowned for the victory of their struggle and passion—there the triumphant virgins, who subdued the lust of the flesh and of the body by the strength of their continency—there are merciful men rewarded, who by feeding and helping the poor have done the works of righteousness—who, keeping the Lord's precepts, have transferred their earthly patrimonies to the heavenly treasuries. To these, beloved brethren, let us hasten with an eager desire; let us crave quickly to be with them, and quickly to come to Christ. May God behold this our eager desire; may the Lord Christ look upon this purpose of our mind and faith, He who will give the larger rewards of His glory to those whose desires in respect of Himself were greater!

Treatise VIII.
On Works and Alms.
Argument.—He Powerfully Exhorts to the Manifestation of Faith by Works and Enforces the Wisdom of Offerings to the Church and of Bounty to the Poor as the Best Investment of a Christian's Estate. This

He Proves Out of Many Scriptures.

1. Many and great, beloved brethren, are the divine benefits wherewith the large and abundant mercy of God the Father and Christ both has labored and is always laboring for our salvation: that the Father sent the Son to preserve us and give us life, in order that He might restore us; and that the Son was willing to be sent and to become the Son of man, that He might make us sons of God; humbled Himself, that He might raise up the people who before were prostrate; was wounded that He might heal our wounds; served, that He might draw out to liberty those who were in bondage; underwent death, that He might set forth immortality to mortals. These are many and great boons of divine compassion. But, moreover, what is that providence, and how great the clemency, that by a plan of salvation it is provided for us, that more abundant care should be taken for preserving man after he is already redeemed! For when the Lord at His advent had cured those wounds which Adam had borne, and had healed the old poisons of the serpent, He gave a law to the sound man and bade him sin no more, lest a worse thing should befall the sinner. We had been limited and shut up into a narrow space by the commandment of innocence. Nor would the infirmity and weakness of human frailty have any resource, unless the divine mercy, coming once more in aid, should open some way of securing salvation by pointing out works of justice and mercy, so that by almsgiving we may wash away whatever foulness we subsequently contract.

2. The Holy Spirit speaks in the sacred Scriptures, and says, "By almsgiving and faith sins are purged." Not assuredly those sins which had been previously contracted, for those are purged by the blood and

sanctification of Christ. Moreover, He says again, "As water extinguishes fire, so almsgiving quenches sin." Here also it is shown and proved, that as in the laver of saving water the fire of Gehenna is extinguished, so by almsgiving and works of righteousness the flame of sins is subdued. And because in baptism remission of sins is granted once for all, constant and ceaseless labor, following the likeness of baptism, once again bestows the mercy of God. The Lord teaches this also in the Gospel. For when the disciples were pointed out, as eating and not first washing their hands, He replied and said, "He that made that which is within, made also that which is without. But give alms, and behold all things are clean unto you;" teaching hereby and showing, that not the hands are to be washed, but the heart, and that the foulness from inside is to be done away rather than that from outside; but that he who shall have cleansed what is within has cleansed also that which is without; and that if the mind is cleansed, a man has begun to be clean also in skin and body. Further, admonishing, and showing whence we may be clean and purged, He added that alms must be given. He who is pitiful teaches and warns us that pity must be shown; and because He seeks to save those whom at a great cost He has redeemed, He teaches that those who, after the grace of baptism, have become foul, may once more be cleansed.

3. Let us then acknowledge, beloved brethren, the wholesome gift of the divine mercy; and let us, who cannot be without some wound of conscience, heal our wounds by the spiritual remedies for the cleansing and purging of our sins. Nor let anyone so flatter himself with the notion of a pure and immaculate heart, as, in dependence on his own innocence, to think that the

medicine needs not to be applied to his wounds; since it is written, "Who shall boast that he hath a clean heart, or who shall boast that he is pure from sins?" And again, in his epistle, John lays it down, and says, "If we say that we have no sin, we deceive ourselves, and the truth is not in us." But if no one can be without sin, and whoever should say that he is without fault is either proud or foolish, how needful, how kind is the divine mercy, which, knowing that there are still found some wounds in those that have been healed, even after their healing, has given wholesome remedies for the curing and healing of their wounds anew!

4. Finally, beloved brethren, the divine admonition in the Scriptures, as well old as new, has never failed, has never been silent in urging God's people always and everywhere to works of mercy; and in the strain and exhortation of the Holy Spirit, everyone who is instructed into the hope of the heavenly kingdom is commanded to give alms. God commands and prescribes to Isaiah: "Cry," says He, "with strength, and spare not. Lift up thy voice as a trumpet, and declare to my people their transgressions, and to the house of Jacob their sins." And when He had commanded their sins to be charged upon them, and with the full force of His indignation had set forth their iniquities, and had said, that not even though they should use supplications, and prayers, and fasting, should they be able to make atonement for their sins; nor, if they were clothed in sackcloth and ashes, be able to soften God's anger, yet in the last part showing that God can be appeased by almsgiving alone, he added, saying, "Break thy bread to the hungry, and bring the poor that are without a home into thy house. If thou sees the naked, clothe him; and despise not the household of thine own

seed. Then shall thy light break forth in season, and thy garments shall arise speedily; and righteousness shall go before thee, and the glory of God shall surround thee. Then shalt thou cry, and God shall hear thee; whilst yet thou art speaking, He shall say, Here I am."

5. The remedies for propitiating God are given in the words of God Himself; the divine instructions have taught what sinners ought to do, that by works of righteousness God is satisfied, that with the deserts of mercy sins are cleansed. And in Solomon we read, "Shut up alms in the heart of the poor, and these shall intercede for thee from all evil." And again: "Whoso stopped his ears that he may not hear the weak, he also shall call upon God, and there will be none to hear him." For he shall not be able to deserve the mercy of the Lord, who himself shall not have been merciful; nor shall he obtain aught from the divine pity in his prayers, who shall not have been humane towards the poor man's prayer. And this also the Holy Spirit declares in the Psalms, and proves, saying, Blessed is he that is considerate of the poor and needy; the Lord will deliver him in the evil day." Remembering which precepts, Daniel, when king Nebuchadnezzar was in anxiety, being frightened by an adverse dream, gave him, for the turning away of evils, a remedy to obtain the divine help, saying, "Wherefore, O king, let my counsel be acceptable to thee; and redeem thy sins by almsgivings, and thine unrighteousness by mercies to the poor, and God will be patient to thy sins." And as the king did not obey him, he underwent the misfortunes and mischiefs which he had seen, and which he might have escaped and avoided had he redeemed his sins by almsgiving. Raphael the angel also witnesses the like, and exhorts that alms should be freely and liberally

bestowed, saying, "Prayer is good, with fasting and alms; because alms do deliver from death, and it purges away sins." He shows that our prayers and fasting are of less avail, unless they are aided by almsgiving; that entreaties alone are of little force to obtain what they seek, unless they be made sufficient by the addition of deeds and good works. The angel reveals, and manifests, and certifies that our petitions become efficacious by almsgiving, that life is redeemed from dangers by almsgiving, that souls are delivered from death by almsgiving.

6. Neither, beloved brethren, are we so bringing forward these things, as that we should not prove what Raphael the angel said, by the testimony of the truth. In the Acts of the Apostles the faith of the fact is established; and that souls are delivered by almsgiving not only from the second, but from the first death, is discovered by the evidence of a matter accomplished and completed. When Tabitha, being greatly given to good works and to bestowing alms, fell sick and died, Peter was summoned to her lifeless body; and when he, with apostolic humanity, had come in haste, there stood around him widows weeping and entreating, showing the cloaks, and coats, and all the garments which they had previously received, and praying for the deceased not by their words, but by her own deeds. Peter felt that what was asked in such a way might be obtained, and that Christ's aid would not be wanting to the petitioners, since He Himself was clothed in the clothing of the widows. When, therefore, falling on his knees, he had prayed, and—fit advocate for the widows and poor—had brought to the Lord the prayers entrusted to him, turning to the body, which was now lying washed on the bier, he said, "Tabitha, in the name of Jesus Christ, arise!" Nor did He fail to bring aid

to Peter, who had said in the Gospel, that whatever should be asked in His name should be given. Therefore death is suspended, and the spirit is restored, and, to the marvel and astonishment of all, the revived body is quickened into this worldly light once more; so effectual were the merits of mercy, so much did righteous works avail! She who had conferred upon suffering widows the help needful to live, deserved to be recalled to life by the widows' petition.

7. Therefore in the Gospel, the Lord, the Teacher of our life and Master of eternal salvation, quickening the assembly of believers, and providing for them forever when quickened, among His divine commands and precepts of heaven, commands and prescribes nothing more frequently than that we should devote ourselves to almsgiving, and not depend on earthly possessions, but rather layup heavenly treasures. "Sell," says He, "your goods, and give alms." And again: "Lay not up for yourselves treasures upon the earth, where moth and rust do corrupt, and where thieves break through and steal. But lay up for yourselves treasures in heaven, where neither moth nor rust doth corrupt, and where thieves do not break through nor steal. For where thy treasure is, there will thy heart be also." And when He wished to set forth a man perfect and complete by the observation of the law, He said, "If thou wilt be perfect, go and sell that thou hast, and give to the poor, and thou shalt have treasure in heaven; and come and follow me." Moreover, in another place He says that a merchant of the heavenly grace, and a gainer of eternal salvation, ought to purchase the precious pearl—that is, eternal life—at the price of the blood of Christ, from the amount of his patrimony, parting with all his wealth for it. He says: "The kingdom

of heaven is like unto a merchantman seeking goodly pearls. And when he found a precious pearl, he went away and sold all that he had, and bought it."

8. In fine, He calls those the children of Abraham whom He sees to be laborious in aiding and nourishing the poor. For when Zacchæus said, "Behold, the half of my goods I give to the poor; and if I have done any wrong to any man, I restore fourfold," Jesus answered and said, "That salvation has this day come to this house, for that he also is a son of Abraham." For if Abraham believed in God, and it was counted unto him for righteousness, certainly he who gives alms according to God's precept believes in God, and he who has the truth of faith maintains the fear of God; moreover, he who maintains the fear of God considers God in showing mercy to the poor. For he labors thus because he believes—because he knows that what is foretold by God's word is true, and that the Holy Scripture cannot lie—that unfruitful trees, that is, unproductive men, are cut off and cast into the fire, but that the merciful are called into the kingdom. He also, in another place, calls laborious and fruitful men faithful; but He denies faith to unfruitful and barren ones, saying, "If ye have not been faithful in the unrighteous mammon, who will commit to you that which is true? And if ye have not been faithful in that which is another man's, who shall give you that which is your own?"

9. If you dread and fear, lest, if you begin to act thus abundantly, your patrimony being exhausted with your liberal dealing, you may perchance be reduced to poverty; be of good courage in this respect, be free from care: that cannot be exhausted whence the service of Christ is supplied, whence the heavenly work is celebrated. Neither do I vouch for this on my own

authority; but I promise it on the faith of the Holy Scriptures, and on the authority of the divine promise. The Holy Spirit speaks by Solomon, and says, "He that giveth unto the poor shall never lack, but he that turns away his eye shall be in great poverty;" showing that the merciful and those who do good works cannot want, but rather that the sparing and barren hereafter come to want. Moreover, the blessed Apostle Paul, full of the grace of the Lord's inspiration, says: "He that ministered seed to the sower, shall both minister bread for your food, and shall multiply your seed sown, and shall increase the growth of the fruits of your righteousness, that in all things ye may be enriched." And again: "The administration of this service shall not only supply the wants of the saints, but shall be abundant also by many thanksgivings unto God;" because, while thanks are directed to God for our almsgivings and labors, by the prayer of the poor, the wealth of the doer is increased by the retribution of God. And the Lord in the Gospel, already considering the hearts of men of this kind, and with prescient voice denouncing faithless and unbelieving men, bears witness, and says: "Take no thought, saying, What shall we eat? or, What shall we drink? or, Wherewithal shall we be clothed? For these things the Gentiles seek. And your Father knows that ye have need of all these things. Seek first the kingdom of God, and His righteousness; and all these things shall be added unto you." He says that all these things shall be added and given to them who seek the kingdom and righteousness of God. For the Lord says, that when the day of judgment shall come, those who have labored in His Church are admitted to receive the kingdom.

10. You are afraid lest perchance your estate

should fail, if you begin to act liberally from it; and you do not know, miserable man that you are, that while you are fearing lest your family property should fail you, life itself, and salvation, are failing; and whilst you are anxious lest any of your wealth should be diminished, you do not see that you yourself are being diminished, in that you are a lover of mammon more than of your own soul; and while you fear, lest for the sake of yourself, you should lose your patrimony, you yourself are perishing for the sake of your patrimony. And therefore the apostle well exclaims, and says: "We brought nothing into this world, neither indeed can we carry anything out. Therefore, having food and clothing, let us therewith be content. For they who will be rich fall into temptation and a snare, and into many and hurtful desires, which drown a man in perdition and in destruction. For covetousness is a root of all evils, which some desiring, have made shipwreck from the faith, and pierced themselves through with many sorrows."

11. Are you afraid that your patrimony perchance may fall short, if you should begin to do liberally from it? Yet when has it ever happened that resources could fail the righteous man, since it is written, "The Lord will not slay with famine the righteous soul?" Elias in the desert is fed by the ministry of ravens; and a meal from heaven is made ready for Daniel in the den, when shut up by the king's command for a prey to the lions; and you are afraid that food should be wanting to you, laboring and deserving well of the Lord, although He Himself in the Gospel bears witness, for the rebuke of those whose mind is doubtful and faith small, and says: "Behold the fowls of heaven, that they sow not, nor reap, nor gather into barns; and your heavenly Father feeds them: are you not of more

value than they?" God feeds the fowls, and daily food is afforded to the sparrows; and to creatures which have no sense of things divine there is no want of drink or food. Thinks thou that to a Christian—thinks thou that to a servant of the Lord—thinks thou that to one given up to good works—thinks thou that to one that is dear to his Lord, anything will be wanting?

12. Unless you imagine that he who feeds Christ is not himself fed by Christ, or that earthly things will be wanting to those to whom heavenly and divine things are given, whence this unbelieving thought, whence this impious and sacrilegious consideration? What does a faithless heart do in the home of faith? Why is he who does not altogether trust in Christ named and called a Christian? The name of Pharisee is more fitting for you. For when in the Gospel the Lord was discoursing concerning almsgiving, and faithfully and wholesomely warned us to make to ourselves friends of our earthly lucre by provident good works, who might afterwards receive us into eternal dwellings, the Scripture added after this, and said, "But the Pharisees heard all these things, who were very covetous, and they derided Him." Some suchlike we see now in the Church, whose closed ears and darkened hearts admit no light from spiritual and saving warnings, of whom we need not wonder that they contemn the servant in his discourses, when we see the Lord Himself despised by such.

13. Wherefore do you applaud yourself in those vain and silly conceits, as if you were withheld from good works by fear and solicitude for the future? Why do you lay out before you certain shadows and omens of a vain excuse? Yea, confess what is the truth; and since you cannot deceive those who know, utter forth the secret and

hidden things of your mind. The gloom of barrenness has besieged your mind; and while the light of truth has departed thence, the deep and profound darkness of avarice has blinded your carnal heart. You are the captive and slave of your money; you are bound with the chains and bonds of covetousness; and you whom Christ had once loosed, are once more in chains. You keep your money, which, when kept, does not keep you. You heap up a patrimony which burdens you with its weight; and you do not remember what God answered to the rich man, who boasted with a foolish exultation of the abundance of his exuberant harvest: "Thou fool," said He, "this night thy soul is required of thee; then whose shall those things be which thou hast provided?" Why do you watch in loneliness over your riches? why for your punishment do you heap up the burden of your patrimony, that, in proportion as you are rich in this world, you may become poor to God? Divide your returns with the Lord your God; share your gains with Christ; make Christ a partner with you in your earthly possessions, that He also may make you a fellow heir with Him in His heavenly kingdom.

14. You are mistaken, and are deceived, whosoever you are, that think yourself rich in this world. Listen to the voice of your Lord in the Apocalypse, rebuking men of your stamp with righteous reproaches: "Thou sayest," says He, "I am rich, and increased with goods, and have need of nothing; and knows not that thou art wretched, and miserable, and poor, and blind, and naked. I counsel thee to buy of me gold tried in the fire, that thou mayest be rich; and white raiment, that thou mayest be clothed, and that the shame of thy nakedness may not appear in thee; and anoint thine eyes with eye-salve, that thou mayest see." You, therefore, who are rich

and wealthy, buy for yourself of Christ gold tried by fire; that you may be pure gold, with your filth burnt out as if by fire, if you are purged by almsgiving and righteous works. Buy for yourself white raiment, that you who had been naked according to Adam, and were before frightful and unseemly, may be clothed with the white garment of Christ. And you who are a wealthy and rich matron in Christ's Church, anoint your eyes, not with the collyrium of the devil, but with Christ's eye-salve, that you may be able to attain to see God, by deserving well of God, both by good works and character.

15. But you who are such as this, cannot labor in the Church. For your eyes, overcast with the gloom of blackness, and shadowed in night, do not see the needy and poor. You are wealthy and rich, and do you think that you celebrate the Lord's Supper, not at all considering the offering, who come to the Lord's Supper without a sacrifice, and yet take part of the sacrifice which the poor man has offered? Consider in the Gospel the widow that remembered the heavenly precepts, doing good even amidst the difficulties and straits of poverty, casting two mites, which were all that she had, into the treasury; whom when the Lord observed and saw, regarding her work not for its abundance, but for its intention, and considering not how much, but from how much, she had given, He answered and said, "Verily I say unto you, that that widow hath cast in more than they all into the offerings of God. For all these have, of that which they had in abundance, cast in unto the offerings of God; but she of her penury hath cast in all the living that she had." Greatly blessed and glorious woman, who even before the day of judgment hast merited to be praised by the voice of the Judge! Let the rich be ashamed of their barrenness and

unbelief. The widow, the widow needy in means, is found rich in works. And although everything that is given is conferred upon widows and orphans, she gives, whom it behooved to receive, that we may know thence what punishment, awaits the barren rich man, when by this very instance even the poor ought to labor in good works. And in order that we may understand that their labors are given to God, and that whoever performs them deserves well of the Lord, Christ calls this "the offerings of God," and intimates that the widow has cast in two farthings into the offerings of God, that it may be more abundantly evident that he who hath pity on the poor lends to God.

16. But neither let the consideration, dearest brethren, restrain and recall the Christian from good and righteous works, that any one should fancy that he could be excused for the benefit of his children; since in spiritual expenditure we ought to think of Christ, who has declared that He receives them; and not prefer our fellow-servants, but the Lord, to our children, since He Himself instructs and warns us, saying, "He that loveth father or mother more than me is not worthy of me, and he that loveth son or daughter more than me is not worthy of me." Also in Deuteronomy, for the strengthening of faith and the love of God, similar things are written: "Who say," he saith, "unto their father or mother, I have not known thee; neither did they acknowledge their children, these have observed Thy words, and kept Thy covenant." For if we love God with our whole heart, we ought not to prefer either our parents or children to God. And this also John lays down in his epistle, that the love of God is not in them whom we see unwilling to labor for the poor. "Whoso," says he, "hath this world's goods, and sees his brother have need, and shut up his bowels from him, how

dwelleth the love of God in him?" For if by almsgiving to the poor we are lending to God—and when it is given to the least it is given to Christ—there is no ground for any one preferring earthly things to heavenly, nor for considering human things before divine.

17. Thus that widow in the third book of Kings, when in the drought and famine, having consumed everything, she had made of the little meal and oil which was left, a cake upon the ashes, and, having used this, was about to die with her children, Elias came and asked that something should first be given him to eat, and then of what remained that she and her children should eat. Nor did she hesitate to obey; nor did the mother prefer her children to Elias in her hunger and poverty. Yea, there is done in God's sight a thing that pleases God: promptly and liberally is presented what is asked for. Neither is it a portion out of abundance, but the whole out of a little, that is given, and another is fed before her hungry children; nor in penury and want is food thought of before mercy; so that while in a saving work the life according to the flesh is contemned, the soul according to the spirit is preserved. Therefore Elias, being the type of Christ, and showing that according to His mercy He returns to each their reward, answered and said: "Thus saith the Lord, The vessel of meal shall not fail, and the cruse of oil shall not be diminished, until the day that the Lord giveth rain upon the earth." According to her faith in the divine promise, those things which she gave were multiplied and heaped up to the widow; and her righteous works and deserts of mercy taking augmentations and increase, the vessels of meal and oil were filled. Nor did the mother take away from her children what she gave to Elias, but rather she conferred upon her children what she did

kindly and piously. And she did not as yet know Christ; she had not yet heard His precepts; she did not, as redeemed by His cross and passion, repay meat and drink for His blood. So that from this it may appear how much he sins in the Church, who, preferring himself and his children to Christ, preserves his wealth, and does not share an abundant estate with the poverty of the needy.

18. Moreover, also, (you say) there are many children at home; and the multitude of your children checks you from giving yourself freely to good works. And yet on this very account you ought to labor the more, for the reason that you are the father of many pledges. There are the more for whom you must beseech the Lord. The sins of many have to be redeemed, the consciences of many to be cleansed, the souls of many to be liberated. As in this worldly life, in the nourishment and bringing up of children, the larger the number the greater also is the expense; so also in the spiritual and heavenly life, the larger the number of children you have, the greater ought to be the outlay of your labors. Thus also Job offered numerous sacrifices on behalf of his children; and as large as was the number of the pledges in his home, so large also was the number of victims given to God. And since there cannot daily fail to be sins committed in the sight of God, there wanted not daily sacrifices wherewith the sins might be cleansed away. The Holy Scripture proves this, saying: "Job, a true and righteous man, had seven sons and three daughters, and cleansed them, offering for them victims to God according to the number of them, and for their sins one calf." If then, you truly love your children, if you show to them the full and paternal sweetness of love, you ought to be the more charitable, that by your righteous works you may commend your children to God.

19. Neither should you think that he is father to your children who is both changeable and infirm, but you should obtain Him who is the eternal and unchanging Father of spiritual children. Assign to Him your wealth which you are saving up for your heirs. Let Him be the guardian for your children; let Him be their trustee; let Him be their protector, by His divine majesty, against all worldly injuries. The state neither takes away the property entrusted to God, nor does the exchequer intrude on it, nor does any forensic calumny overthrow it. That inheritance is placed in security which is kept under the guardianship of God. This is to provide for one's dear pledges for the coming time; this is with paternal affection to take care for one's future heirs, according to the faith of the Holy Scripture, which says: "I have been young, and now am old; yet have I not seen the righteous forsaken, nor his seed wanting bread. All the day long he is merciful, and lends; and his seed is blessed." And again: "He who walketh without reproach in his integrity shall leave blessed children after him." Therefore you are an unfair and traitorous father, unless you faithfully consult for your children, unless you look forward to preserving them in religion and true piety. You who are careful rather for their earthly than for their heavenly estate, rather to commend your children to the devil than to Christ, are sinning twice, and allowing a double and twofold crime, both in not providing for your children the aid of God their Father, and in teaching your children to love their property more than Christ.

20. Be rather such a father to your children as was Tobias. Give useful and saving precepts to your pledges, such as he gave to his son; command your children what he also commanded his son, saying: "And now, my son, I

command thee, serve God in truth, and do before Him that which pleases Him; and command thy sons, that they exercise righteousness and alms, and be mindful of God, and bless His name always." And again: "All the days of thy life, most dear son, have God in your mind, and be not willing to transgress His commandments. Do righteousness all the days of thy life, and be not willing to walk in the way of iniquity; because if thou deal truly, there will be respect of thy works. Give alms of thy substance, and turn not away thy face from any poor man. So shall it be, that neither shall the face of God be turned away from thee. As thou hast, my son, so do. If thy substance is abundant, give alms of it the more. If thou hast little, communicate of that little. And fear not when thou does alms; for thou lays up a good reward for thyself against the day of necessity, because that alms do deliver from death, and suffered not to come into Gehenna. Alms is a good gift to all that give it, in the sight of the most high God."

21. What sort of gift is it, beloved brethren, whose setting forth is celebrated in the sight of God? If, in a gift of the Gentiles, it seems a great and glorious thing to have proconsuls or emperors present, and the preparation and display is the greater among the givers, in order that they may please the higher classes; how much more illustrious and greater is the glory to have God and Christ as the spectators of the gift! How much more sumptuous the preparation and more liberal the expense to be set forth in that case, when the powers of heaven assemble to the spectacle, when all the angels come together: where it is not a four-horsed chariot or a consulship that is sought for the giver, but life eternal is bestowed; nor is the empty and fleeting favor of the rabble grasped at, but the

perpetual reward of the kingdom of heaven is received!

22. And that the indolent and the barren, and those, who by their covetousness for money do nothing in respect of the fruit of their salvation, may be the more ashamed, and that the blush of dishonor and disgrace may the more strike upon their sordid conscience, let each one place before his eyes the devil with his servants, that is, with the people of perdition and death, springing forth into the midst, and provoking the people of Christ with the trial of comparison—Christ Himself being present, and judging—in these words: "I, for those whom thou sees with me, neither received buffets, nor bore scourging, nor endured the cross, nor shed my blood, nor redeemed my family at the price of my suffering and blood; but neither do I promise them a celestial kingdom, nor do I recall them to paradise, having again restored to them immortality. But they prepare for me gifts how precious! how large! with how excessive and tedious labor procured! and that, with the most sumptuous devices either pledging or selling their means in the procuring of the gift! and, unless a competent manifestation followed, they are cast out with scoffing and hissing, and by the popular fury sometimes they are almost stoned! Show, O Christ, such givers as these of Thine—those rich men, those men affluent with abounding wealth—whether in the Church wherein Thou presides and beholds, they set forth a gift of that kind,—having pledged or scattered their riches, yea, having transferred them, by the change of their possessions for the better, into heavenly treasures! In those spectacles of mine, perishing and earthly as they are, no one is fed, no one is clothed, no one is sustained by the comfort either of any meat or drink. All things, between the madness of the

exhibitor and the mistake of the spectator, are perishing in a prodigal and foolish vanity of deceiving pleasures. There, in Thy poor, Thou art clothed and fed; Thou promised eternal life to those who labor for Thee; and scarcely are Thy people made equal to mine that perish, although they are honored by Thee with divine wages and heavenly rewards.

23. What do we reply to these things, dearest brethren? With what reason do we defend the minds of rich men, overwhelmed with a profane barrenness and a kind of night of gloom? With what excuse do we acquit them, seeing that we are less than the devil's servants, so as not even moderately to repay Christ for the price of His passion and blood? He has given us precepts; what His servants ought to do He has instructed us; promising a reward to those that are charitable, and threatening punishment to the unfruitful. He has set forth His sentence. He has before announced what He shall judge. What can be the excuse for the laggard? what the defense for the unfruitful? But when the servant does not do what is commanded, the Lord will do what He threatens, seeing that He says: "When the Son of man shall come in His glory, and all the angels with Him, then shall He sit in the throne of His glory: and before Him shall be gathered all nations; and He shall separate them one from another, as a shepherd divides his sheep from the goats: and He shall set the sheep on His right hand, but the goats on the left. Then shall the King say unto them that shall be on His right hand, Come, you blessed of my Father, receive the kingdom that is prepared for you from the foundation of the world. For I was hungered, and you gave me to eat: I was thirsty, and you gave me to drink: I was a stranger, and you took me in: naked, and you clothed me: I was

sick, and you visited me: I was in prison, and you came to me. Then shall the righteous answer Him, saying, Lord, when did we see You hungered, and fed You? thirsty, and gave You drink? When did we see You a stranger, and took You in? naked, and clothed You? Or when did we see You sick, and in prison, and came unto You? Then shall the King answer and say unto them, Verily I say unto you, Insomuch as you did it to one of the least of these my brethren, you did it unto me. Then shall He say also unto those that shall be at His left hand, Depart from me, you cursed, into everlasting fire, which my Father hath prepared for the devil and his angels. For I was hungered, and you gave me not to eat: I was thirsty, and you gave me not to drink: I was a stranger, and you took me not in: naked, and you clothed me not: sick, and in prison, and you visited me not. Then shall they also answer Him, saying, Lord, when did we see You hungered, or athirst, or a stranger, or naked, or sick, or in prison, and ministered not unto You? And He shall answer them, Verily I say unto you, In so far as you did it not to one of the least of these, you did it not unto me. And these shall go away into everlasting burning: but the righteous into life eternal." What more could Christ declare unto us? How more could He stimulate the works of our righteousness and mercy, than by saying that whatever is given to the needy and poor is given to Himself, and by saying that He is aggrieved unless the needy and poor be supplied? So that he who in the Church is not moved by consideration for his brother, may yet be moved by contemplation of Christ; and he who does not think of his fellow-servant in suffering and in poverty, may yet think of his Lord, who abides in that very man whom he is despising.

24. And therefore, dearest brethren, whose fear is inclined towards God, and who having already despised and trampled underfoot the world, have lifted up your mind to things heavenly and divine, let us with full faith, with devoted mind, with continual labor, give our obedience, to deserve well of the Lord. Let us give to Christ earthly garments, that we may receive heavenly raiment; let us give food and drink of this world, that we may come with Abraham, and Isaac, and Jacob to the heavenly banquet. That we may not reap little, let us sow abundantly. Let us, while there is time, take thought for our security and eternal salvation, according to the admonition of the Apostle Paul, who says: "Therefore, while we have time, let us labor in what is good unto all men, but especially to them that are of the household of faith. But let us not be weary in well-doing, for in its season we shall reap."

25. Let us consider, beloved brethren, what the congregation of believers did in the time of the apostles, when at the first beginnings the mind flourished with greater virtues, when the faith of believers burned with a warmth of faith as yet new. Then they sold houses and farms, and gladly and liberally presented to the apostles the proceeds to be dispensed to the poor; selling and alienating their earthly estate, they transferred their lands thither where they might receive the fruits of an eternal possession, and there prepared homes where they might begin an eternal habitation. Such, then, was the abundance in labors, as was the agreement in love, as we read in the Acts of the Apostles: "And the multitude of them that believed acted with one heart and one soul; neither was there any distinction among them, nor did they esteem anything their own of the goods which

belonged to them, but they had all things common." This is truly to become sons of God by spiritual birth; this is to imitate by the heavenly law the equity of God the Father. For whatever is of God is common in our use; nor is anyone excluded from His benefits and His gifts, so as to prevent the whole human race from enjoying equally the divine goodness and liberality. Thus the day equally enlightens, the sun gives radiance, the rain moistens, the wind blows, and the sleep is one to those that sleep, and the splendor of the stars and of the moon is common. In which example of equality, he who, as a possessor in the earth, shares his returns and his fruits with the fraternity, while he is common and just in his gratuitous bounties, is an imitator of God the Father.

26. What, dearest brethren, will be that glory of those who labor charitably—how great and high the joy when the Lord begins to number His people, and, distributing to our merits and good works the promised rewards, to give heavenly things for earthly, eternal things for temporal, great things for small; to present us to the Father, to whom He has restored us by His sanctification; to bestow upon us immortality and eternity, to which He has renewed us by the quickening of His blood; to bring us anew to paradise, to open the kingdom of heaven, in the faith and truth of His promise! Let these things abide firmly in our perceptions, let them be understood with full faith, let them be loved with our whole heart, let them be purchased by the magnanimity of our increasing labors. An illustrious and divine thing, dearest brethren, is the saving labor of charity; a great comfort of believers, a wholesome guard of our security, a protection of hope, a safeguard of faith, a remedy for sin, a thing placed in the power of the doer, a thing both great and easy, a crown of

peace without the risk of persecution; the true and greatest gift of God, needful for the weak, glorious for the strong, assisted by which the Christian accomplishes spiritual grace, deserves well of Christ the Judge, accounts God his debtor. For this palm of works of salvation let us gladly and readily strive; let us all, in the struggle of righteousness, run with God and Christ looking on; and let us who have already begun to be greater than this life and the world, slacken our course by no desire of this life and of this world. If the day shall find us, whether it be the day of reward or of persecution, furnished, if swift, if running in this contest of charity, the Lord will never fail of giving a reward for our merits: in peace He will give to us who conquer, a white crown for our labors; in persecution, He will accompany it with a purple one for our passion.

Treatise IX.
On the Advantage of Patience.

Argument.—Cyprian Himself Briefly Sets Forth the Occasion of This Treatise at the Conclusion of His Epistle to Jubaianus as Follows: "Charity of Spirit, the Honor of Our College, the Bond of Faith, and Priestly Concord, are Maintained by Us with Patience and Gentleness. For This Reason, Moreover, We Have, with the Best of Our Poor Abilities, by the Permission and Inspiration of the Lord, Written a Pamphlet 'On the Benefit of Patience,' Which, for the Sake of Our Mutual Love, We Have Transmitted to You." a.d. 256.

1. As I am about to speak, beloved brethren, of patience, and to declare its advantages and benefits, from what point should I rather begin than this, that I see that even at this time, for your audience of me, patience is

needful, as you cannot even discharge this duty of hearing and learning without patience? For wholesome discourse and reasoning are then effectually learnt, if what is said be patiently heard. Nor do I find, beloved brethren, among the rest of the ways of heavenly discipline wherein the path of our hope and faith is directed to the attainment of the divine rewards, anything of more advantage, either as more useful for life or more helpful to glory, than that we who are laboring in the precepts of the Lord with the obedience of fear and devotion, should especially, with our whole watchfulness, be careful of patience.

2. Philosophers also profess that they pursue this virtue; but in their case the patience is as false as their wisdom also is. For whence can he be either wise or patient, who has neither known the wisdom nor the patience of God? since He Himself warns us, and says of those who seem to themselves to be wise in this world, "I will destroy the wisdom of the wise, and I will reprove the understanding of the prudent." Moreover, the blessed Apostle Paul, filled with the Holy Spirit, and sent forth for the calling and training of the heathen, bears witness and instructs us, saying, "See that no man despoil you through philosophy and vain deceit, after the tradition of men, after the elements of the world, and not after Christ, because in Him dwelleth all the fulness of divinity." And in another place he says: "Let no man deceive himself; if any man among you thinketh himself to be wise, let him become a fool to this world, that he may become wise. For the wisdom of this world is foolishness with God. For it is written, I will rebuke the wise in their own craftiness." And again: "The Lord knows the thoughts of the wise, that they are foolish." Wherefore if the wisdom among them be not true, the patience also cannot be true.

For if he is wise who is lowly and meek—but we do not see that philosophers are either lowly or meek, but greatly pleasing themselves, and, for the very reason that they please themselves, displeasing God—it is evident that the patience is not real among them where there is the insolent audacity of an affected liberty, and the immodest boastfulness of an exposed and half-naked bosom.

3. But for us, beloved brethren, who are philosophers, not in words, but in deeds, and do not put forward our wisdom in our garb, but in truth—who are better acquainted with the consciousness, than with the boast, of virtues—who do not speak great things, but live them,—let us, as servants and worshippers of God, show, in our spiritual obedience, the patience which we learn from heavenly teachings. For we have this virtue in common with God. From Him patience begins; from Him its glory and its dignity take their rise. The origin and greatness of patience proceed from God as its author. Man ought to love the thing which is dear to God; the good which the Divine Majesty loves, it commends. If God is our Lord and Father, let us imitate the patience of our Lord as well as our Father; because it behooves servants to be obedient, no less than it becomes sons not to be degenerate.

4. But what and how great is the patience in God, that, most patiently enduring the profane temples and the images of earth, and the sacrilegious rites instituted by men, in contempt of His majesty and honor, He makes the day to begin and the light of the sun to arise alike upon the good and the evil; and while He waters the earth with showers, no one is excluded from His benefits, but upon the righteous equally with the unrighteous He bestows His undiscriminating rains. We see that with undistinguishing

equality of patience, at God's behest, the seasons minister to the guilty and the guiltless, the religious and the impious—those who give thanks and the unthankful; that the elements wait on them; the winds blow, the fountains flow, the abundance of the harvests increases, the fruits of the vineyards ripen, the trees are loaded with apples, the groves put on their leaves, the meadows their verdure; and while God is provoked with frequent, yea, with continual offences, He softens His indignation, and in patience waits for the day of retribution, once for all determined; and although He has revenge in His power, He prefers to keep patience for a long while, bearing, that is to say, mercifully, and putting off, so that, if it might be possible, the long protracted mischief may at some time be changed, and man, involved in the contagion of errors and crimes, may even though late be converted to God, as He Himself warns and says, "I do not will the death of him that dies, so much as that he may return and live." And again, "Return unto me, saith the Lord." And again: "Return to the Lord your God; for He is merciful, and gracious, and patient, and of great pity, and who inclines His judgment towards the evils inflicted." Which, moreover, the blessed apostle referring to, and recalling the sinner to repentance, sets forward, and says: "Or despises thou the riches of His goodness, and forbearance, and long-suffering, not knowing that the patience and goodness of God leadeth thee to repentance? But after thy hardness and impenitent heart thou treasures up unto thyself wrath in the day of wrath and of revelation of the righteous judgment of God, who shall render to everyone according to his works." He says that God's judgment is just, because it is tardy, because it is long and greatly deferred, so that by the long patience of God man may be benefited for life eternal. Punishment is then executed on the impious and the sinner, when repentance for the sin can no longer avail.

5. And that we may more fully understand, beloved brethren, that patience is a thing of God, and that whoever is gentle, and patient, and meek, is an imitator of God the Father; when the Lord in His Gospel was giving precepts for salvation, and, bringing forth divine warnings, was instructing His disciples to perfection, He laid it down, and said, "Ye have heard that it is said, Thou shalt love thy neighbor, and have thine enemy in hatred. But I say unto you, Love your enemies, and pray for them which persecute you; that ye may be the children of your Father which is in heaven, who makes His sun to rise on the good and on the evil, and rains upon the just and on the unjust. For if ye love them which love you, what reward shall ye have? do not even the publicans the same? And if ye shall salute your brethren only, what do ye more (than others)? do not even the heathens do the same thing? Be ye therefore perfect, even as your Father in heaven is perfect." He said that the children of God would thus become perfect. He showed that they were thus completed and taught that they were restored by a heavenly birth, if the patience of God our Father dwell in us—if the divine likeness, which Adam had lost by sin, be manifested and shine in our actions. What a glory is it to become like to God! what and how great a felicity, to possess among our virtues, that which may be placed on the level of divine praises!

6. Nor, beloved brethren, did Jesus Christ, our God and Lord, teach this in words only; but He fulfilled it also in deeds. And because He had said that He had come down for this purpose, that He might do the will of His

Father; among the other marvels of His virtues, whereby He showed forth the marks of a divine majesty, He also maintained the patience of His Father in the constancy of His endurance. Finally, all His actions, even from His very advent, are characterized by patience as their associate; in that, first of all, coming down from that heavenly sublimity to earthly things, the Son of God did not scorn to put on the flesh of man, and although He Himself was not a sinner, to bear the sins of others. His immortality being in the meantime laid aside, He suffers Himself to become mortal, so that the guiltless may be put to death for the salvation of the guilty. The Lord is baptized by the servant; and He who is about to bestow remission of sins, does not Himself disdain to wash His body in the laver of regeneration. For forty days He fasts, by whom others are feasted. He is hungry, and suffers famine, that they who had been in hunger of the word and of grace may be satisfied with heavenly bread. He wrestles with the devil tempting Him; and content only to have overcome the enemy, He strives no farther than by words. He ruled over His disciples not as servants in the power of a master; but, kind and gentle, He loved them with a brotherly love. He deigned even to wash the apostles' feet, that since the Lord is such among His servants, He might teach, by His example, what a fellow servant ought to be among his peers and equals. Nor is it to be wondered at, that among the obedient He showed Himself such, since He could bear Judas even to the last with a long patience—could take meat with His enemy—could know the household foe, and not openly point him out, nor refuse the kiss of the traitor. Moreover, in bearing with the Jews, how great equanimity and how great patience, in turning the unbelieving to the faith by persuasion, in soothing the unthankful by concession, in answering gently to the contradictors, in bearing the proud with clemency, in yielding with humility to the persecutors, in wishing to gather together the slayers of the prophets, and those who were always rebellious against God, even to the very hour of His cross and passion!

7. And moreover, in His very passion and cross, before they had reached the cruelty of death and the effusion of blood, what infamies of reproach were patiently heard, what mocking of contumely were suffered, so that He received the spitting of insulters, who with His spittle had a little before made eyes for a blind man; and He in whose name the devil and his angels is now scourged by His servants, Himself suffered scourging! He was crowned with thorns, who crowns martyrs with eternal flowers. He was smitten on the face with palms, who gives the true palms to those who overcome. He was despoiled of His earthly garment, who clothes others in the vesture of immortality. He was fed with gall, who gave heavenly food. He was given to drink of vinegar, who appointed the cup of salvation. That guiltless, that just One,—nay, He who is innocency itself and justice itself,—is counted among transgressors, and truth is oppressed with false witnesses. He who shall judge is judged; and the Word of God is led silently to the slaughter. And when at the cross, of the Lord the stars are confounded, the elements are disturbed, the earthquakes, night shuts out the day, the sun, that he may not be compelled to look on the crime of the Jews, withdraws both his rays and his eyes, He speaks not, nor is moved, nor declares His majesty even in His very passion itself. Even to the end, all things are borne perseveringly and

constantly, in order that in Christ a full and perfect patience may be consummated.

8. And after all these things, He still receives His murderers, if they will be converted and come to Him; and with a saving patience, He who is benignant to preserve, closes His Church to none. Those adversaries, those blasphemers, those who were always enemies to His name, if they repent of their sin, if they acknowledge the crime committed, He receives, not only to the pardon of their sin, but to the reward of the heavenly kingdom. What can be said more patient, what more merciful? Even he is made alive by Christ's blood who has shed Christ's blood. Such and so great is the patience of Christ; and had it not been such and so great, the Church would never have possessed Paul as an apostle.

9. But if we also, beloved brethren, are in Christ; if we put Him on, if He is the way of our salvation, who follow Christ in the footsteps of salvation, let us walk by the example of Christ, as the Apostle John instructs us, saying, "He who saith he abides in Christ, ought himself also to walk even as He walked." Peter also, upon whom by the Lord's condescension the Church was founded, lays it down in his epistle, and says, "Christ suffered for us, leaving you an example, that ye should follow His steps, who did no sin, neither was deceit found in His mouth; who, when He was reviled, reviled not again; when He suffered, threatened not, but gave Himself up to him that judged Him unjustly."

10. Finally, we find that both patriarchs and prophets, and all the righteous men who in their preceding likeness wore the figure of Christ, in the praise of their virtues were watchful over nothing more than that they should preserve patience with a strong and steadfast

equanimity. Thus Abel, who first initiated and consecrated the origin of martyrdom, and the passion of the righteous man, makes no resistance nor struggles against his fratricidal brother, but with lowliness and meekness he is patiently slain. Thus Abraham, believing God, and first of all instituting the root and foundation of faith, when tried in respect of his son, does not hesitate nor delay, but obeys the commands of God with all the patience of devotion. And Isaac, prefigured as the likeness of the Lord's victim, when he is presented by his father for immolation, is found patient. And Jacob, driven forth by his brother from his country, departs with patience; and afterwards with greater patience, he suppliantly brings him back to concord with peaceful gifts, when he is even more impious and persecuting. Joseph, sold by his brethren and sent away, not only with patience pardons them, but even bountifully and mercifully bestows gratuitous supplies of corn on them when they come to him. Moses is frequently contemned by an ungrateful and faithless people, and almost stoned; and yet with gentleness and patience he entreats the Lord for those people. But in David, from whom, according to the flesh, the nativity of Christ springs, how great and marvelous and Christian is the patience, that he often had it in his power to be able to kill king Saul, who was persecuting him and desiring to slay him; and yet, chose rather to save him when placed in his hand, and delivered up to him, not repaying his enemy in turn, but rather, on the contrary, even avenging him when slain! In fine, so many prophets were slain, so many martyrs were honored with glorious deaths, who all have attained to the heavenly crowns by the praise of patience. For the crown of sorrows and sufferings cannot be received unless patience in sorrow and suffering precedes it.

11. But that it may be more manifestly and fully known how useful and necessary patience is, beloved brethren; let the judgment of God be pondered, which even in the beginning of the world and of the human race, Adam, forgetful of the commandment, and a transgressor of the given law, received. Then we shall know how patient in this life we ought to be who are born in such a state, that we labor here with afflictions and contests. "Because," says He, "thou hast hearkened to the voice of thy wife, and hast eaten of the tree of which alone I had charged thee that thou shouldest not eat, cursed shall be the ground in all thy works: in sorrow and in groaning shalt thou eat of it all the days of thy life. Thorns and thistles shall it give forth to thee, and thou shalt eat the food of the field. In the sweat of thy face shalt thou eat thy bread, till thou return into the ground from which thou was taken: for dust thou art, and to dust shalt thou go." We are all tied and bound with the chain of this sentence, until, death being expunged, we depart from this life. In sorrow and groaning we must of necessity be all the days of our life: it is necessary that we eat our bread with sweat and labor.

12. Whence every one of us, when he is born and received in the inn of this world, takes his beginning from tears; and, although still unconscious and ignorant of all things, he knows nothing else in that very earliest birth except to weep. By a natural foresight, the un☐trained soul laments the anxieties and labors of the mortal life, and even in the beginning bears witness by its wails and groans to the storms of the world which it is entering. For the sweat of the brow and labor is the condition of life so long as it lasts. Nor can there be supplied any

consolations to those that sweat and toil other than patience; which consolations, while in this world they are fit and necessary for all men, are especially so for us who are more shaken by the siege of the devil, who, daily standing in the battle-field, are wearied with the wrestling of an inveterate and skillful enemy; for us who, besides the various and continual battles of temptations, must also in the contest of persecutions forsake our patrimonies, undergo imprisonment, bear chains, spend our lives, endure the sword, the wild beasts, fires, crucifixions—in fine, all kinds of torments and penalties, to be endured in the faith and courage of patience; as the Lord Himself instructs us, and says, "These things have I spoken unto you, that in me ye might have peace. But in the world ye shall have tribulation; yet be confident, for I have overcome the world." And if we who have renounced the devil and the world, suffer the tribulations and mischiefs of the devil and the world with more frequency and violence, how much more ought we to keep patience, wherewith as our helper and ally, we may bear all mischievous things!

13. It is the wholesome precept of our Lord and Master: "He that endures," saith He, "unto the end, the same shall be saved;" and again, "If ye continue," saith He, "in my word, ye shall be truly my disciples; and ye shall know the truth, and the truth shall make you free." We must endure and persevere, beloved brethren, in order that, being admitted to the hope of truth and liberty, we may attain to the truth and liberty itself; for that very fact that we are Christians is the substance of faith and hope. But that hope and faith may attain to their result, there is need of patience. For we are not following after present glory, but future, according to what Paul the apostle also

warns us, and says, "We are saved by hope; but hope that is seen is not hope: for what a man sees, why doth he hope for? But if we hope for that which we see not, then do we by patience wait for it." Therefore, waiting and patience are needful, that we may fulfil that which we have begun to be, and may receive that which we believe and hope for, according to God's own showing. Moreover, in another place, the same apostle instructs the righteous and the doers of good works, and 488 them who lay up for themselves treasures in heaven with the increase of the divine usury, that they also should be patient; and teaches them, saying, "Therefore, while we have time, let us labor in that which is good unto all men, but especially to them who are of the household of faith. But let us not faint in well-doing, for in its season we shall reap." He admonishes that no man should impatiently faint in his labor, that none should be either called off or overcome by temptations and desist in the midst of the praise and in the way of glory; and the things that are past perish, while those which have begun cease to be perfect; as it is written, "The righteousness of the righteous shall not deliver him in whatever day he shall transgress;" and again, "Hold that which thou hast, that another take not thy crown." Which word exhorts us to persevere with patience and courage, so that he who strives towards the crown with the praise now near at hand, may be crowned by the continuance of patience.

14. But patience, beloved brethren, not only keeps watch over what is good, but it also repels what is evil. In harmony with the Holy Spirit, and associated with what is heavenly and divine, it struggles with the defense of its strength against the deeds of the flesh and the body, wherewith the soul is assaulted and taken. Let us look

briefly into a few things out of many, that from a few the rest also may be understood. Adultery, fraud, manslaughter, are mortal crimes. Let patience be strong and steadfast in the heart; and neither is the sanctified body and temple of God polluted by adultery, nor is the innocence dedicated to righteousness stained with the contagion of fraud; nor, after the Eucharist carried in it, is the hand spotted with the sword and blood.

15. Charity is the bond of brotherhood, the foundation of peace, the holdfast and security of unity, which is greater than both hope and faith, which excels both good works and martyrdoms, which will abide with us always, eternal with God in the kingdom of heaven. Take from it patience; and deprived of it, it does not endure. Take from it the substance of bearing and of enduring, and it continues with no roots nor strength. The apostle, finally, when he would speak of charity, joined to it endurance and patience. "Charity," he says, "is large-souled; charity is kind; charity envies not, is not puffed up, is not provoked, thinketh not evil; loveth all things, believeth all things, hopes all things, bears all things." Thence he shows that it can tenaciously persevere, because it knows how to endure all things. And in another place: "Forbearing one another," he says, "in love, using every effort to keep the unity of the spirit in the bond of peace." He proved that neither unity nor peace could be kept unless brethren should cherish one another with mutual toleration and should keep the bond of concord by the intervention of patience.

16. What beyond;—that you should not swear nor curse; that you should not seek again your goods when taken from you; that, when you receive a buffet, you should give your other cheek to the smiter; that you

should forgive a brother who sins against you, not only seven times, but seventy times seven times, but, moreover, all his sins altogether; that you should love your enemies; that you should offer prayer for your adversaries and persecutors? Can you accomplish these things unless you maintain the steadfastness of patience and endurance? And this we see done in the case of Stephen, who, when he was slain by the Jews with violence and stoning, did not ask for vengeance for himself, but for pardon for his murderers, saying, "Lord, lay not this sin to their charge." It behooved the first martyr of Christ thus to be, who, fore running the martyrs that should follow him in a glorious death, was not only the preacher of the Lord's passion, but also the imitator of His most patient gentleness. What shall I say of anger, of discord, of strife, which things ought not to be found in a Christian? Let there be patience in the breast, and these things cannot have place there; or should they try to enter, they are quickly excluded and depart, that a peaceful abode may continue in the heart, where it delights the God of peace to dwell. Finally, the apostle warns us, and teaches, saying: "Grieve not the Holy Spirit of God, in whom ye are sealed unto the day of redemption. Let all bitterness, and anger, and wrath, and clamor, and blasphemy, be put away from you." For if the Christian have departed from rage and carnal contention as if from the hurricanes of the sea and have already begun to be tranquil and meek in the harbor of Christ, he ought to admit neither anger nor discord within his breast, since he must neither return evil for evil, nor bear hatred.

17. And moreover, also, for the varied ills of the flesh, and the frequent and severe torments of the body, wherewith the human race is daily wearied and harassed,

patience is necessary. For since in that first transgression of the commandment strength of body departed with immortality, and weakness came on with death—and strength cannot be received unless when immortality also has been received—it behooves us, in this bodily frailty and weakness, always to struggle and to fight. And this struggle and encounter cannot be sustained but by the strength of patience. But as we are to be examined and searched out, diverse sufferings are introduced; and a manifold kind of temptation is inflicted by the losses of property, by the heat of fevers, by the torments of wounds, by the loss of those dear to us. Nor does anything distinguish between the unrighteous and the righteous more than that in affliction the unrighteous man impatiently complains and blasphemes, while the righteous is proved by his patience, as it is written: "In pain endure, and in thy low estate have patience; for gold and silver are tried in the fire."

18. Thus Job was searched out and proved and was raised up to the very highest pinnacle of praise by the virtue of patience. What darts of the devil were sent forth against him! what tortures were put in use! The loss of his estate is inflicted, the privation of a numerous offspring is ordained for him. The master, rich in estate, and the father, richer in children, is on a sudden neither master nor father! The wasting of wounds is added; and, moreover, an eating pest of worms consumes his festering and wasting limbs. And that nothing at all should remain that Job did not experience in his trials, the devil arms his wife also, making use of that old device of his wickedness, as if he could deceive and mislead all by women, even as he did in the beginning of the world. And yet Job is not broken down by his severe and repeated

conflicts, nor the blessing of God withheld from being declared in the midst of those difficulties and trials of his, by the victory of patience. Tobias also, who, after the sublime works of his justice and mercy, was tried with the loss of his eyes, in proportion as he patiently endured his blindness, in that proportion deserved greatly of God by the praise of patience.

19. And, beloved brethren, that the benefit of patience may still more shine forth, let us consider, on the contrary, what mischief impatience may cause. For as patience is the benefit of Christ, so, on the other hand, impatience is the mischief of the devil; and as one in whom Christ dwells and abides is found patient, so he appears always impatient whose mind the wickedness of the devil possesses. Briefly let us look at the very beginnings. The devil suffered with impatience that man was made in the image of God. Hence he was the first to perish and to ruin others. Adam, contrary to the heavenly command with respect to the deadly food, by impatience fell into death; nor did he keep the grace received from God under the guardianship of patience. And in order that Cain should put his brother to death, he was impatient of his sacrifice and gift; and in that Esau descended from the rights of the first-born to those of the younger, he lost his priority by impatience for the pottage. Why were the Jewish people faithless and ungrateful in respect of the divine benefits? Was it not the crime of impatience, that they first departed from God? Not being able to bear the delays of Moses conferring with God, they dared to ask for profane gods, that they might call the head of an ox and an earthen image leaders of their march; nor did they ever desist from their impatience, until, impatient always of docility and of divine admonition, they put to death

their prophets and all the righteous men, and plunged even into the crime of the crucifixion and blood shedding of the Lord. Moreover, impatience makes heretics in the Church, and, after the likeness of the Jews, drives them in opposition to the peace and charity of Christ as rebels, to hostile and raging hatred. And, not at length to enumerate single cases, absolutely everything which patience, by its works, builds up to glory, impatience casts down into ruin.

20. Wherefore, beloved brethren, having diligently pondered both the benefits of patience and the evils of impatience, let us hold fast with full watchfulness the patience whereby we abide in Christ, that with Christ we may attain to God; which patience, copious and manifold, is not restrained by narrow limits, nor confined by strait boundaries. The virtue of patience is widely manifest, and its fertility and liberality proceed indeed from a source of one name but are diffused by overflowing streams through many ways of glory; nor can anything in our actions avail for the perfection of praise, unless from this it receives the substance of its perfection. It is patience which both commends and keeps us to God. It is patience, too, which assuages anger, which bridles the tongue, governs the mind, guards peace, rules discipline, breaks the force of lust, represses the violence of pride, extinguishes the fire of enmity, checks the power of the rich, soothes the want of the poor, protects a blessed integrity in virgins, a careful purity in widows, in those who are united and married a single affection. It makes men humble in prosperity, brave in adversity, gentle towards wrongs and contempt. It teaches us quickly to pardon those who wrong us; and if you yourself do wrong, to entreat long and earnestly. It resists

temptations, suffers persecutions, perfects passions and martyrdoms. It is patience which firmly fortifies the foundations of our faith. It is this which lifts up on high the increase of our hope. It is this which directs our doing, that we may hold fast the way of Christ while we walk by His patience. It is this that makes us to persevere as sons of God, while we imitate our Father's patience.

21. But since I know, beloved brethren, that very many are eager, either on account of the burden or the pain of smarting wrongs, to be quickly avenged of those who act harshly and rage against them, we must not withhold the fact in the furthest particular, that placed as we are in the midst of these storms of a jarring world, and, moreover, the persecutions both of Jews or Gentiles, and heretics, we may patiently wait for the day of (God's) vengeance, and not hurry to revenge our suffering with a querulous haste, since it is written, "Wait ye upon me, saith the Lord, in the day of my rising up for a testimony; for my judgment is to the congregations of the nations, that I may take hold on the kings, and pour out upon them my fury." The Lord commands us to wait, and to bear with brave patience the day of future vengeance; and He also speaks in the Apocalypse, saying, "Seal not the sayings of the prophecy of this book: for now the time is at hand for them that persevere in injuring to injure, and for him that is filthy to be filthy still; but for him that is righteous to do things still more righteous, and likewise for him that is holy to do things still more holy. Behold, I come quickly; and my reward is with me, to render to every man according to his deeds." Whence also the martyrs, crying out and hastening with grief breaking forth to their revenge, are bidden still to wait, and to give patience for the times to be fulfilled and the martyrs to be

completed. "And when He had opened," says he, "the fifth seal, I saw under the altar of God the souls of them that were slain for the word of God, and for their testimony; and they cried with a loud voice, saying, How long, O Lord, holy and true, dost Thou not judge and avenge our blood on them that dwell on the earth? And there were given to them each white robes; and it was said unto them that they should rest yet for a little season, until the number of their fellow-servants and brethren is fulfilled, who afterwards shall be slain after their example."

22. But when shall come the divine vengeance for the righteous blood, the Holy Spirit declares by Malachi the prophet, saying, "Behold, the day of the Lord cometh, burning as an oven; and all the aliens and all the wicked shall be stubble; and the day that cometh shall burn them up, saith the Lord." And this we read also in the Psalms, where the approach of God the Judge is announced as worthy to be reverenced for the majesty of His judgment: "God shall come manifest, our God, and shall not keep silence; a fire shall burn before Him, and round about Him a great tempest. He shall call the heaven above, and the earth beneath, that He may separate His people. Gather His saints together unto Him, who establish His covenant in sacrifices; and the heavens shall declare His righteousness, for God is the Judge." And Isaiah foretells the same things, saying: "For, behold, the Lord shall come like a fire, and His chariot as a storm, to render vengeance in anger; for in the fire of the Lord they shall be judged, and with His sword shall they be wounded." And again: "The Lord God of hosts shall go forth, and shall crumble the war to pieces; He shall stir up the battle, and shall cry out against His enemies with strength, I have held my

peace; shall I always hold my peace?"

23. But who is this that says that he has held his peace before, and will not hold his peace forever? Surely it is He who was led as a sheep to the slaughter; and as a lamb before its shearer is without voice, so He opened not His mouth. Surely it is He who did not cry, nor was His voice heard in the streets. Surely He who was not rebellious, neither contradicted, when He offered His back to stripes, and His cheeks to the palms of the hands; neither turned away His face from the foulness of spitting. Surely it is He who, when He was accused by the priests and elders, answered nothing, and, to the wonder of Pilate, kept a most patient silence. This is He who, although He was silent in His passion, yet by and by will not be silent in His vengeance. This is our God, that is, not the God of all, but of the faithful and believing; and He, when He shall come manifest in His second advent, will not be silent. For although He came first shrouded in humility, yet He shall come manifest in power.

24. Let us wait for Him, beloved brethren, our Judge and Avenger, who shall equally avenge with Himself the congregation of His Church, and the number of all the righteous from the beginning of the world. Let him who hurries, and is too impatient for his revenge, consider that even He Himself is not yet avenged who is the Avenger. God the Father ordained His Son to be adored; and the Apostle Paul, mindful of the divine command, lays it down, and says: "God hath exalted Him, and given Him a name which is above every name, that in the name of Jesus every knee should bow, of things heavenly, and things earthly, and things beneath." And in the Apocalypse the angel withstands John, who wishes to worship him, and says: "See thou do it not; for I am thy

fellow-servant, and of thy brethren. Worship Jesus the Lord." How great is the Lord Jesus, and how great is His patience, that He who is adored in heaven is not yet avenged on earth! Let us, beloved brethren, consider His patience in our persecutions and sufferings; let us give an obedience full of expectation to His advent; and let us not hasten, servants as we are, to be defended before our Lord with irreligious and immodest eagerness. Let us rather press onward and labor, and, watching with our whole heart, and steadfast to all endurance, let us keep the Lord's precepts; so that when that day of anger and vengeance shall come, we may not be punished with the impious and sinners, but may be honored with the righteous and those that fear God.

Treatise X.
On Jealousy and Envy.
Argument.—After Pointing Out that Jealousy or Envy is a Sin All the More Heinous in Proportion as Its Wickedness is Hidden, and that Its Origin is to Be Traced to the Devil, He Gives Illustrations of Envy from the Old Testament, and Gathers, by Reference to Special Vices, that Envy is the Root of All Wickedness. Therefore with Reason Was Fraternal Hatred Forbidden Not in One Place Only, But by Christ and His Apostles. Finally, Exhorting to the Love of One's Enemies by God's Example, He Dissuades from the Sin of Envy, by Urging the Rewards Set Before the Indulgence of Love.

1. To be jealous of what you see to be good, and to be envious of those who are better than yourself, seems, beloved brethren, in the eyes of some people to be a slight and petty wrong; and, being thought trifling and of small account, it is not feared; not being feared, it is contemned;

being contemned, it is not easily shunned: and it thus becomes a dark and hidden mischief, which, as it is not perceived so as to be guarded against by the prudent, secretly distresses incautious minds. But, moreover, the Lord bade us be prudent, and charged us to watch with careful solicitude, lest the adversary, who is always on the watch and always lying in wait, should creep stealthily into our breast, and blow up a flame from the sparks, magnifying small things into the greatest; and so, while soothing the unguarded and careless with a milder air and a softer breeze, should stir up storms and whirlwinds, and bring about the destruction of faith and the shipwreck of salvation and of life. Therefore, beloved brethren, we must be on our guard, and strive with all our powers to repel, with solicitous and full watchfulness, the enemy, raging and aiming his darts against every part of our body in which we can be stricken and wounded, in accordance with what the Apostle Peter, in his epistle, forewarns and teaches, saying, "Be sober, and watch; because your adversary the devil, as a roaring lion, goes about seeking any one to devour."

2. He goes about every one of us; and even as an enemy besieging those who are shut up (in a city), he examines the walls, and tries whether there is any part of the walls less firm and less trustworthy, by entrance through which he may penetrate to the inside. He presents to the eyes seductive forms and easy pleasures, that he may destroy chastity by the sight. He tempts the ears with harmonious music, that by the hearing of sweet sounds he may relax and enervate Christian vigor. He provokes the tongue by reproaches; he instigates the hand by exasperating wrongs to the recklessness of murder; to make the cheat, he presents dishonest gains; to take

captive the soul by money, he heaps together mischievous hoards; he promises earthly honors, that he may deprive of heavenly ones; he makes a show of false things, that he may steal away the true; and when he cannot hiddenly deceive, he threatens plainly and openly, holding forth the fear of turbulent persecution to vanquish God's servants—always restless, and always hostile, crafty in peace, and fierce in persecution.

3. Wherefore, beloved brethren, against all the devil's deceiving snares or open threatening, the mind ought to stand arrayed and armed, ever as ready to repel as the foe is ever ready to attack. And since those darts of his which creep on us in concealment are more frequent, and his more hidden and secret hurling of them is the more severely and frequently effectual to our wounding, in proportion as it is the less perceived, let us also be watchful to understand and repel these, among which is the evil of jealousy and envy. And if any one closely looks into this, he will find that nothing should be more guarded against by the Christian, nothing more carefully watched, than being taken captive by envy and malice, that none, entangled in the blind snares of a deceitful enemy, in that the brother is turned by envy to hatred of his brother, should himself be unwittingly destroyed by his own sword. That we may be able more fully to collect and more plainly to perceive this, let us recur to its fount and origin. Let us consider whence arises jealousy, and when and how it begins. For so mischievous an evil will be more easily shunned by us, if both the source and the magnitude of that same evil be known.

4. From this source, even at the very beginnings of the world, the devil was the first who both perished (himself) and destroyed (others). He who was sustained in

angelic majesty, he who was accepted and beloved of God, when he beheld man made in the image of God, broke forth into jealousy with malevolent envy—not hurling down another by the instinct of his jealousy before he himself was first hurled down by jealousy, captive before he takes captive, ruined before he ruins others. While, at the instigation of jealousy, he robs man of the grace of immortality conferred, he himself has lost that which he had previously been. How great an evil is that, beloved brethren, whereby an angel fell, whereby that lofty and illustrious grandeur could be defrauded and overthrown, whereby he who deceived was himself deceived! Thenceforth envy rages on the earth, in that he who is about to perish by jealousy obeys the author of his ruin, imitating the devil in his jealousy; as it is written, "But through envy of the devil death entered into the world." Therefore they who are on his side imitate him.

5. Hence, in fine, began the primal hatreds of the new brotherhood, hence the abominable fratricides, in that the unrighteous Cain is jealous of the righteous Abel, in that the wicked persecutes the good with envy and jealousy. So far prevailed the rage of envy to the consummation of that deed of wickedness, that neither the love of his brother, nor the immensity of the crime, nor the fear of God, nor the penalty of the sin, was considered. He was unrighteously stricken who had been the first to show righteousness; he endured hatred who had not known how to hate; he was impiously slain, who, dying, did not resist. And that Esau was hostile to his brother Jacob, arose from jealousy also. For because the latter had received his father's blessing, the former was inflamed to a persecuting hatred by the brands of jealousy. And that Joseph was sold by his brethren, the

reason of their selling him proceeded from envy. When in simplicity, and as a brother to brethren, he set forth to them the prosperity which had been shown to him in visions, their malevolent disposition broke forth into envy. Moreover, that Saul the king hated David, so as to seek by often repeated persecutions to kill him—innocent, merciful, gentle, patient in meekness—what else was the provocation save the spur of jealousy? Because, when Goliath was slain, and by the aid and condescension of God so great an enemy was routed, the wondering people burst forth with the suffrage of acclamation into praises of David, Saul through jealousy conceived the rage of enmity and persecution. And, not to go to the length of numbering each one, let us observe the destruction of a people that perished once for all. Did not the Jews perish for this reason, that they chose rather to envy Christ than to believe Him? Disparaging those great works which He did, they were deceived by blinding jealousy, and could not open the eyes of their heart to the knowledge of divine things.

6. Considering which things, beloved brethren, let us with vigilance and courage fortify our hearts dedicated to God against such a destructiveness of evil. Let the death of others avail for our safety; let the punishment of the unwise confer health upon the prudent. Moreover, there is no ground for anyone to suppose that evil of that kind is confined in one form or restrained within brief limits in a narrow boundary. The mischief of jealousy, manifold and fruitful, extends widely. It is the root of all evils, the fountain of disasters, the nursery of crimes, the material of transgressions. Thence arises hatred, thence proceeds animosity. Jealousy inflames avarice, in that one cannot be content with what is his own, while he sees

another wealthier. Jealousy stirs up ambition, when one sees another more exalted in honors. When jealousy darkens our perceptions and reduces the secret agencies of the mind under its command, the fear of God is despised, the teaching of Christ is neglected, the day of judgment is not anticipated. Pride inflates, cruelty embitters, faithlessness prevaricates, impatience agitates, discord rages, anger grows hot; nor can he who has become the subject of a foreign authority any longer restrain or govern himself. By this the bond of the Lord's peace is broken; by this is violated brotherly charity; by this truth is adulterated, unity is divided; men plunge into heresies and schisms when priests are disparaged, when bishops are envied, when a man complains that he himself was not rather ordained, or disdains to suffer that another should be put over him. Hence the man who is haughty through jealousy, and perverse through envy, kicks, hence he revolts, in anger and malice the opponent, not of the man, but of the honor.

 7. But what a gnawing worm of the soul is it, what a plague-spot of our thoughts, what a rust of the heart, to be jealous of another, either in respect of his virtue or of his happiness; that is, to hate in him either his own deserving or the divine benefits—to turn the advantages of others into one's own mischief—to be tormented by the prosperity of illustrious men—to make other people's glory one's own penalty, and, as it were, to apply a sort of executioner to one's own breast, to bring the tormentors to one's own thoughts and feelings, that they may tear us with intestine pangs, and may smite the secret recesses of the heart with the hoof of malevolence. To such, no food is joyous, no drink can be cheerful. They are ever sighing, and groaning, and grieving; and since envy is never put

off by the envious, the possessed heart is rent without intermission day and night. Other ills have their limit; and whatever wrong is done, is bounded by the completion of the crime. In the adulterer the offence ceases when the violation is perpetrated; in the case of the robber, the crime is at rest when the homicide is committed; and the possession of the booty puts an end to the rapacity of the thief; and the completed deception places a limit to the wrong of the cheat. Jealousy has no limit; it is an evil continually enduring, and a sin without end. In proportion as he who is envied has the advantage of a greater success, in that proportion the envious man burns with the fires of jealousy to an increased heat.

8. Hence the threatening countenance, the lowering aspect, pallor in the face, trembling on the lips, gnashing of the teeth, mad words, unbridled reviling, a hand prompt for the violence of slaughter; even if for the time deprived of a sword, yet armed with the hatred of an infuriate mind. And accordingly the Holy Spirit says in the Psalms: "Be not jealous against him who walketh prosperously in his way." And again: "The wicked shall observe the righteous and shall gnash upon him with his teeth. But God shall laugh at him; for He sees that his day is coming." The blessed Apostle Paul designates and points out these when he says, "The poison of asps is under their lips, and their mouth is full of cursing and bitterness. Their feet are swift to shed blood, destruction and misery are in their ways, who have not known the way of peace; neither is the fear of God before their eyes."

9. The mischief is much more trifling, and the danger less, when the limbs are wounded with a sword. The cure is easy where the wound is manifest; and when

the medicament is applied, the sore that is seen is quickly brought to health. The wounds of jealousy are hidden and secret; nor do they admit the remedy of a healing cure, since they have shut themselves in blind suffering within the lurking-places of the conscience. Whoever you are that is envious and malignant, observe how crafty, mischievous, and hateful you are to those whom you hate. Yet you are the enemy of no one's well-being more than your own. Whoever he is whom you persecute with jealousy, can evade and escape you. You cannot escape yourself. Wherever you may be, your adversary is with you; your enemy is always in your own breast; your mischief is shut up within; you are tied and bound with the links of chains from which you cannot extricate yourself; you are captive under the tyranny of jealousy; nor will any consolations help you. It is a persistent evil to persecute a man who belongs to the grace of God. It is a calamity without remedy to hate the happy.

10. And therefore, beloved brethren, the Lord, taking thought for this risk, that none should fall into the snare of death through jealousy of his brother, when His disciples asked Him which among them should be the greatest, said, "Who soever shall be least among you all, the same shall be great." He cut off all envy by His reply. He plucked out and tore away every cause and matter of gnawing envy. A disciple of Christ must not be jealous, must not be envious. With us there can be no contest for exaltation; from humility we grow to the highest attainments; we have learnt in what way we may be pleasing. And finally, the Apostle Paul, instructing and warning, that we who, illuminated by the light of Christ, have escaped from the darkness of the conversation of night, should walk in the deeds and works of light, writes

and says, "The night has passed over, and the day is approaching let us therefore cast away the works of darkness, and let us put upon us the armor of light. Let us walk honestly, as in the day; not in rioting and drunkenness, not in lusts and wantonness, not in strife and jealousy." If the darkness has departed from your breast, if the night is scattered therefrom, if the gloom is chased away, if the brightness of day has illuminated your senses, if you have begun to be a man of light, do those things which are Christ's, because Christ is the Light and the Day.

11. Why do you rush into the darkness of jealousy? why do you enfold yourself in the cloud of malice? why do you quench all the light of peace and charity in the blindness of envy? why do you return to the devil, whom you had renounced? why do you stand like Cain? For that he who is jealous of his brother, and has him in hatred, is bound by the guilt of homicide, the Apostle John declares in his epistle, saying, "Whosoever hated his brother is a murderer; and ye know that no murderer hath life abiding in him." And again: "He that saith he is in the light, and hated his brother, is in darkness even until now, and walketh in darkness, and knows not whither he goes, because that darkness hath blinded his eyes." Whosoever hates, says he, his brother, walketh in darkness, and knows not whither he goes. For he goes unconsciously to Gehenna, in ignorance and blindness; he is hurrying into punishment, departing, that is, from the light of Christ, who warns and says, "I am the light of the world. He that followed me shall not walk in darkness but shall have the light of life." But he follows Christ who stands in His precepts, who walks in the way of His teaching, who follows His footsteps and His ways,

who imitates that which Christ both did and taught; in accordance with what Peter also exhorts and warns, saying, "Christ suffered for us, leaving you an example that ye should follow His steps."

12. We ought to remember by what name Christ calls His people, by what title He names His flock. He calls them sheep, that their Christian innocence may be like that of sheep; He calls them lambs, that their simplicity of mind may imitate the simple nature of lambs. Why does the wolf lurk under the garb of sheep? why does he who falsely asserts himself to be a Christian, dishonor the flock of Christ? To put on the name of Christ, and not to go in the way of Christ, what else is it but a mockery of the divine name, but a desertion of the way of salvation; since He Himself teaches and says that he shall come unto life who keeps His commandments, and that he is wise who hears and does His words; that he, moreover, is called the greatest doctor in the kingdom of heaven who thus does and teaches; that, then, will be of advantage to the preacher what has been well and usefully preached, if what is uttered by his mouth is fulfilled by deeds following? But what did the Lord more frequently instill into His disciples, what did He more charge to be guarded and observed among His saving counsels and heavenly precepts, than that with the same love wherewith He Himself loved the disciples, we also should love one another? And in what manner does he keep either the peace or the love of the Lord, who, when jealousy intrudes, can neither be peaceable nor loving?

13. Thus also the Apostle Paul, when he was urging the merits of peace and charity, and when he was strongly asserting and teaching that neither faith nor alms, nor even the passion itself of the confessor and the

martyr, would avail him, unless he kept the requirements of charity entire and inviolate, added, and said: "Charity is magnanimous, charity is kind, charity envies not;" teaching, doubtless, and showing that whoever is magnanimous, and kind, and averse from jealousy and rancor, such a one can maintain charity. Moreover, in another place, when he was advising that the man who has already become filled with the Holy Spirit, and a son of God by heavenly birth, should observe nothing but spiritual and divine things, he lays it down, and says: "And I indeed, brethren, could not speak unto you as unto spiritual, but as unto carnal, even as unto babes in Christ. I have fed you with milk, not with meat: for ye were not able hitherto; moreover, neither now are ye able. For ye are yet carnal: for whereas there are still among you jealousy, and contention, and strife, are ye not carnal, and walk as men?"

14. Vices and carnal sins must be trampled down, beloved brethren, and the corrupting plague of the earthly body must be trodden under foot with spiritual vigor, lest, while we are turned back again to the conversation of the old man, we be entangled in deadly snares, even as the apostle, with foresight and wholesomeness, forewarned us of this very thing, and said: "Therefore, brethren, let us not live after the flesh; for if ye live after the flesh, ye shall begin to die; but if ye, through the Spirit, mortify the deeds of the flesh, ye shall live. For as many as are led by the Spirit of God, they are the sons of God." If we are the sons of God, if we are already beginning to be His temples, if, having received the Holy Spirit, we are living holily and spiritually, if we have raised our eyes from earth to heaven, if we have lifted our hearts, filled with God and Christ, to things above and divine, let us do

nothing but what is worthy of God and Christ, even as the apostle arouses and exhorts us, saying: "If ye be risen with Christ, seek those things which are above, where Christ is sitting at the right hand of God; occupy your minds with things that are above, not with things which are upon the earth. For ye are dead, and your life is hidden with Christ in God. But when Christ, who is your life, shall appear, then shall ye also appear with Him in glory." Let us, then, who in baptism have both died and been buried in respect of the carnal sins of the old man, who have risen again with Christ in the heavenly regeneration, both think upon and do the things which are Christ's, even as the same apostle again teaches and counsels, saying: "The first man is of the dust of the earth; the second man is from heaven. Such as he is from the earth, such also are they who are from the earth and such as He the heavenly is, such also are they who are heavenly. As we have borne the image of him who is of the earth, let us also bear the image of Him who is from heaven." But we cannot bear the heavenly image, unless in that condition wherein we have already begun to be, we show forth the likeness of Christ.

  15. For this is to change what you had been, and to begin to be what you were not, that the divine birth might shine forth in you, that the godly discipline might respond to God, the Father, that in the honor and praise of living, God may be glorified in man; as He Himself exhorts, and warns, and promises to those who glorify Him a reward in their turn, saying, "Them that glorify me I will glorify, and he who despises me shall be despised." For which glorification the Lord, forming and preparing us, and the Son of God instilling the likeness of God the Father, says in His Gospel: "Ye have heard that it hath been said, Thou

shalt love thy neighbor, and hate thine enemy. But I say unto you, Love your enemies, and pray for them which persecute you; that ye may be the children of your Father which is in heaven, who makes His sun to rise on the good and on the evil, and sends rain upon the just and on the unjust." If it is a source of joy and glory to men to have children like to themselves—and it is more agreeable to have begotten an offspring then when the remaining progeny responds to the parent with like lineaments—how much greater is the gladness in God the Father, when any one is so spiritually born that in his acts and praises the divine eminence of race is announced! What a palm of righteousness is it, what a crown to be such a one as that the Lord should not say of you, "I have begotten and brought up children, but they have despised me!" Let Christ rather applaud you, and invite you to the reward, saying, "Come, ye blessed of my Father, receive the kingdom which is prepared for you from the beginning of the world."

16. The mind must be strengthened, beloved brethren, by these meditations. By exercises of this kind it must be confirmed against all the darts of the devil. Let there be the divine reading in the hands, the Lord's thoughts in the mind; let constant prayer never cease at all; let saving labor persevere. Let us be always busied in spiritual actions, that so often as the enemy approaches, however often he may try to come near, he may find the breast closed and armed against him. For a Christian man's crown is not only that which is received in the time of persecution: peace also has its crowns, wherewith the victors, from a varied and manifold engagement, are crowned, when their adversary is prostrated and subdued. Overcoming lust is the palm of continency. To have

resisted against anger, against injury, is the crown of patience. It is a triumph over avarice to despise money. It is the praise of faith, by trust in the future, to suffer the adversity of the world. And he who is not haughty in prosperity, obtains glory for his humility; and he who is disposed to the mercifulness of cherishing the poor, obtains the retribution of a heavenly treasure; and he who knows not to be jealous, and who with one heart and in meekness loves his brethren, is honored with the recompense of love and peace. In this course of virtues we daily run; to these palms and crowns of justice we attain without intermission of time.

17. To these rewards that you also may come who had been possessed with jealousy and rancor, cast away all that malice wherewith you were before held fast, and be reformed to the way of eternal life in the footsteps of salvation. Tear out from your breast thorns and thistles, that the Lord's seed may enrich you with a fertile produce, that the divine and spiritual cornfield may abound to the plentifulness of a fruitful harvest. Cast out the poison of gall, cast out the virus of discords. Let the mind which the malice of the serpent had infected be purged; let all bitterness which had settled within be softened by the sweetness of Christ. If you take both meat and drink from the sacrament of the cross, let the wood which at Mara availed in a figure for sweetening the taste, avail to you in reality for soothing your softened breast; and you shall not strive for a medicine for your increasing health. Be cured by that whereby you had been wounded. Love those whom you previously had hated; favor those whom you envied with unjust disparagements. Imitate good men, if you are able to follow them; but if you are not able to follow them, at least rejoice with them, and

congratulate those who are better than you. Make yourself a sharer with them in united love; make yourself their associate in the alliance of charity and the bond of brotherhood. Your debts shall be remitted to you when you yourself shall have forgiven. Your sacrifices shall be received when you shall come in peace to God. Your thoughts and deeds shall be directed from above, when you consider those things which are divine and righteous, as it is written: "Let the heart of a man consider righteous things, that his steps may be directed by the Lord."

18. And you have many things to consider. Think of paradise, whither Cain does not enter, who by jealousy slew his brother. Think of the heavenly kingdom, to which the Lord does not admit any but those who are of one heart and mind. Consider that those alone can be called sons of God who are peacemakers, who in heavenly birth and by the divine law are made one and respond to the likeness of God the Father and of Christ. Consider that we are standing under the eyes of God, that we are pursuing the course of our conversation and our life, with God Himself looking on and judging, that we may then at length be able to attain to the result of beholding Him, if we now delight Him who sees us, by our actions, if we show ourselves worthy of His favor and indulgence; if we, who are always to please Him in His kingdom, previously please Him in the world.

Treatise XI.
Exhortation to Martyrdom, Addressed to Fortunatus. Preface.
1. You have desired, beloved Fortunatus that, since the burden of persecutions and afflictions is lying heavy upon us, and in the ending and completion of the

world the hateful time of Antichrist is already beginning to draw near, I would collect from the sacred Scriptures some exhortations for preparing and strengthening the minds of the brethren, whereby I might animate the soldiers of Christ for the heavenly and spiritual contest. I have been constrained to obey your so needful wish, so that as much as my limited powers, instructed by the aid of divine inspiration, are sufficient, some arms, as it were, and defenses might be brought forth from the Lord's precepts for the brethren who are about to fight. For it is little to arouse God's people by the trumpet call of our voice, unless we confirm the faith of believers, and their valor dedicated and devoted to God, by the divine readings.

2. But what more fitly or more fully agrees with my own care and solicitude, than to prepare the people divinely entrusted to me, and an army established in the heavenly camp, by assiduous exhortations against the darts and weapons of the devil? For he cannot be a soldier fitted for the war who has not first been exercised in the field; nor will he who seeks to gain the crown of contest be rewarded on the racecourse, unless he first considers the use and skillfulness of his powers. It is an ancient adversary and an old enemy with whom we wage our battle: six thousand years are now nearly completed since the devil first attacked man. All kinds of temptation, and arts, and snares for his overthrow, he has learned by the very practice of long years. If he finds Christ's soldier unprepared, if unskilled, if not careful and watching with his whole heart; he circumvents him if ignorant, he deceives him incautious, he cheats him inexperienced. But if a man, keeping the Lord's precepts, and bravely adhering to Christ, stands against him, he must needs be

conquered, because Christ, whom that man confesses, is unconquered.

3. And that I might not extend my discourse, beloved brother, to too great a length, and fatigue my hearer or reader by the abundance of a too diffuse style, I have made a compendium; so that the titles being placed first, which everyone ought both to know and to have in mind, I might subjoin sections of the Lord's word, and establish what I had proposed by the authority of the divine teaching, in such wise as that I might not appear to have sent you my own treatise so much, as to have suggested material for others to discourse on; a proceeding which will be of advantage to individuals with increased benefit. For if I were to give a man a garment finished and ready, it would be my garment that another was making use of, and probably the thing made for another would be found little fitting for his figure of stature and body. But now I have sent you the very wool and the purple from the Lamb, by whom we were redeemed and quickened; which, when you have received, you will make into a coat for yourself according to your own will, and the rather that you will rejoice in it as your own private and special garment. And you will exhibit to others also what we have sent, that they themselves may be able to finish it according to their will; so that that old nakedness being covered, they may all bear the garments of Christ robed in the sanctification of heavenly grace.

4. Moreover also, beloved brethren, I have considered it a useful and wholesome plan in an exhortation so needful as that which may make martyrs, to cut off all delays and tardiness in our words, and to put away the windings of human discourse, and set down only those things which God speaks, wherewith Christ exhorts

His servants to martyrdom. Those divine precepts themselves must be supplied, as it were, for arms for the combatants. Let them be the incitements of the warlike trumpet; let them be the clarion-blast for the warriors. Let the ears be roused by them; let the minds be prepared by them; let the powers both of soul and body be strengthened to all endurance of suffering. Let us only who, by the Lord's permission, have given the first baptism to believers, also prepare each one for the second; urging and teaching that this is a baptism greater in grace, more lofty in power, more precious in honor—a baptism wherein angels baptize—a baptism in which God and His Christ exult—a baptism after which no one sins any more—a baptism which completes the increase of our faith—a baptism which, as we withdraw from the world, immediately associates us with God. In the baptism of water is received the remission of sins, in the baptism of blood the crown of virtues. This thing is to be embraced and desired, and to be asked for in all the entreaties of our petitions, that we who are God's servants should be also His friends.

Heads of the Following Book.

1. Therefore, in exhorting and preparing our brethren, and in arming them with firmness of virtue and faith for the heralding forth of the confession of the Lord, and for the battle of persecution and suffering, we must declare, in the first place, that the idols which man makes for himself are not gods. For things which are made are not greater than their maker and fashioner; nor can these things protect and preserve anybody, which themselves

perish out of their temples, unless they are preserved by man. But neither are those elements to be worshipped which serve man according to the disposition and ordinance of God.

2. The idols being destroyed, and the truth concerning the elements being manifested, we must show that God only is to be worshipped.

3. Then we must add, what is God's threatening against those who sacrifice to idols.

4. Besides, we must teach that God does not easily pardon idolaters.

5. And that God is so angry with idolatry, that He has even commanded those to be slain who persuade others to sacrifice and serve idols.

6. After this we must subjoin, that being redeemed and quickened by the blood of Christ, we ought to prefer nothing to Christ, because He preferred nothing to us, and on our account preferred evil things to good, poverty to riches, servitude to rule, death to immortality; that we, on the contrary, in our sufferings are preferring the riches and delights of paradise to the poverty of the world, eternal dominion and kingdom to the slavery of time, immortality to death, God and Christ to the devil and Antichrist.

7. We must urge also, that when snatched from the jaws of the devil, and freed from the snares of this world, if they begin to be in difficulty and trouble, they must not desire to return again to the world, and so lose the advantage of their withdrawal therefrom.

8. That we must rather urge on and persevere in faith and virtue, and in completion of heavenly and spiritual grace, that we may attain to the palm and to the crown.

9. For that afflictions and persecutions are brought about for this purpose, that we may be proved.

10. Neither must we fear the injuries and penalties of persecutions, because greater is the Lord to protect than the devil to assault.

11. And lest anyone should be frightened and troubled at the afflictions and persecutions which we suffer in this world, we must prove that it was before foretold that the world would hold us in hatred, and that it would arouse persecutions against us; that from this very thing, that these things come to pass, is manifest the truth of the divine promise, in recompenses and rewards which shall afterwards follow; that it is no new thing which happens to Christians, since from the beginning of the world the good have suffered, and have been oppressed and slain by the unrighteous.

12. In the last place, it must be laid down what hope and what reward await the righteous and martyrs after the struggles and the sufferings of this time, and that we shall receive more in the reward of our suffering than what we suffer here in the passion itself.

On the Exhortation to Martyrdom.

1. That idols are not gods, and that the elements are not to be worshipped in the place of gods.

In the cxiiith Psalm it is shown that "the idols of the heathen are silver and gold, the work of men's hands. They have a mouth, and speak not; eyes have they, and see not. They have ears and hear not; neither is there any breath in their mouth. Let those that make them be made like unto them." Also in the Wisdom of Solomon: "They counted all the idols of the nations to be gods, which neither have the use of eyes to see, nor noses to draw breath, nor ears to hear, nor fingers on their hands to handle; and as for their feet, they are slow to go. For man made them, and he that borrowed his own spirit fashioned them; but no man can make a god like unto himself. For, since he is mortal, he works a dead thing with wicked hands; for he himself is better than the things which he worshipped, since he indeed lived once, but they never." In Exodus also: "Thou shalt not make to thee an idol, nor the likeness of anything." Moreover, in Solomon, concerning the elements: "Neither by considering the works did they acknowledge who was the work master; but deemed either fire, or wind, or the swift air, or the circle of the stars, or the violent water, or the sun, or the moon, to be gods. On account of whose beauty, if they thought this, let them know how much more beautiful is the Lord than they. Or if they admired their powers and operations, let them understand by them, that He that made these mighty things is mightier than they."

2. That God alone must be worshipped.

"As it is written, Thou shalt worship the Lord thy God, and Him only shalt thou serve." Also in Exodus: "Thou shalt have none other gods beside me." Also in Deuteronomy: "See ye, see ye that I am He, and that there is no God beside me. I will kill, and will make alive; I will smite, and I will heal; and there is none who can deliver out of mine hands." In the Apocalypse, moreover: "And I saw another angel fly in the midst of heaven, having the everlasting Gospel to preach over the earth, and over all nations, and tribes, and tongues, and peoples, saying with a loud voice, Fear God rather, and give glory to Him: for the hour of His judgment is come; and worship Him that made heaven and earth, and the sea, and all that therein is." So also the Lord, in His Gospel, makes mention of the first and second commandment, saying, "Hear, O Israel, The Lord thy God is one God;" and, "Thou shalt love thy Lord with all thy heart, and with all thy soul, and with all thy strength. This is the first; and the second is like unto it, Thou shalt love thy neighbor as thyself. On these two commandments hang all the law and the prophets." And once more: "And this is life eternal, that they may know Thee, the only and true God, and Jesus Christ, whom Thou hast sent."

3. What is God's threatening against those who sacrifice to idols?

In Exodus: "He that sacrifices unto any gods but the Lord only, shall be rooted out." Also in Deuteronomy: "They sacrificed unto demons, and not to God." In Isaiah also: "They worshipped those which their fingers have made; and the mean man was bowed down, and the great man was humbled: and I will not forgive them." And again: "To them hast thou poured out drink-offerings, and to them thou hast offered sacrifices. For these, therefore, shall I not be angry, saith the Lord?" In Jeremiah also: "Walk ye not after other gods, to serve them; and worship them not, and provoke me not in the works of your hands, to destroy you." In the Apocalypse too: "If any man worship the beast and his image, and receive his mark in his forehead or in his hand, he shall also drink of the wine of the wrath of God, which is mixed in the cup of His wrath, and shall be punished with fire and brimstone before the eyes of the holy angels, and before the eyes of the Lamb: and the smoke of their torments shall ascend for ever and ever: and they shall have no rest day or night, whosoever worship the beast and his image."

4. That God does not easily pardon idolaters.

Moses in Exodus prays for the people, and does not obtain his prayer, saying: "I pray, O Lord, this people hath sinned a great sin. They have made them gods of gold. And now, if Thou forgives them their sin, forgive it; but if not, blot me out of the book which Thou hast written. And the Lord said unto Moses, If any one hath sinned against me, him will I blot out of my book." Moreover, when Jeremiah besought for the people, the Lord speaks to him, saying: "And pray not thou for this people, and entreat not for them in prayer and supplication; because I will not hear in the time wherein they shall call upon me in the time of their affliction." Ezekiel also denounces this same anger of God upon those who sin against God and says: "And the word of the Lord came unto me, saying, Son of man, whatsoever land sinned against me, by committing an offence, I will stretch forth mine hand upon it, and will crush the support of the bread thereof; and I will send into it famine, and I will take away from it man and beast. And though these three men were in the midst of it, Noah, Daniel, and Job, they shall not deliver sons nor daughters; they themselves only shall be delivered." Likewise in the first book of Kings: "If a man sin by offending against another, they shall beseech the Lord for him; but if a man sin against God, who shall entreat for him?"

5. That God is so angry against idolatry, that He has even enjoined those to be slain who persuade others to sacrifice and serve idols.

In Deuteronomy: "But if thy brother, or thy son, or thy daughter, or thy wife which is in thy bosom, or thy friend which is the fellow of thine own soul, should ask thee secretly, saying, Let us go and serve other gods, the gods of the nations, thou shalt not consent unto him, and thou shalt not hearken unto him, neither shall thine eye spare him, neither shalt thou conceal him, declaring thou shalt declare concerning him. Thine hand shall be upon him first of all to put him to death, and afterwards the hand of all the people; and they shall stone him, and he shall die, because he hath sought to turn thee away from the Lord thy God." And again the Lord speaks, and says, that neither must a city be spared, even though the whole city should consent to idolatry: "Or if thou shalt hear in one of the cities which the Lord thy God shall give thee, to dwell there, saying, Let us go and serve other gods, which thou hast not known, slaying thou shalt kill all who are in the city with the slaughter of the sword, and burn the city with fire, and it shall be without habitation forever. Moreover, it shall no longer be rebuilt, that the Lord may be turned from the indignation of His anger. And He will show thee mercy, and He will pity thee, and will multiply thee, if thou wilt hear the voice of the Lord thy God, and wilt observe His precepts." Remembering which precept and its force, Mattathias slew him who had approached the altar to sacrifice. But if before the coming of Christ these precepts concerning the worship of God and the despising of idols were observed, how much more should they be regarded since Christ's advent; since He, when He came, not only exhorted us with words, but with deeds also, but after all wrongs and contumelies, suffered also, and was crucified, that He might teach us to suffer and to die by His example, that there might be no excuse for a man not to suffer for Him, since He suffered for us; and that since He suffered for the sins of others, much rather ought each to suffer for his own sins. And therefore in the Gospel He threatens and says: "Whosoever shall confess me before men, him will I also confess before my Father which is in heaven; but whosoever shall deny me before men, him will I also deny before my Father which is in heaven." The Apostle Paul also says: "For if we die with Him, we shall also live with Him; if we suffer, we shall also reign with Him; if we deny Him, He also will deny us." John too: "Whosoever denies the Son, the same hath not the Father; he that acknowledges the Son, hath both the Son and the Father." Whence the Lord exhorts and strengthens us to contempt of death, saying: "Fear not them which kill the body, but are not able to kill the soul; but rather fear Him which is able to kill soul and body in Gehenna." And again: "He that loves his life shall lose it; and he who hates his life in this world, shall keep it unto life eternal."

6. That, being redeemed and quickened by the blood of Christ, we ought to prefer nothing to Christ.

In the Gospel the Lord speaks and says: "He that loveth father or mother more than me, is not worthy of me; and he that loveth son or daughter more than me, is not worthy of me; and he that takes not his cross and follows me, is not worthy of me." So also it is written in Deuteronomy: "They who say to their father and their mother, I have not known thee, and have not acknowledged their own children, these have kept Thy precepts, and have observed Thy covenant." Moreover, the Apostle Paul says: "Who shall separate us from the love of Christ? shall tribulation, distress, or persecution, or hunger, or nakedness, or peril, or sword? As it is written, Because for Thy sake we are killed all the day long, we are counted as sheep for the slaughter. Nay, in all these things we overcome on account of Him who hath loved us." And again: "Ye are not your own, for ye are bought with a great price. Glorify and bear God in your body." And again: "Christ died for all, that both they which live may not henceforth live unto themselves, but unto Him which died for them, and rose again."

7. That those who are snatched from the jaws of the devil, and delivered from the snares of this world, ought not again to return to the world, lest they should lose the advantage of their withdrawal therefrom.

In Exodus the Jewish people, prefigured as a shadow and image of us, when, with God for their guardian and avenger, they had escaped the most severe slavery of Pharaoh and of Egypt—that is, of the devil and the world—faithless and ungrateful in respect of God, murmur against Moses, looking back to the discomforts of the desert and of their labor; and, not understanding the divine benefits of liberty and salvation, they seek to return to the slavery of Egypt—that is, of the world whence they had been drawn forth—when they ought rather to have trusted and believed on God, since He who delivers His people from the devil and the world, protects them also when delivered. "Wherefore hast thou thus done with us," say they, "in casting us forth out of Egypt? It is better for us to serve the Egyptians than to die in this wilderness. And Moses said unto the people, Trust, and stand fast, and see the salvation which is from the Lord, which He shall do to you to-day. The Lord Himself shall fight for you, and ye shall hold your peace." The Lord, admonishing us of this in His Gospel, and teaching that we should not return again to the devil and to the world, which we have renounced, and whence we have escaped, says: "No man looking back, and putting his hand to the plough, is fit for the kingdom of God." And again: "And let him that is in the field not return back. Remember

Lot's wife." And lest anyone should be retarded by any covetousness of wealth or attraction of his own people from following Christ, He adds, and says: "He that forsakes not all that he hath, cannot be my disciple."

8. That we must press on and persevere in faith and virtue, and in completion of heavenly and spiritual grace, that we may attain to the palm and the crown.

In the book of Chronicles: "The Lord is with you so long as ye also are with Him; but if ye forsake Him, He will forsake you." In Ezekiel also: "The righteousness of the righteous shall not deliver him in what day soever he may transgress." Moreover, in the Gospel the Lord speaks, and says: "He that shall endure to the end, the same shall be saved." And again: "If ye shall abide in my word, ye shall be my disciples indeed; and ye shall know the truth, and the truth shall make you free." Moreover, forewarning us that we ought always to be ready, and to stand firmly equipped and armed, He adds, and says: "Let your loins be girded about, and your lamps burning, and ye yourselves like unto men that wait for their lord when he shall return from the wedding, that when he cometh and knocks they may open unto him. Blessed are those servants whom their lord, when he cometh, shall find watching." Also the blessed Apostle Paul, that our faith may advance and grow, and attain to the highest point, exhorts us, saying: "Know ye not, that they which run in a race run all indeed, yet one receives the prize? So run, that ye may obtain. And they, indeed, that they may receive a corruptible crown; but ye an incorruptible." And again: "No man that wars for God binds himself to anxieties of this world, that he may be able to please Him to whom he hath approved himself. Moreover, also, if a man should contend, he will not be crowned unless he have fought lawfully." And again: "Now I beseech you, brethren, by the mercy of God, that ye constitute your bodies a living sacrifice, holy, acceptable unto God; and be not conformed to this world, but be ye transformed in the renewing of your spirit, that ye may prove what is the will of God, good, and acceptable, and perfect." And again: "We are children of God: but if children, then heirs; heirs indeed of God, but joint heirs with Christ, if we suffer together, that we may also be glorified together." And in the Apocalypse the same exhortation of divine preaching speaks, saying, "Hold fast that which thou hast, lest another take thy crown;" which example of perseverance and persistence is pointed out in Exodus, when Moses, for the overthrow of Amalek, who bore the type of the devil, raised up his open hands in the sign and sacrament of the cross, and could not conquer his adversary unless when he had steadfastly persevered in the sign with hands continually lifted up. "And it came to pass," says he, "when Moses raised up his hands, Israel prevailed; but when he let down his hands, Amalek grew mighty. And they took a stone and placed it under him, and he sate thereon. And Aaron and Hur held up his hands on the one side and on the other side, and Moses' hands were made steady even to the going down of the sun. And Jesus routed Amalek and all his people. And the Lord said unto Moses, Write this, and let it be a memorial in a book, and tell it in the ears of Jesus; because in destroying I will destroy the remembrance of Amalek from under heaven."

9. That afflictions and persecutions arise for the sake of our being proved.

In Deuteronomy, "The Lord your God proves you, that He may know if ye love the Lord your God with all your heart, and with all your soul, and with all your strength." And again, Solomon: "The furnace proves the potter's vessel, and righteous men the trial of tribulation." Paul also testifies similar things, and speaks, saying: "We glory in the hope of the glory of God. And not only so, but we glory in tribulations also; knowing that tribulation worketh patience, and patience experience, and experience hope; and hope makes not ashamed, because the love of God is shed abroad in our hearts by the Holy Spirit who is given unto us." And Peter, in his epistle, lays it down, and says: "Beloved, be not surprised at the fiery heat which falls upon you, which happens for your trial; and fail not, as if some new thing were happening unto you. But as often as ye communicate with the sufferings of Christ, rejoice in all things, that also in the revelation made of His glory you may rejoice with gladness. If ye be reproached in the name of Christ, happy are ye; because the name of the majesty and power of the Lord rested upon you; which indeed according to them is blasphemed, but according to us is honored."

10. That injuries and penalties of persecutions are not to be feared by us, because greater is the Lord to protect than the devil to assault.

John, in his epistle, proves this, saying: "Greater is He who is in you than he that is in the world." Also in the cxviith Psalm: "I will not fear what man can do unto me; the Lord is my helper." And again: "These in chariots, and those in horses; but we will glory in the name of the Lord our God. They themselves are bound, and they have fallen; but we have risen up and stand upright." And even more strongly the Holy Spirit, teaching and showing that the army of the devil is not to be feared, and that, if the foe should declare war against us, our hope consists rather in that war itself; and that by that conflict the righteous attain to the reward of the divine abode and eternal salvation,—lays down in the twenty-sixth Psalm, and says: "Though an host should be arrayed against me, my heart shall not fear; though war should rise up against me, in that will I put my hope. One hope have I sought of the Lord, this will I require; that I may dwell in the house of the Lord all the days of my life." Also in Exodus, the Holy Scripture declares that we are rather multiplied and increased by afflictions, saying: "And the more they afflicted them, so much the more they became greater, and waxed stronger." And in the Apocalypse, divine protection is promised to our sufferings. "Fear nothing of these things," it says, "which thou shalt suffer." Nor does anyone else promise us security and protection, than He who also speaks by Isaiah the prophet, saying: "Fear not; for I have redeemed thee, and called thee by thy name: thou art mine. And if thou passes through the water, I am with thee, and the rivers shall not overflow thee. And if thou passes through the fire, thou shalt not be burned, and the flame shall not burn thee; for I, the Lord thy God, the Holy One of Israel, am He who makes thee safe." Who also promises in the Gospel that divine help shall not be wanting to God's servants in persecutions, saying: "But when they shall deliver you up, take no thought how or what ye shall speak. For it shall be given you in that hour what ye shall speak. For it is not ye who speak, but the Spirit of your Father who speaks in you." And again: "Settle it in your hearts not to meditate before how to answer. For I will give you a mouth and wisdom, which your adversaries shall not be able to resist." As in Exodus God speaks to Moses when he delayed and trembled to go to the people, saying: "Who hath given a mouth to man? and who hath made the stammerer? and who the deaf man? and who the seeing, and the blind man? Have not I, the Lord God? And now go, and I will open thy mouth, and will instruct thee what thou shalt say." Nor is it difficult for God to open the mouth of a man devoted to Himself, and to inspire constancy and confidence in speech to His confessor; since in the book of Numbers He made even a she-ass to speak against the prophet Balaam. Wherefore in persecutions let no one think what danger the devil is bringing in, but let him indeed consider what help God affords; nor let human mischief overpower the mind, but let divine protection strengthen the faith; since everyone, according to the Lord's promises and the deserving of his faith, receives so much from God's help as he thinks that he receives. Nor is there anything which the Almighty is not able to grant, unless the failing faith of the receiver be deficient and give way.

11. That it was before predicted that the world would hold us in abhorrence, and that it would stir up persecutions against us, and that no new thing is happening to the Christians, since from the beginning of the world the good have suffered, and the righteous have been oppressed and slain by the unrighteous.

The Lord in the Gospel forewarns and foretells, saying: "If the world hates you, know that it first hated me. If ye were of the world, the world would love what is its own: but because ye are not of the world, and I have chosen you out of the world, therefore the world hates you. Remember the word that I spoke unto you, The servant is not greater than his master. If they have persecuted me, they will persecute you also." And again: "The hour will come, that everyone that kills you will think that he does God service; but they will do this because they have not known the Father nor me. But these things have I told you, that when the hour shall come ye may remember them, because I told you." And again: "Verily, verily, I say unto you, That ye shall weep and lament, but the world shall rejoice; ye shall be sorrowful, but your sorrow shall be turned into joy." And again: "These things have I spoken unto you, that in me ye may have peace; but in the world ye shall have tribulation: but be of good confidence, for I have overcome the world." And when He was interrogated by His disciples concerning the sign of His coming, and of the consummation of the world, He answered and said: "Take care lest any deceive you: for many shall come in my name, saying, I am Christ; and shall deceive many. And ye shall begin to hear of wars, and rumors of wars; see that ye be not troubled: for these things must needs come to pass, but the end is not yet. For nation shall rise against nation, and kingdom against kingdom: and there shall be famines, and earthquakes, and pestilences, in every place. But all these things are the beginnings of travailing. Then they shall deliver you up into affliction and shall kill you: and ye shall be hateful to all nations for my name's sake. And then shall many be offended, and shall betray one another, and shall hate one another. And many false prophets shall arise and shall seduce many; and because wickedness shall abound, the love of many shall wax cold. But he who shall endure to the end, the same shall be saved. And this Gospel of the kingdom shall be preached through all the world, for a testimony to all nations; and then shall come the end. When, therefore, ye shall see the abomination of desolation which is spoken of by Daniel the prophet, standing in the holy place (let him who reads understand), then let them which are in Judea flee to the mountains; and let him which is on the house-roof not go down to take anything from the house; and let him who is in the field not return back to carry away his clothes. But woe to them that are pregnant, and to those that are giving suck in those days! But pray ye that your flight be not in the winter, nor on the Sabbath-day: for there shall be great tribulation, such as has not arisen from the beginning of the world until now, neither shall arise. And unless those days should be shortened, no flesh should be saved; but for the elect's sake those days shall be shortened. Then if anyone shall say unto you, Lo, here is Christ, or, Lo, there; believe him not. For there shall arise false Christs, and false prophets, and shall show great signs and wonders, to cause error, if it be possible, even to the elect. But take ye heed: behold, I have foretold you all things. If, therefore, they shall say to you, Lo, he is in the desert; go not forth: lo, he is in the sleeping chambers; believe it not. For as the flashing of lightning goes forth from the east, and appears even to the west, so also shall the coming of the Son of man be. Wheresoever the carcass shall be, there shall the eagles be gathered together. But immediately after the affliction of those days the sun shall be darkened, and the moon shall not give her light, and the stars shall fall from heaven, and the powers of heaven shall be moved: and then shall appear the sign of the Son of man in heaven: and all the tribes of the earth shall lament and shall see the Son of man coming in the clouds of heaven with great power and glory. And He shall send His angels with a great trumpet, and they shall gather together His elect from the four winds, from the heights of heaven, even into the farthest bounds thereof." And these are not new or sudden things which are now happening to Christians; since the good and righteous, and those who are devoted to God in the law of innocence and the fear of true religion, advance always through afflictions, and wrongs, and the severe and manifold penalties of troubles, in the hardship of a narrow path. Thus, at the very beginning of the world, the righteous Abel was the first to be slain by his brother; and Jacob was driven into exile, and Joseph was sold, and king Saul persecuted the merciful David; and king Ahab endeavored to oppress Elias, who firmly and bravely asserted the majesty of God. Zacharias the priest was slain between the temple and the altar, that himself might there become a sacrifice where he was accustomed to offer sacrifices to God. So many martyrdoms of the righteous have, in fact, often been celebrated; so many examples of faith and virtue have been set forth to future generations. The three youths, Ananias, Azarias, and Misäel, equal in age, agreeing in love, steadfast in faith, constant in virtue, stronger than the flames and penalties that urged them, proclaim that they only obey God, that they know Him alone, that they worship Him alone, saying: "O king Nebuchadnezzar, there is no need for us to answer thee in this matter. For the God whom we serve is able to deliver us out of the furnace of burning fire; and He will deliver us from thy hands, O king. And if not, be it known unto thee, that we do not serve thy gods, and we do not adore the golden image which thou hast set up." And Daniel, devoted to God, and filled with the Holy Spirit, exclaims and says: "I worship nothing but the Lord my God, who founded the heaven and the earth." Tobias also, although under a royal and tyrannical slavery, yet in feeling and spirit free, maintains his confession to God, and sublimely announces both the divine power and majesty, saying: "In the land of my captivity I confess to

Him, and I show forth His power in a sinful nation." What, indeed, do we find in the Maccabees of seven brethren, equals alike in their lot of birth and virtues, filling up the number seven in the sacrament of a perfected completion? Seven brethren were thus associating in martyrdom. As the first seven days in the divine arrangement containing seven thousand of years, as the seven spirits and seven angels which stand and go in and out before the face of God, and the seven branched lamp in the tabernacle of witness, and the seven golden candlesticks in the Apocalypse, and the seven columns in Solomon upon which Wisdom built her house; so here also the number seven of the brethren, embracing, in the quantity of their number, the seven churches, as likewise in the first book of Kings we read that the barren hath borne seven. And in Isaiah seven women lay hold on one man, whose name they ask to be called upon them. And the Apostle Paul, who refers to this lawful and certain number, writes to the seven churches. And in the Apocalypse the Lord directs His divine and heavenly precepts to the seven churches and their angels, which number is now found in this case, in the seven brethren, that a lawful consummation may be completed. With the seven children is manifestly associated also the mother, their origin and root, who subsequently begat seven churches, she herself having been first, and alone founded upon a rock by the voice of the Lord. Nor is it of no account that in their sufferings the mother alone is with her children. For martyrs who witness themselves as the sons of God in suffering are now no more counted as of any father but God, as in the Gospel the Lord teaches, saying, "Call no man your father upon earth; for one is your Father, which is in heaven."

But what utterances of confessions did they herald forth! how illustrious, how great proofs of faith did they afford! The king Antiochus, their enemy—yea, in Antiochus Antichrist was set forth—sought to pollute the mouths of martyrs, glorious and unconquered in the spirit of confession, with the contagion of swine's flesh; and when he had severely beaten them with whips, and could prevail nothing, commanded iron plates to be heated, which being heated and made to glow, he commanded him who had first spoken, and had more provoked the king with the constancy of his virtue and faith, to be brought up and roasted, his tongue having first been pulled out and cut off, which had confessed God; and this happened the more gloriously to the martyr. For the tongue which had confessed the name of God, ought itself first to go to God. Then in the second, sharper pains having been devised, before he tortured the other limbs, he tore off the skin of his head with the hair, doubtless with a purpose in his hatred. For since Christ is the head of the man, and God is the head of Christ, he who tore the head in the martyr was persecuting God and Christ in that head. But he, trusting in his martyrdom, and promising to himself from the retribution of God the reward of resurrection, exclaimed and said, "Thou indeed impotently destroys us out of this present life; but the King of the world will raise us up, who die for His laws, unto the eternal resurrection of life." The third being challenged, quickly put forth his tongue; for he had learned from his brother to despise the punishment of cutting off the tongue. Moreover, he firmly held forth his hands to be cut off, greatly happy in such a mode of punishment, since it was his lot to imitate, by stretching forth his hands, the form of his Lord's passion. And also the fourth, with like virtue, despising the tortures, and answering, to restrain the king, with a heavenly voice exclaimed, and said, "It is better that those who are given to death by men should wait for hope from God, to be raised up by Him again to eternal life. For to thee there shall be no resurrection to life." The fifth, besides treading underfoot the torments of the king, and his severe and various tortures, by the strength of faith, animated to prescience also and knowledge of future events by the Spirit of divinity, foretold to the king the wrath of God, and the vengeance that should swiftly follow. "Having power," said he, "among men, though thou art corruptible, thou does what thou wilt. But think not that our race is forsaken of God. Abide, and see His great power, how He will torment thee and thy seed." What alleviation was that to the martyr! how substantial a comfort in his sufferings, not to consider his own torments, but to predict the penalties of his tormentor! But in the sixth, not his bravery only, but also his humility, is to be set forth; that the martyr claimed nothing to himself, nor even made an account of the honor of his own confession with proud words, but rather ascribed it to his sins that he was suffering persecution from the king, while he attributed to God that afterwards he should be avenged. He taught that martyrs are modest, that they were confident of vengeance, and boasted nothing in their suffering. "Do not," said he, "needlessly err; for we on our own account suffer these things, as sinning against our God. But think not thou that thou shalt be unpunished, who dares to fight against God." Also the admirable mother, who, neither broken down by the weakness of her sex, nor moved by her manifold bereavement, looked upon her dying children with cheerfulness, and did not reckon those things punishments of her darlings, but glories, giving as great a witness to God by the virtue of her eyes, as her children had given by the tortures and suffering of their limbs; when, after the punishment and slaying of six, there remained one of the brethren, to whom the king promised riches, and power, and many things, that his cruelty and ferocity might be soothed by the satisfaction of even one being subdued, and asked that the mother would entreat that her son might be cast down with herself; she entreated, but it was as became a mother of martyrs—as became one who was mindful of the law and of God—as became one who loved her sons not delicately, but bravely. For she entreated, but it was that he would confess God. She entreated that the brother would not be separated from his brothers in the alliance of praise and glory; then only considering herself the mother of seven sons, if it should happen to her to have brought forth seven sons, not to the world, but to God. Therefore arming him, and strengthening him, and so bearing her son by a more blessed birth, she said, "O son, pity me that bare thee ten months in the womb, and gave thee milk for three years, and nourished thee and brought thee up to this age; I pray thee, O son, look upon the heaven and the earth; and having considered all the things which are in them, understand that out of nothing God made these things and the human race. Therefore, O son, do not fear that executioner; but being made worthy of thy brethren, receive death, that in the same mercy I may receive thee with thy brethren." The mother's praise was great in her exhortation to virtue, but greater in the fear of God and in the truth of faith, that she promised nothing to herself or her son from the honor of the six martyrs, nor believed that the prayer of the brothers would avail for the salvation of one who should deny, but rather persuaded him to become a sharer in their suffering, that in the day of judgment he might be found with his brethren. After this the mother also dies with her children; for neither was anything else becoming, than that she who had borne and made martyrs, should be joined in the fellowship of glory with them, and that she herself should follow those whom she had sent before to God. And lest any, when the opportunity either of a certificate or of any such matter is offered to him whereby he may deceive, should embrace the wicked part of deceivers, let us not be silent, moreover, about Eleazar, who, when an opportunity was offered him by the ministers of the king, that having received the flesh which it was allowable for him to partake of, he might pretend, for the misguiding of the king, that he ate those things which were forced upon him from the sacrifices and unlawful meats, would not consent to this deception, saying that it was fitting neither for his age nor nobility to feign that, whereby others would be scandalized and led into error; if they should think that Eleazar, being ninety years old, had left and betrayed the law of God, and had gone over to the manner of aliens; and that it was not of so much consequence to gain the short moments of life, and so incur eternal punishment from an offended God. And he having been long tortured, and now at length reduced to extremity, while he was dying in the midst of stripes and tortures, groaned and said, "O Lord, that hast the holy knowledge, it is manifest that although I might be delivered from death, I suffer the severest pains of body, being beaten with scourges; but with my mind, on account of Thy fear, I willingly suffer these things." Assuredly his faith was sincere and his virtue sound, and abundantly pure, not to have regarded king Antiochus, but God the Judge, and to have known that it could not avail him for salvation if he should mock and deceive man, when God, who is the judge of our con science, and who only is to be feared, cannot at all be mocked nor deceived. If, therefore, we also live as dedicated and devoted to God—if we make our way over the ancient and sacred footsteps of the righteous, let us go through the same proofs of sufferings, the same testimonies of passions, considering the glory of our time the greater on this account, that while ancient examples may be numbered, yet that subsequently, when the abundance of virtue and faith was in excess, the Christian martyrs cannot be numbered, as the Apocalypse testifies and says: "After these things I beheld a great multitude, which no man could number, of every nation, and of every tribe, and people, and language, standing in the sight of the throne and of the Lamb; and they were clothed in white robes, and palms were in their hands; and they said with a loud voice, Salvation to our God, who sits upon the throne, and unto the Lamb! And one of the elders answered and said unto me, Who are those which are arrayed in white robes, and whence come they? And I said unto him, My lord, thou knows. And he said unto me, These are they who have come out of great tribulation, and have washed their robes, and made them white in the blood of the Lamb. Therefore are they before the throne of God and serve Him day and night in His temple." But if the assembly of the Christian martyrs is shown and proved to be so great, let no one think it a hard or a difficult thing to become a martyr, when he sees that the crowd of martyrs cannot be numbered.

12. What hope and reward remains for the righteous and for martyrs after the conflicts and sufferings

of this present time,

The Holy Spirit shows and predicts by Solomon, saying: "And although in the sight of men they suffered torments, yet their hope is full of immortality. And having been troubled in a few things, they shall be in many happily ordered, because God has tried them, and has found them worthy of Himself. As gold in the furnace, He hath tried them; and as whole burnt offerings of sacrifice, He hath received them, and in its season there will be respect of them. They will shine and run about as sparks in a place set with reeds. They shall judge the nations and have dominion over the peoples; and their Lord shall reign forever." In the same also our vengeance is described, and the repentance of those who persecute and molest us is announced. "Then," saith he, "shall the righteous stand in great constancy before such as have afflicted them, and who have taken away their labors; when they see it, they shall be troubled with a horrible fear: and they shall marvel at the suddenness of their unexpected salvation, saying among themselves, repenting and groaning for anguish of spirit, These are they whom we had sometime in derision and as a proverb of reproach. We fools counted their life madness, and their end to be without honor. How are they numbered among the children of God, and their lot is among the saints! Therefore have we erred from the way of truth, and the light of righteousness hath not shined unto us, and the sun hath not risen upon us. We have been wearied in the way of unrighteousness and perdition, and have walked through hard deserts, but have not known the way of the Lord. What hath pride profited us, or what hath the boasting of riches brought to us? All these things have passed away like a shadow." Likewise in the cxvth Psalm is shown the price and the reward of suffering: "Precious," it says, "in the sight of the Lord is the death of His saints." In the cxxvth Psalm also is expressed the sadness of the struggle, and the joy of the retribution: "They who sow," it says, "in tears, shall reap in joy. As they walked, they walked and wept, casting their seeds; but as they come again, they shall come in exultation, bearing their sheaves." And again, in the cxviiith Psalm: "Blessed are those that are undefiled in the way, who walk in the law of the Lord. Blessed are they who search His testimonies, and seek Him out with their whole heart." Moreover, the Lord in the Gospel, Himself the avenger of our persecution and the rewarder of our suffering, says: "Blessed are they who suffer persecution for righteousness' sake, for theirs is the kingdom of heaven." And again: "Blessed shall ye be when men shall hate you, and shall separate you, and shall expel you, and shall revile your name as evil, for the Son of man's sake. Rejoice ye in that day, and leap for joy; for, behold, your reward is great in heaven." And once more: "Whosoever shall lose his life for my sake, the same shall save it." Nor do the rewards of the divine promise attend those alone who are reproached and slain; but if the passion itself be wanting to the faithful, while their faith has remained sound and unconquered, and having forsaken and contemned all his possessions, the Christian has shown that he is following Christ, even he also is honored by Christ among the martyrs, as He Himself promises and says: "There is no man that leaves house, or land, or parents, or brethren, or wife, or children, for the kingdom of God's sake, but shall receive seven times as much in this present time, and in the world to come eternal life." In the Apocalypse also He says the same thing: "And I saw," saith he, "the souls of them that were slain for the name of Jesus and the word of God." And when he had placed those who were slain in the first place, he added, saying: "And whosoever had not worshipped the image of the beast, neither had received his mark upon their forehead or in their hand;" all these he joins together, as seen by him at one time in the same place, and says, "And they lived and reigned with Christ." He says that all live and reign with Christ, not only who have been slain; but even whosoever, standing in firmness of the faith and in the fear of God, have not worshipped the image of the beast, and have not consented to his deadly and sacrilegious edicts.

13. That we receive more as the reward of our suffering than what we endure here in the suffering itself,

The blessed Apostle Paul proves; who by the divine condescension, being caught up into the third heaven and into paradise, testifies that he heard unspeakable words, who boasts that he saw Jesus Christ by the faith of sight, who professes that which he both learnt and saw with the greater truth of consciousness, and says: "The sufferings of this present time are not worthy to be compared with the coming glory which shall be revealed in us." Who, then, does not with all his powers labor to attain to such a glory that he may become the friend of God, that he may at once rejoice with Christ, that after earthly tortures and punishments he may receive divine rewards? If to soldiers of this world it is glorious to return in triumph to their country when the foe is vanquished, how much more excellent and greater is the glory, when the devil is overcome, to return in triumph to paradise, and to bring back victorious trophies to that place whence Adam was ejected as a sinner, after casting down him who formerly had cast him down; to offer to God the most acceptable gift—an uncorrupted faith, and an unyielding virtue of mind, an illustrious praise of devotion; to accompany Him when He shall come to receive vengeance from His enemies, to stand at His side when He shall sit to judge, to become co-heir of Christ, to be made equal to the angels; with the patriarchs, with the apostles, with the prophets, to rejoice in the possession of the heavenly kingdom! Such thoughts as these, what persecution can conquer, what tortures can overcome? The brave and steadfast mind, founded in religious meditations, endures; and the spirit abides unmoved against all the terrors of the devil and the threats of the world, when it is strengthened by the sure and solid faith of things to come. In persecutions, earth is shut up, but heaven is opened; Antichrist is threatening, but Christ is protecting; death is brought in, but immortality follows; the world is taken away from him that is slain, but paradise is set forth to him restored; the life of time is extinguished, but the life of eternity is realized. What a dignity it is, and what a security, to go gladly from hence, to depart gloriously in the midst of afflictions and tribulations; in a moment to close the eyes with which men and the world are looked upon, and at once to open them to look upon God and Christ! Of such a blessed departure how great is the swiftness! You shall be suddenly taken away from earth, to be placed in the heavenly kingdoms. It behooves us to embrace these things in our mind and consideration, to meditate on these things day and night. If persecution should fall upon such a soldier of God, his virtue, prompt for battle, will not be able to be overcome. Or if his call should come to him before, his faith shall not be without reward, seeing it was prepared for martyrdom; without loss of time, the reward is rendered by the judgment of God. In persecution, the warfare,—in peace, the purity of conscience, is crowned.

Treatise XII.
Three Books of Testimonies Against the Jews.

Cyprian to his son Quirinus, greeting. It was necessary, my beloved son, that I should obey your spiritual desire, which asked with most urgent petition for those divine teachings wherewith the Lord has condescended to teach and instruct us by the Holy Scriptures, that, being led away from the darkness of error, and enlightened by His pure and shining light, we may keep the way of life through the saving sacraments. And indeed, as you have asked, so has this discourse been arranged by me; and this treatise has been ordered in an abridged compendium, so that I should not scatter what was written in too diffuse an abundance, but, as far as my poor memory suggested, might collect all that was necessary in selected and connected heads, under which I may seem, not so much to have treated the subject, as to have afforded material for others to treat it. Moreover, to readers also, brevity of the same kind is of very great advantage, in that a treatise of too great length dissipates the understanding and perception of the reader, while a tenacious memory keeps that which is read in a more exact compendium. But I have comprised in my undertaking two books of equally moderate length: one wherein I have endeavored to show that the Jews, according to what had before been foretold, had departed from God, and had lost God's favor, which had been given them in past time, and had been promised them for the future; while the Christians had succeeded to their place, deserving well of the Lord by faith, and coming out of all nations and from the whole world. The second book likewise contains the sacrament of Christ, that He has come who was announced according to the Scriptures, and has done and perfected all those things whereby He was foretold as being able to be perceived and known. And these things may be of advantage to you meanwhile, as you read, for forming the first lineaments of your faith. More strength will be given you, and the intelligence of the heart will be affected more and more, as you examine more fully the Scriptures, old and new, and read through the complete volumes of the spiritual books. For now we have filled a small measure from the divine fountains, which in the meantime we would send to you. You will be able to drink more plentifully, and to be more abundantly satisfied, if you also approach to drink together with us at the same springs of the divine fulness. I bid you, beloved son, always heartily farewell.

First Book.
Heads.
1. That the Jews have fallen under the heavy wrath of God, because they have departed from the Lord, and have followed idols.
2. Also because they did not believe the prophets and put them to death.
3. That it was previously foretold that they would neither know the Lord, nor understand nor receive Him.
4. That the Jews would not understand the Holy Scriptures, but that they would be intelligible in the last times, after Christ had come.
5. That the Jews could understand nothing of the Scriptures unless they first believed on Christ.

6. That they would lose Jerusalem and leave the land which they had received.

7. That they would also lose the Light of the Lord.

8. That the first circumcision of the flesh was made void, and a second circumcision of the spirit was promised instead.

9. That the former law, which was given by Moses, was about to cease.

10. That a new law was to be given.

11. That another dispensation and a new covenant was to be given.

12. That the old baptism was to cease, and a new one was to begin.

13. That the old yoke was to be made void, and a new yoke was to be given.

14. That the old pastors were to cease, and new ones to begin.

15. That Christ should be God's house and temple, and that the old temple should pass away, and a new one should begin.

16. That the old sacrifice should be made void, and a new one should be celebrated.

17. That the old priesthood should cease, and a new priest should come who should be forever.

18. That another prophet, such as Moses, was promised, to wit, who should give a new testament, and who was rather to be listened to.

19. That two peoples were foretold, the elder and the younger; that is, the ancient people of the Jews, and the new one which should be of us.

20. That the Church, which had previously been barren, should have more sons from among the Gentiles than the synagogue had had before.

21. That the Gentiles should rather believe in Christ.

22. That the Jews should lose the bread and the cup of Christ, and all His grace; while we should receive them, and that the new name of Christians should be blessed in the earth.

23. That rather the Gentiles than the Jews should attain to the kingdom of heaven.

24. That by this alone the Jews could obtain pardon of their sins, if they wash away the blood of Christ slain in His baptism, and, passing over into the Church, should obey His precepts.

Testimonies.

1. That the Jews have fallen under the heavy wrath of God because they have forsaken the Lord, and have followed idols.

In Exodus the people said to Aaron: "Arise and make us gods which shall go before us: because as for this man Moses, who brought us out of Egypt, we know not what has become of him." In the same place also Moses says to the Lord: "O Lord, I pray thee, this people have sinned a great sin. They have made to themselves gods of gold and silver. And now, if thou wilt forgive them their sin, forgive; but if not, blot me out of the book which Thou hast written. And the Lord said unto Moses, If any one hath sinned against me, him will I blot out of my book." Likewise in Deuteronomy: They sacrificed unto demons, and not unto God." In the book of Judges too: "And the children of Israel did evil in the sight of the Lord God of their fathers, who brought them out of the land of Egypt, and followed the gods of the peoples that were round about them, and offended the Lord, and forsook God, and served Baal." Also in the same place: "And the children of Israel added again to do evil in the sight of the Lord, and served Baal and the gods of the strangers, and forsook the Lord, and served Him not." In Malachi: "Judah is forsaken and has become an abomination in Israel and in Jerusalem, because Judah has profaned the holiness of the Lord in those things wherein He hath loved, and courted strange gods. The Lord will cut off the man who doeth this, and he shall be made base in the tabernacles of Jacob."

2. Also because they did not believe the prophets and put them to death.

In Jeremiah the Lord says: "I have sent unto you my servants the prophets. Before the daylight I sent them (and ye heard me not, and did not listen with your ears), saying, Let every one of you be converted from his evil way, and from your most wicked desires; and ye shall dwell in that land which I have given you and your fathers for ever and ever." And again: "Go not after other gods, to serve them, and do not worship them; and provoke me not to anger in the works of your hands to scatter you abroad; and ye have not hearkened unto me." Also in the third book of the Kings, Elias saith unto the Lord: "In being jealous I have been jealous for the Lord God Almighty; because the children of Israel have forsaken Thee, have demolished Thine altars, and have slain Thy prophets with the sword; and I have remained solitary, and they seek my life, to take it away from me." In Ezra also: "They have fallen away from Thee, and have cast Thy law behind their backs, and have killed Thy prophets which testified against them that they should return to Thee.

3. That it was previously foretold that they would neither know the Lord, nor understand, nor receive Him.

In Isaiah: "Hear, O heaven, and give ear, O earth: for the Lord hath spoken; I have begotten and brought up children, but they have rejected me. The ox knows his owner, and the ass his master's crib: but Israel hath not known me, and my people hath not perceived me. Ah sinful nation, a people filled with sins, a wicked seed, corrupting children: ye have forsaken the Lord, and have sent that Holy One of Israel into anger." In the same also the Lord says: "Go and tell this people, Ye shall hear with the ear, and shall not understand; and seeing, ye shall see, and shall not perceive. For the heart of this people hath waxed gross, and they hardly hear with their ears, and they have shut up their eyes, lest haply they should see with their eyes, and hear with their ears, and understand with their heart, and should return, and I should heal them." Also in Jeremiah the Lord says: "They have forsaken me, the fountain of living water, and have dug for themselves worn-out cisterns, which could not hold water." Moreover, in the same: "Behold, the word of the Lord has become unto them a reproach, and they do not wish for it." Again in the same the Lord says: "The kite knows his time, the turtle, and the swallow; the sparrows of the field keep the time of their coming in; but my people doth not know the judgment of the Lord. How say you, We are wise, and the law of the Lord is with us? The false measurement has been made vain; the scribes are confounded; the wise men have trembled, and been taken, because they have rejected the word of the Lord." In Solomon also: "Evil men seek me and shall not find me; for they held wisdom in hatred and did not receive the word of the Lord." Also in the twenty-seventh Psalm: "Render to them their deserving, because they have not perceived in the works of the Lord." Also in the eighty-first Psalm: "They have not known, neither have they understood; they shall walk on in darkness." In the Gospel, too, according to John: "He came unto His own, and His own received Him not. As many as received Him, to them gave He power to become the sons of God who believe on His name."

4. That the Jews would not understand the Holy Scriptures, but that they would be intelligible in the last times, after that Christ had come.

In Isaiah: "And all these words shall be unto you as the words of a book that is sealed, which, if you shall give to a man that knows letters to read, he shall say, I cannot read, for it is sealed. But in that day the deaf shall hear the words of the book, and they who are in darkness and in a cloud; the eyes of the blind shall see." Also in Jeremiah: "In the last of the days ye shall know those things." In Daniel, moreover: "Secure the words, and seal the book until the time of consummation, until many learn, and knowledge is fulfilled, because when there shall be a dispersion they shall know all these things." Likewise in the first Epistle of Paul to the Corinthians: "Brethren, I would not that ye should be ignorant, that all our fathers were under the cloud." Also in the second Epistle to the Corinthians: "Their minds are blinded even unto this day, by this same veil, which is taken away in Christ, while this same veil remains in the reading of the Old Testament, which is not unveiled, because it is made void in Christ; and even to this day, if at any time Moses is read, the veil is upon their heart. But by and by, when they shall be turned unto the Lord, the veil shall be taken away." In the Gospel, the Lord after His resurrection says: "These are the words which I spoke unto you while I was yet with you, that all things must be fulfilled which are written in the law of Moses, and in the prophets, and in the Psalms, concerning me. Then opened He their understanding, that they might understand the Scriptures; and said unto them, That thus it is written, and thus it behooved Christ to suffer, and to rise again from the dead the third day; and that repentance and remission of sins should be preached in His name even among all nations."

5. That the Jews could understand nothing of the Scriptures unless they first believed in Christ.

In Isaiah: "And if ye will not believe, neither will ye understand." Also the Lord in the Gospel: "For if ye believe not that I am He, ye shall die in your sins." Moreover, that righteousness should subsist by faith, and that in it was life, was predicted in Habakkuk: "Now the just shall live by faith of me." Hence Abraham, the father of the nations, believed; in Genesis: "Abraham believed in God, and it was counted unto him for righteousness." In like manner, Paul to the Galatians: "Abraham believed in God, and it was counted unto him for righteousness. Ye know, therefore, that they which are of faith, the same are children of Abraham. But the Scripture, foreseeing that God justifies the heathens by faith, foretold to Abraham that all nations should be blessed in him. Therefore they who are of faith are blessed with faithful Abraham."

6. That the Jews should lose Jerusalem and should leave the land which they had received.

In Isaiah: "Your country is desolate, your cities

are burned with fire: your land, strangers shall devour it in your sight; and the daughter of Zion shall be left deserted, and overthrown by foreign peoples, as a cottage in a vineyard, and as a keeper's lodge in a garden of cucumbers, as a city which is besieged. And unless the Lord of Sabaoth had left us a seed, we should have been as Sodom, and we should have been like unto Gomorrah." Also in the Gospel the Lord says: "Jerusalem, Jerusalem, that kills the prophets, and stones them that are sent unto thee, how often would I have gathered thy children as a hen gathered her chickens under her wings, and thou wouldst not! Behold, your house shall be left unto you desolate."

7. Also that they should lose the Light of the Lord.

In Isaiah: "Come you and let us walk in the light of the Lord. For He hath sent away His people, the house of Israel." In His Gospel also, according to John: "That was the true light which lighted every man that cometh into this world. He was in this world, and the world was made by Him, and the world knew Him not." Moreover, in the same place: "He that believeth not is judged already, because he hath not believed in the name of the only begotten Son of God. And this is the judgment, that light is come into the world, and men loved darkness rather than light."

8. That the first circumcision of the flesh is made void, and the second circumcision of the spirit is promised instead.

In Jeremiah: "Thus saith the Lord to the men of Judah, and to them who inhabit Jerusalem, Renew newness among you, and do not sow among thorns: circumcise yourselves to your God, and circumcise the foreskin of your heart; lest my anger go forth like fire, and burn you up, and there be none to extinguish it." Also Moses says: "In the last days God will circumcise thy heart, and the heart of thy seed, to love the Lord thy God." Also in Jesus the son of Nave: "And the Lord said unto Jesus, Make thee small knives of stone, very sharp, and set about to circumcise the children of Israel for the second time." Paul also, to the Colossians: "Ye are circumcised with the circumcision not made with hands in the putting off of the flesh, but with the circumcision of Christ." Also, because Adam was first made by God uncircumcised, and righteous Abel, and Enoch, who pleased God and was translated; and Noah, who, when the world and men were perishing on account of transgressions, was chosen alone, that in him the human race might be preserved; and Melchizedek, the priest according to whose order Christ was promised. Then, because that sign did not avail women, but all are sealed by the sign of the Lord.

9. That the former law which was given by Moses was to cease.
In Isaiah: "Then shall they be manifest who seal the law, that they may not learn; and he shall say, I wait upon the Lord, who turned away His face from the house of Jacob, and I shall trust in Him." In the Gospel also: "All the prophets and the law prophesied until John."

10. That a new law was to be given.
In Micah: "For the law shall go forth out of Sion, and the word of the Lord from Jerusalem. And He shall

judge among many peoples, and He shall subdue and uncover strong nations." Also in Isaiah: "For from Sion shall go forth the law, and the word of the Lord from Jerusalem; and He shall judge among the nations." Likewise in the Gospel according to Matthew: "And behold a voice out of the cloud, saying, This is my beloved Son, in whom I am well pleased; hear ye Him."

11. That another dispensation and a new covenant was to be given.

In Jeremiah: "Behold, the days come, saith the Lord, and I will complete for the house of Israel, and for the house of Judah, a new testament, not according to the testament which I ordered with their fathers in that day in which I took hold of their hands to bring them out of the land of Egypt, because they remained not in my testament, and I disregarded them, saith the Lord: Because this is the testament which I will establish with the house of Israel after those days, saith the Lord: I will give them my laws, and into their minds I will write them; and I will be to them for a God, and they shall be to me for a people; and they shall not teach every man his brother, saying, Know the Lord: for all shall know me, from the least even to the greatest of them: for I will be merciful to their iniquities, and will no more be mindful of their sins."

12. That the old baptism should cease, and a new one should begin.

In Isaiah: "Therefore remember ye not the former things, neither reconsider the ancient things. Behold, I make new the things which shall now arise, and ye shall know it; and I will make in the desert a way, and rivers in a dry place, to give drink to my chosen race, my people whom I acquired, that they should show forth my praises." In the same also: "If they thirst, He will lead them through the deserts; He will bring forth water from the rock; the rock shall be cloven, and the water shall flow and my people shall drink." Moreover, in the Gospel according to Matthew, John says: "I indeed baptize you with water unto repentance: but He that cometh after me is mightier than I, whose shoes I am not worthy to bear; He shall baptize you with the Holy Ghost, and with fire." Also according to John: "Except a man be born of water, and of the Spirit, he cannot enter into the kingdom of God. For that which is born of the flesh is flesh, and that which is born of the Spirit is spirit."

13. That the old yoke should be made void, and a new yoke should be given.

In the second Psalm: "For what purpose have the heathen raged, and the people imagined vain things? The kings of the earth stood up, and the rulers have gathered together against the Lord, and against His Christ. Let us break their bonds asunder and cast away their yoke from us." Likewise in the Gospel according to Matthew, the Lord says: "Come unto me, all ye that labor and are burdened, and I will cause you to rest. Take my yoke upon you and learn of me; for I am meek and lowly in heart: and ye shall find rest unto your souls. For my yoke is excellent, and my burden is light." In Jeremiah: "In that day I will shatter the yoke from their neck and will burst their fetters; and they shall not labor for others, but they shall labor for the Lord God; and I will raise up David a king unto them."

14. That the old pastors should cease, and new ones begin.

In Ezekiel: "Wherefore thus saith the Lord, Behold, I am above the shepherds; and I will require my sheep from their hands, and I will turn them away from feeding my sheep; and they shall feed them no more, and I will deliver my sheep from their mouth, and I will feed them with judgment." In Jeremiah the Lord says: "And I will give you shepherds according to my own heart, and they shall feed you with the food of discipline." In Jeremiah, moreover: "Hear the word of the Lord, ye nations, and tell it to the islands which are afar off. Say, He that scattered Israel will gather him, and will keep him as a shepherd his flock: for the Lord hath redeemed Jacob, and taken him out from the hand of him that was stronger than he."

15. That Christ should be the house and temple of God, and that the old temple should cease, and the new one should begin.

In the second book of Kings: "And the word of the Lord came to Nathan, saying, Go and tell my servant David, Thus saith the Lord, Thou shalt not build me an house to dwell in; but it shall be, when thy days shall be fulfilled, and thou shalt sleep with thy fathers, I will raise up thy seed after thee, which shall come from thy bowels, and I will make ready his kingdom. He shall build me a house in my name, and I will raise up his throne forever; and I will be to him for a father, and he shall be to me for a son: and his house shall obtain confidence, and his kingdom for evermore in my sight." Also in the Gospel the Lord says: "There shall not be left in the temple one stone upon another that shall not be thrown down." And

"After three days another shall be raised up without hands."

16. That the ancient sacrifice should be made void, and a new one should be celebrated.

In Isaiah: "For what purpose to me is the multitude of your sacrifices? saith the Lord: I am full; I will not have the burnt sacrifices of rams, and fat of lambs, and blood of bulls and goats. For who hath required these things from your hands?" Also in the forty-ninth Psalm: "I will not eat the flesh of bulls, nor drink the blood of goats. Offer to God the sacrifice of praise and pay your vows to the Most High. Call upon me in the day of trouble, and I will deliver thee: and thou shalt glorify me." In the same Psalm, moreover: "The sacrifice of praise shall glorify me: therein is the way in which I will show him the salvation of God." In the fourth Psalm too: "Sacrifice the sacrifice of righteousness, and hope in the Lord." Likewise in Malachi: "I have no pleasure concerning you, saith the Lord, and I will not have an accepted offering from your hands. Because from the rising of the sun, even unto the going down of the same, my name is glorified among the Gentiles; and in every place odors of incense are offered to my name, and a pure sacrifice, because great is my name among the nations, saith the Lord."

17. That the old priesthood should cease, and a new priest should come, who should be forever. In the cixth Psalm: "Before the morning star I begat thee. The Lord hath sworn, and He will not repent, Thou art a priest forever, after the order of Melchizedek." Also in the first book of Kings, God says to the priest Eli: "And I will

raise up to me a faithful priest, who shall do all things which are in my heart: and I will build him a sure house; and he shall pass in the presence of my anointed ones for all days. And it shall be, whosoever shall remain in thine house, shall come to worship for an obolus of money, and for one loaf of bread."

18. That another Prophet such as Moses was promised, to wit, one who should give a new testament, and who rather ought to be heard.

In Deuteronomy God said to Moses: "And the Lord said to me, A Prophet will I raise up to them from among their brethren, such as thee, and I will give my word in His mouth; and He shall speak unto them that which I shall command Him. And whosoever shall not hear whatsoever things that Prophet shall speak in my name; I will avenge it." Concerning whom also Christ says in the Gospel according to John: "Search the Scriptures, in which ye think ye have eternal life. These are they which set forth testimony concerning me; and ye will not come to me, that ye might have life. Do not think that I accuse you to the Father: there is one that accuses you, even Moses, on whom ye hope. For if ye had believed Moses, ye would also believe me: for he wrote of me. But if ye believe not his writings, how shall ye believe my words?"

19. That two peoples were foretold, the elder and the younger; that is, the old people of the Jews, and the new one which should consist of us.

In Genesis: "And the Lord said unto Rebekah, Two nations are in thy womb, and two peoples shall be separated from thy belly; and the one people shall overcome the other people; and the elder shall serve the younger." Also in Hosea: "I will call them my people that are not my people, and her beloved that was not beloved. For it shall be, in that place in which it shall be called not my people, they shall be called the sons of the living God."

20. That the Church which before had been barren should have more children from among the Gentiles than what the synagogue had had before.

In Isaiah: "Rejoice, thou barren, that barest not; and break forth and cry, thou that travails not: because many more are the children of the desolate one than of her who hath an husband. For the Lord hath said, Enlarge the place of thy tabernacle, and of thy curtains, and fasten them: spare not, make long thy measures, and strengthen thy stakes: stretch forth yet to thy right hand and to thy left hand; and thy seed shall possess the nations, and shall inhabit the deserted cities. Fear not; because thou shalt overcome nor be afraid because thou art cursed; for thou shalt forget thy eternal confusion." Thus also to Abraham, when his former son was born of a bondwoman, Sarah remained long barren; and late in old age bare her son Isaac, of promise, who was the type of Christ. Thus also Jacob received two wives: the elder Leah, with weak eyes, a type of the synagogue; the younger the beautiful Rachel, a type of the Church, who also remained long barren, and afterwards brought forth Joseph, who also was himself a type of Christ. And in the first of Kings it is said that Elkanah had two wives: Peninnah, with her sons; and Hannah, barren, from whom is born Samuel, not according to the order of generation, but according to the mercy and promise of God, when she had prayed in the temple; and Samuel being born, was a type of Christ. Also in the first book of Kings: "The barren hath borne seven and she that had many children has grown weak." But the seven children are the seven churches. Whence also Paul wrote to seven churches; and the Apocalypse sets forth seven churches, that the number seven may be preserved; as the seven days in which God made the world; as the seven angels who stand and go in and out before the face of God, as Raphael the angel says in Tobit; and the sevenfold lamp in the tabernacle of witness; and the seven eyes of God, which keep watch over the world; and the stone with seven eyes, as Zechariah says; and the seven spirits; and the seven candlesticks in the Apocalypse; and the seven pillars upon which Wisdom hath builded her house in Solomon.

21. That the Gentiles should rather believe in Christ.

In Genesis: "And the Lord God said unto Abraham, Go out from thy country, and from thy kindred, and from thy father's house, and go into that land which I shall show thee: and I will make of thee a great nation, and I will bless thee, and I will magnify thy name; and thou shalt be blessed: and I will bless him that blesses thee, and I will curse him that curses thee: and in thee shall all the tribes of the earth be blessed." On this same point in Genesis: "And Isaac blessed Jacob. Behold, the smell of my son is as the smell of a plentiful field which the Lord hath blessed: and God give thee of the dew of heaven, and of the fertility of the earth, abundance of corn, and wine, and oil: and peoples shall obey thee, and princes shall worship thee: and thou shalt be lord over thy brother, and the sons of thy father shall worship thee; and he that curses thee shall be cursed, and he that blesses thee shall be blessed." On this matter too in Genesis: "But when Joseph saw that his father placed his right hand on the head of Ephraim, it seemed displeasing to him: and Joseph laid hold of his father's hand, to lift it from the head of Ephraim on to the head of Manasseh. Moreover, Joseph said unto his father, Not so, my father: this is my first-born; place thy right hand upon his head. But he would not, and said, I know it, my son, I know it: and he also shall be a people, and he shall be exalted; but his younger brother shall be greater than he, and his seed shall become a multitude of nations." Moreover in Genesis: "Judah, thy brethren shall praise thee: thine hand shall be upon the back of thine enemies; the sons of thy father shall worship thee. Judah is a lion's whelp: from the slender twig, my son, thou hast ascended: thou lay down and sleeps as a lion, and as a lion's whelp. Who shall stir him up? There shalt not fail a prince from Judah, and a leader from his loins, until those things entrusted to him shall come; and he is the hope of the nations: binding his foal unto the vine, and his ass's colt unto the branch of the vine; he shall wash his garments in wine, and his clothing in the blood of the grape: terrible are his eyes with wine, and his teeth are whiter than milk." Hence in Numbers it is written concerning our people: "Behold, the people shall rise up as a lion-like people." In Deuteronomy: "Ye Gentiles shall be for the head; but this unbelieving people shall be for the tail." Also in Jeremiah: "Hear the sound of the trumpet. And they said, We will not hear for this cause the nations shall hear, and they who shall feed their cattle among them." In the seventeenth Psalm: "Thou shalt establish me the head of the nations: a people whom I have not known have served me: at the hearing of the ear they have obeyed me." Concerning this very thing the Lord says in Jeremiah: "Before I formed thee in the belly, I knew thee; and before thou went forth from the womb, I sanctified thee, and established thee as a prophet among the nations." Also in Isaiah: "Behold, I have manifested him for a witness to the nations, a prince and a commander to the peoples." Also in the same: "Nations which have not known Thee shall call upon Thee; and peoples which were ignorant of Thee shall flee to Thee." In the same, moreover: "And in that day there shall be a root of Jesse, which shall rise to rule in all the nations; in Him shall the Gentiles hope: and His rest shall be honor." In the same again: "The land of Zebulon, and the land of Nephtalim, by the way of the sea, and ye others who inhabit the maritime places, and beyond Jordan of the nations. People that walk in darkness, behold ye a great light; ye who dwell in the region of the shadow of death, the light shall shine upon you." Also in the same: "Thus saith the Lord God to Christ my Lord, whose right hand I hold, that the nations may hear Him; and I will break asunder the strength of kings, I will open before Him gates; and cities shall not be shut." Also in the same: "I come to gather together all nations and tongues; and they shall come and see my glory. And I will send out over them a standard, and I will send those that are preserved among them to the nations which are afar off, which have not heard my name nor seen my glory; and they shall declare my glory to the nations." Also in the same: "And in all these things they are not converted; therefore He shall lift up a standard to the nations which are afar, and He will draw them from the end of the earth." Also in the same: "Those who had not been told of Him shall see, and they who have not heard shall understand." Also in the same: "I have been made manifest to those who seek me not: I have been formal of those who asked not after me. I said, Lo, here am I, to a nation that has not called upon my name." Of this same thing, in the Acts of the Apostles, Paul says: "It was necessary that the word of God should first be shown to you; but since ye put it from you, and judged yourselves unworthy of eternal life, lo, we turn to the Gentiles: for thus said the Lord by the Scriptures, Behold, I have set Thee a light among the nations, that Thou shouldest be for salvation even to the ends of the earth."

22. That the Jews would lose while we should receive the bread and the cup of Christ and all His grace, and that the new name of Christians should be blessed in the earth.

In Isaiah: "Thus saith the Lord, Behold, they who serve me shall eat, but ye shall be hungry: behold, they who serve me shall drink, but ye shall be thirsty: behold, they who serve me shall rejoice, but ye shall be confounded; the Lord shall slay you. But to those who serve me a new name shall be named, which shall be blessed in the earth." Also in the same place: "Therefore shall He lift up an ensign to the nations which are afar off, and He will draw them from the end of the earth; and behold, they shall come swiftly with lightness; they shall not hunger nor thirst." Also in the same place: "Behold, therefore, the Ruler, the Lord of Sabaoth, shall take away from Judah and from Jerusalem the healthy man and the strong man, the strength of bread and the strength of water." Likewise in the thirty-third Psalm: "O taste and see how sweet is the Lord. Blessed is the man that hopes in Him. Fear the Lord God, all ye His saints: for there is no want to them that fear Him. Rich men have wanted and have hungered; but they who seek the Lord shall never want any good thing." Moreover, in the Gospel according to John, the Lord says: "I am the bread of life: he that comes to me shall not hunger, and he that trusted in me shall never thirst." Likewise He saith in that place: "If any one thirst, let him come and drink. He that believeth on me, as the Scripture saith, out of his belly shall flow rivers of living water." Moreover, He says in the same place: "Except ye eat the flesh of the Son of man, and drink His blood, ye shall have no life in you."

23. That the Gentiles rather than the Jews attain to the kingdom of heaven.

In the Gospel the Lord says: "Many shall come from the east and from the west, and shall lie down with Abraham, and Isaac, and Jacob, in the kingdom of heaven; but the children of the kingdom shall go out into outer darkness: there shall be weeping and gnashing of teeth."

24. That by this alone the Jews can receive pardon of their sins, if they wash away the blood of Christ slain, in His baptism, and, passing over into His Church, obey His precepts.

In Isaiah the Lord says: "Now I will not release your sins. When ye stretch forth your hands, I will turn away my face from you; and if ye multiply prayers, I will not hear you: for your hands are full of blood. Wash you, make you clean; take away the wickedness from your souls from the sight of mine eyes; cease from your wickedness; learn to do good; seek judgment; keep him who suffers wrong; judge for the orphan, and justify the widow. And come, let us reason together, saith the Lord: and although your sins be as scarlet, I will whiten them as snow; and although they were as crimson, I will whiten them as wool. And if ye be willing and listen to me, ye shall eat of the good of the land; but if ye be unwilling, and will not hear me, the sword shall consume you; for the mouth of the Lord hath spoken these things."

Second Book.
Heads.
1. That Christ is the First-born, and that He is the Wisdom of God, by whom all things were made.
2. That Christ is the Wisdom of God; and about the sacrament of His incarnation, and passion, and cup, and altar, and the apostles who were sent and preached.
3. That Christ also is Himself the Word of God.
4. That the same Christ is God's hand and arm.
5. That the same is Angel and God.
6. That Christ is God.
7. That Christ our God should come as the Illuminator and Savior of the human race.
8. That although from the beginning He had been Son of God, He had yet to be begotten again according to the flesh.
9. That this should be the sign of His nativity, that He should be born of a virgin—man and God—Son of man and of God.
10. That Christ is man and God, compounded of either nature, that He might be a mediator between us and the Father.
11. That He was to be born of the seed of David after the flesh.
12. That He should be born in Bethlehem.

13. That He should come in lowly condition on His first advent.

14. That He was the righteous One whom the Jews should put to death.

15. That He was called a Sheep and a Lamb who would have to be slain, and concerning the sacrament of the passion.

16. That He is also called a Stone.

17. That subsequently that stone should become a mountain, and should fill the whole earth.

18. That in the last times the same mountain should be manifested, upon which the Gentiles should come, and on which the righteous should go up.

19. That He is the Bridegroom, having the Church as His bride, from whom children should be spiritually born.

20. That the Jews should fasten Him to the Cross.

21. That in the passion and the sign of the cross is all virtue and power.

22. That in this sign of the cross is salvation for all who are marked on their foreheads.

23. That at mid-day, during His passion, there should be darkness.

24. That He should not be overcome of death, nor should remain in hell.

25. That He should rise again from hell on the third day.

26. That when He had risen, He should receive from His Father all power, and His power should be eternal.

27. That it is impossible to attain to God the Father, except through the Son Jesus Christ.

28. That He is to come as a Judge.

29. That He is to reign as a King forever.
30. That He is both Judge and King.

Testimonies.

1. That Christ is the First-born, and that He is the Wisdom of God, by whom all things were made.

In Solomon in the Proverbs: "The Lord established me in the beginning of His ways, into His works: before the world He founded me. In the beginning, before He made the earth, and before He appointed the abysses, before the fountains of waters gushed forth, before the mountains were settled, before all the hills, the Lord begot me. He made the countries, and the uninhabitable places, and the uninhabitable bounds under heaven. When He prepared the heaven, I was present with Him; and when He set apart His seat. When He made the strong clouds above the winds, and when He placed the strengthened fountains under heaven, when He made the mighty foundations of the earth, I was by His side, ordering them: I was He in whom He delighted: moreover, I daily rejoiced before His face in all time, when He rejoiced in the perfected earth." Also in the same in Ecclesiasticus: "I went forth out of the mouth of the Most High, first-born before every creature: I made the unwearyingly light to rise in the heavens, and I covered the whole earth with a cloud: I dwelt in the high places, and my throne in the pillar of the cloud: I compassed the circle of heaven, and I penetrated into the depth of the abyss, and I walked on the waves of the sea, and I stood in all the earth; and in every people and in every nation I had the pre-eminence, and by my own strength I have trodden the hearts of all the excellent and the humble: in me is all hope of life and virtue: pass over to me, all ye who desire me." Also in the eighty-eighth Psalm: "And I will establish Him as my first-born, the highest among the kings of the earth. I will keep my mercy for Him forever, and my faithful covenant for Him; and I will establish his seed for ever and ever. If his children forsake my law and walk not in my judgments; if they profane my judgments, and do not observe my precepts, I will visit their wickedness with a rod, and their sins with scourges; but my mercy will I not scatter away from them." Also in the Gospel according to John, the Lord says: "And this is life eternal, that they should know Thee, the only and true God, and Jesus Christ, whom Thou hast sent. I have glorified Thee on the earth: I have finished the work which Thou gives me to do. And now, do Thou glorify me with Thyself, with the glory which I had with Thee before the world was made." Also Paul to the Colossians: "Who is the image of the invisible God, and the first-born of every creature." Also in the same place: "The first born from the dead, that He might in all things become the holder of the pre-eminence." In the Apocalypse too: "I am Alpha and Omega, the beginning and the end. I will give unto Him that is thirsting from the fountain of the water of life freely." That He also is both the wisdom and the power of God, Paul proves in his first Epistle to the Corinthians. "Because the Jews require a sign, and the Greeks seek after wisdom: but we preach Christ crucified, to the Jews indeed a stumbling-block, and to the Gentiles foolishness; but to them that are called, both Jews and Greeks, Christ the power of God and the wisdom of God."

2. That Christ is the Wisdom of God; and concerning the sacrament of His incarnation and of His

passion, and cup and altar; and of the apostles who were sent and preached.

In Solomon in the Proverbs: "Wisdom hath built herself an house, and she has placed under it seven pillars; she has slain her victims; she hath mingled her wine in the goblet, and hath made ready her table, and hath sent her servants, calling with a loud announcement to the cup, saying, Let him who is foolish turn to me: and to them that want understanding she has said, Come, eat of my loaves, and drink the wine which I have mingled for you. Forsake foolishness, and seek wisdom, and correct knowledge by understanding."

3. That the same Christ is the Word of God.

In the forty-fourth Psalm: "My heart hath breathed out a good Word. I tell my works to the King." Also in the thirty-second Psalm: "By the Word of God were the heavens made fast; and all their strength by the breath of His mouth." Also in Isaiah: "A Word completing and shortening in righteousness, because a shortened word will God make in the whole earth." Also in the cvith Psalm: "He sent His Word and healed them." Moreover, in the Gospel according to John: "In the beginning was the Word, and the Word was with God, and God was the Word. The same was in the beginning with God. All things were made by Him, and without Him was nothing made that was made. In Him was life; and the life was the light of men. And the light shineth in darkness; and the darkness com☐prehended it not." Also in the Apocalypse: "And I saw the heaven opened, and lo, a white horse; and he who sate upon him was called Faithful and True, judging rightly and justly; and He made war. And He was covered with a garment sprinkled with blood; and His name is called the Word of God."

4. That Christ is the Hand and Arm of God.

In Isaiah: "Is God's Hand not strong to save? or has He made His ear heavy, that He cannot hear? But your sins separate between you and God; and on account of your sins He turns His face away from you, that He may not pity. For your hands are defiled with blood, and your fingers with sins. Moreover, your lips have spoken wickedness, and your tongue meditates unrighteousness. No one speaks truth, nor is there true judgment: they trust in vanity, and speak emptiness, who conceive sorrow, and bring forth wickedness." Also in the same place: "Lord, who hath believed our report? and to whom is the Arm of God revealed?" Also in the same: "Thus saith the Lord, Heaven is my throne, and the earth is the support of my feet. What house will ye build unto me? or what is the place for my rest? For all these things hath mine hand made." Also in the same: "O Lord God, Thine Arm is high, and they knew it not; but when they know it, they shall be confounded." Also in the same: "The Lord hath revealed His Arm, that holy Arm, in the sight of all nations; all nations, even the ends of the earth, shall see salvation from God." Also in the same place: "Behold, I have made thee as the wheels of a thrashing chariot, new and turned back upon themselves;" and thou shalt thrash the mountains, and shalt beat the hills small, and shalt make them as chaff, and shall winnow them; and the wind shall seize them, and the whirlwind shall scatter them: but thou shalt rejoice in the saints of Israel; and the poor and needy shall exult. For they shall seek water, and there shall be none. For their tongue shall be dry for thirst. I the Lord God, I the God of Israel, will hear them, and will not forsake them; but I will open rivers in the mountains, and fountains in the midst of the fields. I will make the wildernesses watery groves, and a thirsty land into watercourses. I will establish in the land of drought the cedar-tree and the box-tree, and the myrtle and the cypress, and the elm and the poplar, that they may see and acknowledge, and know and believe together, that the Hand of the Lord hath done these things, and the Holy One of Israel hath shown them."

5. That Christ is at once Angel and God.

In Genesis, to Abraham: "And the Angel of the Lord called him from heaven, and said unto him, Abraham, Abraham! And he said, Here am I. And He said, Lay not thine hand upon the lad, neither do thou anything unto him. For now I know that thou fears thy God, and hast not spared thy son, thy beloved son, for my sake." Also in the same place, to Jacob: "And the Angel of the Lord spoke unto me in dreams, I am God, whom thou saw in the place of God where thou anointed me a pillar of stone, and vowed to me a vow." Also in Exodus: "But God went before them by day indeed in a pillar of cloud, to show them the way; and by night in a pillar of fire." And afterwards, in the same place: "And the Angel of God moved forward, which went before the army of the children of Israel." Also in the same place: "Lo, I send my Angel before thy face, to keep thee in the way, that He may lead thee into the land which I have prepared for thee. Observe Him, and obey Him, and be not disobedient to Him, and He will not be wanting to thee. For my Name is in Him." Whence He Himself says in the Gospel: "I came in the name of my Father, and you received me not. When another shall come in his own name, him ye will receive." And again in the cxviith Psalm: "Blessed is He who cometh in the name of the Lord." Also in Malachi: "My covenant of life and peace was with Levi; and I gave him fear, that he should fear me, that he should go from the face of my name. The law of truth was in his mouth, and unrighteousness was not found in his lips. In the peace of the tongue correcting, he walked with us, and turned many away from unrighteousness. Because the lips of the priests shall keep knowledge, and they shall seek the law at His mouth; for He is the Angel of the Almighty."

6. That Christ is God.

In Genesis: "And God said unto Jacob, Arise, and go up to the place of Bethel, and dwell there; and make there an altar to that God who appeared unto thee when thou fled from the face of thy brother Esau." Also in Isaiah: "Thus saith the Lord, the God of Sabaoth, Egypt is wearied; and the merchandise of the Ethiopians, and the tall men of the Sabeans, shall pass over unto Thee, and shall be Thy servants; and shall walk after Thee bound with chains; and shall worship Thee, and shall pray to Thee, because God is in Thee, and there is no other God beside Thee. For Thou art God, and we knew it not, O God of Israel, our Savior. They shall all be confounded and fear who oppose Thee and shall fall into confusion." Likewise in the same: "The voice of one crying in the wilderness, Prepare ye the way of the Lord, make straight the paths of our God. Every channel shall be filled up, and every mountain and hill shall be made low, and all crooked places shall be made straight, and rough places plain; and the glory of the Lord shall be seen, and all flesh shall see the salvation of God, because the Lord hath spoken it." Moreover, in Jeremiah: This is our God, and no other shall be esteemed beside Him, who hath found all the way of knowledge, and hath given it to Jacob His son, and to Israel His beloved. After this He was seen upon earth, and He conversed with men." Also in Zechariah God says: "And they shall cross over through the narrow sea, and they shall smite the waves in the sea, and they shall dry up all the depths of the rivers; and all the haughtiness of the Assyrians shall be confounded, and the scepter of Egypt shall be taken away. And I will strengthen them in the Lord their God, and in His name shall they glory, saith the Lord." Moreover, in Hosea the Lord saith: "I will not do according to the anger of mine indignation, I will not allow Ephraim to be destroyed: for I am God, and there is not a holy man in thee: and I will not enter into the city; I will go after God." Also in the forty-fourth Psalm: "Thy throne, O God, is for ever and ever: the scepter of righteousness is the scepter of Thy kingdom. Thou hast loved righteousness, and hated iniquity: wherefore God, Thy God, hath anointed Thee with the oil of gladness above Thy fellows." So, too, in the forty-fifth Psalm: "Be still, and know that I am God. I will be exalted among the nations, and I will be exalted in the earth." Also in the eighty-first Psalm: "They have not known, neither have they understood: they will walk on in darkness." Also in the sixty-seventh Psalm: "Sing unto God, sing praises unto His name: make a way for Him who goes up into the west: God is His name." Also in the Gospel according to John: "In the beginning was the Word, and the Word was with God, and God was the Word." Also in the same: "The Lord said to Thomas, Reach hither thy finger, and behold my hands: and be not faithless, but believing. Thomas answered and said unto

Him, My Lord and my God. Jesus saith unto him, Because thou hast seen me, thou hast believed: blessed are they who have not seen, and yet have believed." Also Paul to the Romans: "I could wish that I myself were accursed from Christ for my brethren and my kindred according to the flesh: who are Israelites: whose are the adoption, and the glory, and the covenant, and the appointment of the law, and the service (of God), and the promises; whose are the fathers, of whom, according to the flesh, Christ came, who is God over all, blessed for evermore." Also in the Apocalypse: "I am Alpha and Omega, the beginning and the end: I will give to him that is athirst, of the fountain of living water freely. He that overcomes shall possess these things, and their inheritance; and I will be his God, and he shall be my son." Also in the eighty-first Psalm: "God stood in the congregation of gods, and judging gods in the midst." And again in the same place: "I have said, Ye are gods; and ye are all the children of the Highest: but ye shall die like men." But if they who have been righteous, and have obeyed the divine precepts, may be called gods, how much more is Christ, the Son of God, God! Thus He Himself says in the Gospel according to John: "Is it not written in the law, that I said, Ye are gods? If He called them gods to whom the word of God was given, and the Scripture cannot be relaxed, do ye say to Him whom the Father hath sanctified and sent into the world, that thou blasphemes, because I said, I am the Son of God? But if I do not the works of my Father, believe me not; but if I do, and ye will not believe me, believe the works, and know that the Father is in me, and I in Him." Also in the Gospel according to Matthew: "And ye shall call His name Emmanuel, which is, being interpreted, God with us."

7. That Christ our God should come, the Enlightener and Savior of the human race.

In Isaiah: "Be comforted, ye weakened hands; and ye weak knees, be strengthened. Ye who are of a timorous heart, fear not. Our God will recompense judgment, He Himself will come, and will save us. Then shall be opened the eyes of the blind, and the ears of the deaf shall hear. Then the lame man shall leap as a stag, and the tongue of the dumb shall be intelligible; because in the wilderness the water is broken forth, and the stream in the thirsty land." Also in that place: "Not an elder nor an angel, but the Lord Himself shall deliver them; because He shall love them, and shall spare them, and He Himself shall redeem them." Also in the same place: "I the Lord God have called Thee in righteousness, that I may hold Thine hand, and I will comfort Thee; and I have given Thee for a covenant of my people, for a light of the nations; to open the eyes of the blind, to bring forth them that are bound from chains, and those who sit in darkness from the prison-house. I am the Lord God, that is my name. I will not give my glory to another, nor my powers to graven images." Also in the twenty-fourth Psalm: "Show me Thy ways, O Lord, and teach me Thy paths, and lead me unto Thy truth, and teach me; for Thou art the God of my salvation." Whence, in the Gospel according to John, the Lord says: "I am the light of the world. He that will follow me shall not walk in darkness but shall have the light of life." Moreover, in that according to Matthew, the angel Gabriel says to Joseph: "Joseph, thou son of David, fear not to take unto thee Mary thy wife. For that which shall be born to her is of the Holy Ghost. And she shall bring forth a son, and thou shalt call His name Jesus; for

He shall save His people from their sins." Also in that according to Luke: "And Zacharias was filled with the Holy Ghost, and prophesied, saying, Blessed be the Lord God of Israel, who hath foreseen redemption for His people, and hath raised up a horn of salvation for us in the house of His servant David." Also in the same place, the angel said to the shepherds: "Fear not; for, behold, I bring you tidings that unto you is born this day in the city of David a Savior, which is Christ Jesus."

8. That although from the beginning He had been the Son of God, yet He had to be begotten again according to the flesh.

In the second Psalm: "The Lord said unto me, Thou art my Son; this day have I begotten Thee. Ask of me, and I will give Thee the nations for Thine inheritance, and the bounds of the earth for Thy possession." Also in the Gospel according to Luke: "And it came to pass, when Elisabeth heard the salutation of Mary, the babe leaped in her womb; and she was filled with the Holy Ghost, and she cried out with a loud voice, and said, Blessed art thou among women, and blessed is the fruit of thy womb. And whence does this happen to me, that the mother of my Lord should come to me?" Also Paul to the Galatians: "But when the fulness of the time was come, God sent His Son, born of a woman." Also in the Epistle of John: "Every spirit which confesses that Jesus Christ is come in the flesh is of God. But whosoever denies that He is come in the flesh is not of God but is of the spirit of Antichrist."

9. That this should be the sign of His nativity, that He should be born of a virgin—man and God—a son of man and a Son of God.

In Isaiah: "And the Lord went on to speak to Ahaz, saying, Ask thee a sign from the Lord thy God, in the height above and in the depth below. And Ahaz said, I will not ask, and I will not tempt the Lord my God. And He said, Hear ye, therefore, O house of David: it is no trifling contest unto you with men, since God supplies the struggle. On this account God Himself will give you a sign. Behold, a virgin shall conceive, and shall bear a son, and ye shall call His name Emmanuel. Butter and honey shall He eat; before that He knows to prefer the evil, He shall exchange the good." This seed God had foretold would proceed from the woman that should trample on the head of the devil. In Genesis: "Then God said unto the serpent, Because thou hast done this, cursed art thou from every kind of the beasts of the earth. Upon thy breast and thy belly shalt thou crawl, and earth shall be thy food all the days of thy life. And I will place enmity between thee and the woman and her seed. He shall regard thy head, and thou shalt watch his heel."

10. That Christ is both man and God, compounded of both natures, that He might be a Mediator between us and the Father.

In Jeremiah: "And He is man, and who shall know Him?" Also in Numbers: "A Star shall arise out of Jacob, and a man shall rise up from Israel." Also in the same place: "A Man shall go forth out of his seed and shall rule over many nations; and His kingdom shall be exalted as Gog, and His kingdom shall be increased; and God brought Him forth out of Egypt. His glory is as of the unicorn, and He shall eat the nations of His enemies, and shall take out the marrow of their fatness, and will pierce His enemy with His arrows. He couched and lay down as a lion, and as a lion's whelp. Who shall raise Him up? Blessed are they who bless Thee, and cursed are they who curse Thee." Also in Isaiah: "The Spirit of the Lord is upon me; on account whereof He hath anointed me: He hath sent me to tell good tidings to the poor; to heal the bruised in heart, to preach deliverance to the captives, and sight to the blind, to proclaim the acceptable year of the Lord, and the day of retribution." Whence, in the Gospel according to Luke, Gabriel says to Mary: "And the angel, answering, said to her, The Holy Ghost shall come upon thee, and the power of the Highest shall overshadow thee. Wherefore that holy thing which is born of thee shall be called the Son of God." Also in the first Epistle of Paul to the Corinthians: "The first man is of the mud of the earth; the second man is from heaven. As was he from the soil, such are they also that are of the earth; and as is the heavenly, such also are the heavenly. As we have borne the image of him who is of the earth, let us also bear the image of Him who is from heaven."

11. That Christ was to be born of the seed of David, according to the flesh.

In the second of Kings: "And the word of the Lord came to Nathan, saying, Go and tell my servant David, Thus saith the Lord, Thou shalt not build me an house to dwell in; but it shall come to pass, when thy days shall be fulfilled, and thou shalt sleep with thy fathers, I will raise up thy seed after thee who shall come from thy loins, and I will establish His kingdom. He shall build me a house in my name, and I will set up His throne forever; and I will be to Him a Father, and He shall be to me a Son; and His house shall obtain confidence, and His kingdom forever in my sight." Also in Isaiah: "And a rod shall go forth of the root of Jesse, and a flower shall go up from his root; and the Spirit of the Lord shall rest upon Him, the spirit of wisdom and of understanding, the spirit of counsel and might, the spirit of knowledge and piety; and the spirit of the fear of the Lord shall fill Him." Also in the cxxxist Psalm: "God hath sworn the truth unto David himself, and He has not repudiated it; of the fruit of thy belly will I set upon my throne." Also in the Gospel according to Luke: "And the angel said unto her, Fear not, Mary. For thou hast found favor before God. Behold, thou shalt conceive, and shalt bring forth a son, and shalt call His name Jesus. The same shall be great, and He shall be called the Son of the Highest; and the Lord God shall give Him the throne of His father David, and He shall reign over the house of Jacob forever, and of His kingdom there shall be no end." Also in the Apocalypse: "And I saw in the right hand of God, who sate on the throne, a book written within, and on the back sealed with seven seals; and I saw a strong angel proclaiming with a loud voice, Who is worthy to receive the book, and to open its seals? Nor was there anyone either in heaven or upon the earth, or under the earth, who was able to open the book, nor even to look into it. And I wept much because nobody was found worthy to open the book, nor to look into it. And one of the elders said unto me, Weep not; behold, the Lion of the tribe of Judah, the Root of David, hath prevailed to open the book, and to loose its seven seals."

12. That Christ should be born in Bethlehem.

In Micah: "And thou, Bethlehem, house of Ephrata, art not little, that thou should be appointed among the thousands of Judah. Out of thee shall He come forth to me, that He may be a prince in Israel, and His goings forth from the beginning from the days of old." Also in the Gospel: "And when Jesus was born in Bethlehem of Judah, in the days of Herod the king, behold, Magi came from the east to Jerusalem, saying, Where is He that is born King of the Jews? For we have seen His star in the east, and we have come with gifts to worship Him."

13. That Christ was to come in low estate in His first advent.

In Isaiah: "Lord, who hath believed our report, and to whom is the Arm of the Lord revealed? We have declared in His presence as children, as a root in a thirsty ground. There is no form nor glory in Him; and we saw Him, and He had no form nor beauty; but His form was without honor and lacking beyond other men. He was a man set in a plague and knowing how to bear weakness; because His face was turned away, He was dishonored, and was not accounted of. He bears our sins and grieves for us; and we thought that He was in grief, and in wounding, and in affliction; but He was wounded for our transgressions, and He was weakened for our sins. The discipline of our peace was upon Him, and with His bruise we are healed. We all like sheep have gone astray; man has gone out of his way. And God has delivered Him for our sins; and He, because He was afflicted, opened not His mouth." Also in the same: "I am not rebellious, nor do I contradict. I gave my back to the stripes, and my cheeks to the palms of the hands. Moreover, I did not turn away my face from the foulness of spitting, and God was my helper." Also in the same: "He shall not cry, nor will anyone hear His voice in the streets. He shall not break a bruised reed, and a smoking flax He shall not extinguish;

but He shall bring forth judgment in truth. He shall shine forth, and shall not be shaken, until He set judgment in the earth, and in His name shall the nations trust." Also in the twenty-first Psalm: "But I am a worm, and no man; the accursed of man, and the casting away of the people. All they who saw me despised me, and spoke within their lips, and moved their head. He hoped in the Lord, let Him deliver him; let Him save him, since he will have Him." Also in that place: "My strength is dried up like a potsherd, and my tongue is glued to my jaws." Also in Zechariah: "And the Lord showed me Jesus, that great priest, standing before the face of the Angel of the Lord, and the devil was standing at his right hand to oppose him. And Jesus was clothed in filthy garments, and he stood before the face of the Angel Himself; and He answered and said to them who were standing before His face, saying, Take away his filthy garments from him. And he said to him, Behold, I have taken away thine iniquities. And put upon him a priestly garment and set a fair miter upon his head." Also Paul to the Philippians: "Who, being established in the form of God, thought it not robbery that He was equal with God, but emptied Himself, taking the form of a servant, and was made in the likeness of men; and being found in fashion as a man, He humbled Himself, becoming obedient even unto death, even the death of the cross. Wherefore also God exalted Him and gave Him a name which is above every name, that in the name of Jesus every knee should bow, of things in heaven, of things in earth, and of infernal things, and every tongue should confess that Jesus Christ is Lord in the glory of God the Father."

14. That He is the righteous One whom the Jews

should put to death.

In the Wisdom of Solomon: "Let us lay hold of the righteous, because He is disagreeable to us, and is contrary to our works, and reproached us with our transgressions of the law. He professed that He has the knowledge of God and calls Himself the Son of God; He has become to us an exposure of our thoughts; He is grievous unto us even to look upon, because His life is unlike to others, and His ways are changed. We are esteemed by Him as frivolous, and He restrained Himself from our ways, as if from uncleanness; and He extols the last end of the righteous and boasts that He has God for His Father. Let us see, then, if His words are true, and let us try what will come to Him. Let us interrogate Him with reproach and torture, that we may know His reverence and prove His patience. Let us condemn Him with a most shameful death. These things they considered, and erred. For their maliciousness hath blinded them, and they knew not the sacraments of God." Also in Isaiah: "See ye how the righteous perished, and no man understand; and righteous men are taken away, and no man regarded. For the righteous man is taken away from the face of unrighteousness, and his burial shall be in peace." Concerning this very thing it was before foretold in Exodus: "Thou shalt not slay the innocent and the righteous." Also in the Gospel: "Judas, led by penitence, said to the priests and elders, I have sinned, in that I have betrayed the innocent blood."

15. That Christ is called a sheep and a lamb who was to be slain and concerning the sacrament (mystery) of the passion.

In Isaiah: "He was led as a sheep to the slaughter,

and as a lamb before his shearer is dumb, so He opened not His mouth. In His humiliation His judgment was taken away: who shall relate His nativity? Because His life shall be taken away from the earth. By the transgressions of my people He was led to death; and I will give the wicked for His burial, and the rich themselves for His death; because He did no wickedness, nor deceits with His mouth. Wherefore He shall gain many, and shall divide the spoils of the strong; because His soul was delivered up to death, and He was counted among transgressors. And He bare the sins of many, and was delivered for their offences." Also in Jeremiah: "Lord, give me knowledge, and I shall know it: then I saw their meditations. I was led like a lamb without malice to the slaughter; against me they devised a device, saying, Come, let us cast the tree into His bread, and let us erase His life from the earth, and His name shall no more be a remembrance." Also in Exodus God said to Moses: "Let them take to themselves each man a sheep, through the houses of the tribes, a sheep without blemish, perfect, male, of a year old it shall be to you. Ye shall take it from the lambs and from the goats, and all the congregation of the synagogue of the children of Israel shall kill it in the evening; and they shall take of its blood, and shall place it upon the two posts, and upon the threshold in the houses, in the very houses in which they shall eat it. And they shall eat the flesh on the same night, roasted with fire; and they shall eat unleavened bread with bitter herbs. Ye shall not eat of them raw nor dressed in water, but roasted with fire; the head with the feet and the inward parts. Ye shall leave nothing of them to the morning; and ye shall not break a bone of it. But what of it shall be left to the morning shall be burnt with fire. But thus ye shall eat it;

your loins girt, and your sandals on your feet, and your staff in your hands; and ye shall eat it in haste: for it is the Lord's Passover." Also in the Apocalypse: "And I saw in the midst of the throne, and of the four living creatures, and in the midst of the elders, a Lamb standing as if slain, having seven horns and seven eyes, which are the seven spirits of God sent forth throughout all the earth. And He came and took the book from the right hand of God, who sate on the throne. And when He had taken the book, the four living creatures and the four and twenty elders cast themselves before the Lamb, having every one of them harps and golden cups4036 full of odors of supplications, which are the prayers of the saints; and they sang a new song, saying, Worthy art Thou, O Lord, to take the book, and to open its seals: for Thou was slain, and hast redeemed us with Thy blood from every tribe, and tongue, and people, and nation; and Thou hast made us a kingdom unto our God, and hast made us priests, and they shall reign upon the earth." Also in the Gospel: "On the next day John saw Jesus coming to him, and saith, Behold the Lamb of God, and behold Him that taketh away the sins of the world!"

16. That Christ also is called a Stone.

In Isaiah: "Thus saith the Lord, Behold, I place on the foundations of Sion a precious stone, elect, chief, a corner stone, honorable; and he who trusted in Him shall not be confounded." Also in the cxviith Psalm: "The stone which the builders rejected, the same is become the head of the corner. This is done by the Lord, and it is wonderful in our eyes. This is the day which the Lord hath made; let us rejoice and be glad in it. O Lord, save therefore, O Lord, direct therefore. Blessed is He who cometh in the name of the Lord." Also in Zechariah: "Behold, I bring forth my servant. The Orient is his name, because the stone which I have placed before the face of Jesus; upon that one stone are seven eyes." Also in Deuteronomy: "And thou shalt write upon the stone all this law, very plainly." Also in Jesus the son of Nave: "And he took a great stone, and placed it there before the Lord; and Jesus said unto the people, Behold, this stone shall be to you for a testimony, because it hath heard all the things which were spoken by the Lord, which He hath spoken to you to-day; and it shall be for a testimony to you in the last of the days, when ye shall have departed from your God." Also in the Acts of the Apostles, Peter: "Ye princes of the people, and elders of Israel, hearken: Behold, we are this day interrogated by you about the good deed done to the impotent man, by means of which he is made whole. Be it known unto you all, and to all the people of Israel, that in the name of Jesus Christ of Nazareth, whom ye have crucified, whom God hath raised up from the dead, by Him he stands whole in your presence, but by none other. This is the stone which was despised by you builders, which has become the head of the corner. For there is no other name given to men under heaven in which we must be saved." This is the stone in Genesis, which Jacob places at his head, because the head of the man is Christ; and as he slept he saw a ladder reaching to heaven, on which the Lord was placed, and angels were ascending and descending. And this stone he designating Christ consecrated and anointed with the sacrament of unction. This is the stone in Exodus upon which Moses sate on the top of a hill when Jesus the son of Nave fought against Amalek; and by the sacrament of the stone, and the steadfastness of his sitting, Amalek was overcome by Jesus, that is, the devil was overcome by Christ. This is the great stone in the first book of Kings, upon which was placed the ark of the covenant when the oxen brought it back in the cart, sent back and returned by the strangers. Also, this is the stone in the first book of Kings, with which David smote the forehead of Goliath and slew him; signifying that the devil and his servants are thereby thrown down—that part of the head, namely, being conquered which they have not had sealed. And by this seal we also are always safe and live. This is the stone which, when Israel had conquered the aliens, Samuel set up and called its name Ebenezer; that is, the stone that helps.

17. That afterwards this Stone should become a mountain, and should fill the whole earth.

In Daniel: "And behold a very great image; and the aspect of this image was fearful, and it stood erect before thee; whose head was of fine gold, its breast and arms were silver, its belly and thighs were of brass, and its feet were partly indeed of iron, and partly of clay, until that a stone was cut out of the mountain, without the hands of those that should cut it, and struck the image upon the feet of iron and clay, and brake them into small fragments. And the iron, and the clay, and the brass, and the silver, and the gold, was made altogether; and they became small as chaff, or dust in the threshing-floor in summer; and the wind blew them away, so that nothing remained of them. And the stone which struck the image became a great mountain, and filled the whole earth."

18. That in the last times the same mountain

should be manifested, and upon it the Gentiles should come, and on it all the righteous should go up.

In Isaiah: "In the last times the mountain of the Lord shall be revealed, and the house of God upon the tops of the mountains; and it shall be exalted above the hills, and all nations shall come upon it, and many shall walk and say, Come, and let us go up into the mountain of the Lord, and into the house of the God of Jacob; and He will tell us His way, and we will walk in it. For from Sion shall proceed the law, and the word of the Lord from Jerusalem; and He shall judge among the nations, and shall rebuke much people; and they shall beat their swords into ploughshares, and their spears into pruning-hooks, and they shall no more learn to fight." Also in the twenty-third Psalm: "Who shall ascend into the hill of the Lord, or who shall stand in His holy place? He that is innocent in his hands, and of a clean heart; who hath not received his life in vanity, and hath not sworn craftily to his neighbor. He shall receive the blessing from the Lord, and mercy from the God that saves him. This is the generation of those who seek Him, that seek the face of the God of Jacob."

19. That Christ is the Bridegroom, having the Church as His bride, from which spiritual children were to be born.

In Joel: "Blow with the trumpet in Sion; sanctify a fast, and call a healing; assemble the people, sanctify the Church, gather the elders, collect the little ones that suck the breast; let the Bridegroom go forth of His chamber, and the bride out of her closet." Also in Jeremiah: "And I will take away from the cities of Judah, and from the streets of Jerusalem, the voice of the joyous, and the voice of the glad; the voice of the bridegroom, and the voice of the bride." Also in the eighteenth Psalm: "And he is as a bridegroom going forth from his chamber; he exulted as a giant to run his course. From the height of heaven is his going forth, and his circuit even to the end of it; and there is nothing which is hid from his heat." Also in the Apocalypse: "Come, I will show thee the new bride, the Lamb's wife. And he took me in the Spirit to a great mountain, and he showed me the holy city Jerusalem descending out of heaven from God, having the glory of God." Also in the Gospel according to John: "Ye are my witnesses, that I said to them who were sent from Jerusalem to me, that I am not the Christ, but that I am sent before Him. For he who has the bride is the bridegroom; but the friend of the bridegroom is he who stands and hears him with joy and rejoices because of the voice of the bridegroom." The mystery of this matter was shown in Jesus the son of Nave, when he was bidden to put his shoes from off him, doubtless because he himself was not the bridegroom. For it was in the law, that whoever should refuse marriage should put off his shoe, but that he should be shod who was to be the bridegroom: "And it happened, when Jesus was in Jericho, he looked around with his eyes, and saw a man standing before his face, and holding a javelin in his hand, and said, Art thou for us or for our enemies? And he said, I am the leader of the host of the Lord; now draw near. And Jesus fell on his face to the earth, and said to him, Lord, what dost Thou command unto Thy servant. And the leader of the Lord's host said, Loose thy shoe from thy feet, for the place whereon thou stands is holy ground." Also, in Exodus, Moses is bidden to put off his shoe, because he, too, was not the bridegroom: "And there appeared unto him the angel of the Lord in a flame of fire out of a bush; and he saw that the bush burned with fire, but the bush was not consumed. And Moses said, I will pass over and see this great sight, why the bush is not consumed. But when He saw that he drew near to see, the Lord God called him from the bush, saying, Moses, Moses. And he said, What is it? And He said, Draw not nigh hither, unless thou hast loosed thy shoe from off thy feet; for the place on which thou stands is holy ground. And He said unto him, I am the God of thy father, the God of Abraham, and the God of Isaac, and the God of Jacob." This was also made plain in the Gospel according to John: "And John answered them, I indeed baptize with water, but there stands One in the midst of you whom ye know not: He it is of whom I said, The man that cometh after me is made before me, the latchet of whose shoe I am not worthy to unloose." Also according to Luke: "Let your loins be girt, and your lamps burning, and ye like to men that wait for their master when he shall come from the wedding, that when he cometh and knocks, they may open unto him. Blessed are those servants whom their Lord, when He cometh, shall find watching." Also in the Apocalypse: "The Lord God omnipotent reigns: let us be glad and rejoice, and let us give to Him the honor of glory; for the marriage of the Lamb is come, and His wife hath made herself ready."

20. That the Jews would fasten Christ to the cross.
In Isaiah: "I have spread out my hands all day to a people disobedient and contradicting me, who walk in ways that are not good, but after their own sins." Also in Jeremiah: "Come, let us cast the tree into His bread, and let us blot out His life from the earth." Also in

Deuteronomy: "And Thy life shall be hanging (in doubt) before Thine eyes; and Thou shalt fear day and night, and shalt not trust to Thy life." Also in the twenty-first Psalm: "They tore my hands and my feet; they numbered all my bones. And they gazed upon me, and saw me, and divided my garments among them, and upon my vesture they cast a lot. But Thou, O Lord, remove not Thy help far from me; attend unto my help. Deliver my soul from the sword, and my only one from the paw of the dog. Save me from the mouth of the lion, and my lowliness from the horns of the unicorns. I will declare Thy name unto my brethren; in the midst of the Church I will praise Thee." Also in the cxviiith Psalm: "Pierce my flesh with nails through fear of Thee." Also in the cxlth Psalm: "The lifting up of my hands is an evening sacrifice." Of which sacrifice Sophonias said: "Fear from the presence of the Lord God, since His day is near, because the Lord hath prepared His sacrifice, He hath sanctified His elect." Also in Zechariah: "And they shall look upon me, whom they have pierced." Also in the eighty-seventh Psalm: "I have called unto Thee, O Lord, the whole day; I have stretched out my hands unto Thee." Also in Numbers: "Not as a man is God suspended, nor as the son of man does He suffer threats." Whence in the Gospel the Lord says: "As Moses lifted up the serpent in the wilderness, even so must the Son of man be lifted up, that whosoever believeth in the Son may have life eternal."

21. That in the passion and the sign of the cross is all virtue and power.

In Habakkuk: "His virtue covered the heavens, and the earth is full of His praise, and His splendor shall be as the light; there shall be horns in His hands. And there the virtue of His glory was established, and He founded His strong love. Before His face shall go the Word, and shall go forth unto the plains according to His steps." In Isaiah also: "Behold, unto us a child is born, and to us a Son is given, upon whose shoulders shall be government; and His name shall be called the Messenger of a mighty thought." By this sign of the cross also Amalek was conquered by Jesus through Moses. In Exodus Moses said to Jesus: "Choose thee out men, and go forth, and order yourselves with Amalek until the morrow. Behold, I will stand on the top of the hill, and the rod of God in mine hand. And it came to pass, when Moses lifted up his hands, Israel prevailed; but when Moses had let down his hands, Amalek waxed strong. But the hands of Moses were heavy; and they took a stone, and placed it under him, and he sat upon it and Aaron and Hur held up his hands, on the one side and on the other side; and the hands of Moses were made steady even to the setting of the sun. And Jesus routed Amalek and all his people. And the Lord said unto Moses, Write this, that it may be a memorial in a book, and tell it unto the ears of Jesus, that I may utterly destroy the memory of Amalek from under heaven."

22. That in this sign of the Cross is salvation for all people who are marked on their foreheads.

In Ezekiel the Lord says: "Pass through the midst of Jerusalem, and thou shalt mark the sign upon the men's foreheads, who groan and grieve for the iniquities which are done in the midst of them."4080 Also in the same place: "Go and smite, and do not spare your eyes. Have no pity on the old man, and the youth, and the virgin, and slay little children and women, that they may be utterly destroyed. But ye shall not touch any one upon whom the sign is written, and begin with my holy places themselves." Also in Exodus God says to Moses: "And there shall be blood for a sign to you upon the houses wherein ye shall be; and I will look on the blood and will protect you. And there shall not be in you the plague of wasting when I shall smite the land of Egypt." Also in the Apocalypse: "And I saw a Lamb standing on Mount Sion, and with Him a hundred and forty and four thousand; and they had His name and the name of His Father written on their foreheads." Also in the same place: "I am Alpha and Omega, the first and the last, the beginning and the end. Blessed are they that do His commandments, that they may have power over the tree of life."

23. That at mid-day in His passion there should be darkness.

In Amos: "And it shall come to pass in that day, saith the Lord, the sun shall set at noonday, and the day of light shall be darkened; and I will turn your feast-days into grief, and all your songs into lamentation." Also in Jeremiah: "She is frightened that hath borne children, and her soul hath grown weary. Her sun hath gone down while as yet it was mid-day; she hath been confounded and accursed: I will give the rest of them to the sword in the sight of their enemies." Also in the Gospel: "Now from the sixth hour there was darkness over all the earth even to the ninth hour."

24. That He was not to be overcome of death, nor should remain in Hades.

In the twenty-ninth Psalm: "O Lord, Thou hast brought back my soul from hell." Also in the fifteenth

Psalm: "Thou wilt not leave my soul in hell, neither wilt Thou suffer Thine Holy One to see corruption." Also in the third Psalm: "I laid me down and slept, and rose up again, because the Lord helped me." Also according to John: "No man taketh away my life from me; but I lay it down of myself. I have the power of laying it down, and I have the power of taking it again. For this commandment I have received from my Father."

25. That He should rise again from the dead on the third day.

In Hosea: "After two days He will revive us; we shall rise again on the third day." Also in Exodus: "And the Lord said unto Moses, Go down and testify to the people, and sanctify them to-day and to-morrow; and let them wash their garments, and let them be prepared against the day after to-morrow. For on the third day the Lord will come down on Mount Sinai." Also in the Gospel: "A wicked and adulterous generation seeks after a sign; and there shall no sign be given unto it but the sign of the prophet Jonas: for as Jonas was in the whale's belly three days and three nights, so shall the Son of man be three days and three nights in the heart of the earth."

26. That after He had risen again He should receive from His Father all power, and His power should be everlasting.

In Daniel: "I saw in a vision by night, and behold as it were the Son of man, coming in the clouds of heaven, came even to the Ancient of days, and stood in His sight. And they who stood beside Him brought Him before Him: and to Him was given a royal power, and all the kings of the earth by their generation, and all glory obeying Him: and His power is eternal, which shall not be taken away, and His kingdom shall not be destroyed." Also in Isaiah: "Now will I arise, saith the Lord; now will I be glorified, now will I be exalted, now ye shall see, now ye shall understand, now ye shall be confounded. Vain will be the strength of your spirit: the fire shall consume you." Also in the cixth Psalm: "The Lord said unto my Lord, Sit Thou on my right hand, until I make Thine enemies the footstool of Thy feet. God will send the rod of Thy power out of Sion, and Thou shalt rule in the midst of Thine enemies." Also in the Apocalypse: "And I turned and looked to see the voice which spoke with me. And I saw seven golden candlesticks, and in the midst of the candlesticks one like unto the Son of man, clothed with a long garment, and He was girt about the paps with a golden girdle. And His head and His hairs were white as wool or snow, and His eyes as a flame of fire, and His feet like to fine brass from a furnace of fire, and His voice like the sound of many waters. And He had in His right hand seven stars: and out of His mouth went a sharp two-edged sword; and His face shone as the sun in his might. And when I saw Him, I fell at His feet as dead. And He laid His right hand upon me, and said, Fear not; I am the first and the last, and He that lives and was dead; and, lo, I am living for evermore and I have the keys of death and of hell." Likewise in the Gospel, the Lord after His resurrection says to His disciples: "All power is given unto me in heaven and in earth. Go therefore and teach all nations, baptizing them in the name of the Father, and of the Son, and of the Holy Ghost, teaching them to observe all things whatsoever I have commanded you."

27. That it is impossible to attain to God the

Father, except by His Son Jesus Christ.

In the Gospel: "I am the way, and the truth, and the life: no one cometh to the Father but by me." Also in the same place: "I am the door: by me if any man shall enter in, he shall be saved." Also in the same place: "Many prophets and righteous men have desired to see the things which ye see and have not seen them; and to hear those things which ye hear, and have not heard them." Also in the same place: "He that believeth on the Son hath eternal life: he that is not obedient in word to the Son hath not life; but the wrath of God shall abide upon him." Also Paul to the Ephesians: "And when He had come, He preached peace to you, to those which are afar off, and peace to those which are near, because through Him we both have access in one Spirit unto the Father." Also to the Romans: "For all have sinned and fail of the glory of God; but they are justified by His gift and grace, through the redemption which is in Christ Jesus." Also in the Epistle of Peter the apostle: "Christ hath died once for our sins, the just for the unjust, that He might present us to God." Also in the same place: "For in this also was it preached to them that are dead, that they might be raised again." Also in the Epistle of John: "Whosoever denies the Son, the same also hath not the Father. He that confesses the Son, hath both the Son and the Father."

28. That Jesus Christ shall come as a Judge.

In Malachi: "Behold, the day of the Lord cometh, burning as an oven; and all the aliens and all the wicked shall be as stubble; and the day that cometh shall burn them up, saith the Lord." Also in the forty-ninth (or fiftieth) Psalm: "God the Lord of gods hath spoken and called the earth. From the rising of the sun even to the going down thereof, out of Sion is the beauty of His glory. God shall come manifestly, our God, and shall not keep silence. A fire shall burn before Him, and round about Him shall be a great storm. He hath called the heaven above, and the earth, that He may separate His people. Gather together His saints unto Him, those who arrange His covenant with sacrifices. And the heavens shall announce His righteousness, for God is the judge." Also in Isaiah: "The Lord God of strength shall go forth and shall break war in pieces: He shall stir up contest, and shall cry over His enemies with strength. I have been silent; shall I always be silent?" Also in the sixty-seventh Psalm: "Let God arise, and let His enemies be scattered: and let those who hate Him flee from His face. As smoke vanishes, let them vanish: as wax melts from the face of fire, thus let the sinners perish from the face of God. And let the righteous be glad and rejoice in the sight of God: and let them be glad with joyfulness. Sing unto God, sing praises unto His name: make a way to Him who goes up into the west. God is His name. They shall be put to confusion from the face of Him who is the Father of the orphans, and the Judge of the widows. God is in His holy place: God, who makes men to dwell with one mind in an house, bringing forth them that are bound with might, and equally those who provoke unto anger, who dwell in the sepulchers: God, when Thou went forth in the sight of Thy people, in passing into the desert." Also in the eighty-first Psalm: "Arise, O God; judge the earth: for Thou wilt exterminate among all nations." Also in the Gospel according to Matthew: "What have we to do with Thee, Thou Son of David? why art Thou come hither to punish us before the time?" Likewise according to John: "The Father judges nothing, but hath given all judgment to the

Son, that all may honor the Son as they honor the Father. He that honored not the Son, honored not the Father who hath sent Him." So too in the second Epistle of Paul to the Corinthians: "We must all appear before the judgment-seat of Christ, that everyone may bear the things proper to his body, according to those things which he hath done, whether they be good or evil."

29. That He will reign as a King forever.

In Zechariah: "Tell ye the daughter of Zion, Behold, thy King cometh unto thee: just, and having salvation; meek, sitting upon an ass that hath not been tamed." Also in Isaiah: "Who will declare to you that eternal place? He that walks in righteousness, and holds back his hands from gifts; stopping his ears that he may not hear the judgment of blood; and closing his eyes, that he may not see unrighteousness: this man shall dwell in the lofty cavern of the strong rock; bread shall be given him, and his water shall be sure. Ye shall see the King with glory." Likewise in Malachi: "I am a great King, saith the Lord, and my name is illustrious among the nations." Also in the second Psalm: "But I am established as a King by Him upon His holy hill of Zion, announcing His empire." Also in the twenty-first Psalm: "All the ends of the world shall be reminded and shall turn to the Lord: and all the countries of the nations shall worship in Thy sight. For the kingdom is the Lord's: and He shall rule over all nations." Also in the twenty-third Psalm: "Lift up your gates, ye princes; and be ye lifted up, ye everlasting doors; and the King of glory shall come in. Who is this King of glory? The Lord strong and mighty, the Lord strong in battle. Lift up your gates, O ye princes; and be ye lifted up, ye everlasting doors; and the King of glory shall come in. Who is this King of glory? The Lord of hosts, He is the King of glory." Also in the forty-fourth Psalm: "My heart hath breathed forth a good discourse: I tell my works to the king: my tongue is the pen of a writer intelligently writing. Thou art lovely in beauty above the children of men: grace is shed forth on Thy lips, because God hath blessed Thee forever. Be girt with Thy sword on Thy thigh, O most mighty. To Thy honor and to Thy beauty both attend, and direct Thyself, and reign, because of truth, and meekness, and righteousness." Also in the fifth Psalm: "My King, and my God, because unto Thee will I pray. O Lord, in the morning Thou shalt hear my voice; in the morning I will stand before Thee and will contemplate Thee." Also in the ninety-sixth Psalm: "The Lord hath reigned; let the earth rejoice; let the many isles be glad." Moreover, in the forty-fourth Psalm: "The queen stood at thy right hand in a golden garment; she is clothed in many colors. Hear, O daughter, and see, and incline thine ear, and forget thy people and thy father's house; for the King hath desired thy beauty, for He is thy Lord God." Also in the seventy-third Psalm: "But God is our King before the world; He hath wrought salvation in the midst of the earth." Also in the Gospel according to Matthew: "And when Jesus was born in Bethlehem of Judah in the days of Herod the king, behold, Magi from the east came to Jerusalem, saying, Where is He who is born King of the Jews? for we have seen His star in the east, and have come to worship Him." Also, according to John, Jesus said: "My kingdom is not of this world. If my kingdom were of this world, my servants would be in trouble, that I should not be delivered to the Jews; but now is my kingdom not from hence. Pilate said, Art thou a king, then? Jesus answered, Thou sayest that I am a king. For this cause I was born, and for this cause I am come into the world, that I might bear testimony to the truth. Every one that is of the truth heareth my voice."

30. That He Himself is both Judge and King.

In the seventy-first Psalm: "O God, give Thy judgment to the king, and Thy righteousness to the king's son, to judge Thy people in righteousness." Also in the Apocalypse: "And I saw the heaven opened and behold a white horse; and He who sate upon him was called Faithful and True; and He judges justice and righteousness, and makes war. And His eyes were, as it were, a flame of fire, and upon His head were many crowns; and He bare a name written that was known to none other than Himself: and He was clothed with a garment sprinkled with blood, and His name is called the Word of God. And the armies which are in heaven followed Him on white horses, clothed in linen white and clean. And out of His mouth went forth a sword with two edges, that with it He should smite the nations, which He shall shepherd with a rod of iron; and He shall tread the winepress of the wrath of God Almighty. Also He has on His garment and on His thigh the name written, King of kings, and Lord of lords." Likewise in the Gospel: "When the Son of man shall come in His glory, and all the angels with Him, then He shall sit in the throne of His glory; and all nations shall be gathered together before Him, and He shall separate them one from another, even as a shepherd separates the sheep from the goats; and He shall place the sheep at His right hand, but the goats at His left hand. Then shall the King say unto them who shall be at His right hand, Come, ye blessed of my Father, receive the kingdom which is prepared for you from the beginning of the world: for I was hungry, and ye gave me to eat: I was thirsty, and ye gave me to drink: I was a stranger, and ye received me: naked, and ye clothed me: sick, and ye visited me: I was in prison, and ye came unto me. Then shall the righteous answer, and say unto Him, Lord, when saw we Thee hungry, and fed Thee? thirsty, and gave Thee to drink? And when saw we Thee a stranger, and received Thee? naked, and clothed Thee? And when saw we Thee sick, and in prison, and came unto Thee? And the King, answering, shall say unto them, Verily I say unto you, In as far as ye have done it to the least of these my brethren, ye have done it unto me. Then shall He say unto them who shall be on His left hand, Depart from me, ye cursed, into everlasting fire, which my Father hath prepared for the devil and his angels: for I have been hungry, and ye gave me not to eat: I have been thirsty, and ye gave me not to drink: I was a stranger, and ye received me not: naked, and ye clothed me not: sick, and in prison, and ye visited me not. Then shall they also answer and say, Lord, when saw we Thee hungry, or thirsty, or a stranger, or naked, or sick, or in prison, and have not ministered unto Thee? And He shall answer unto them, Verily I say unto you, Inasmuch as ye have not done it to one of the least of these, ye have not done it unto me. And these shall go away into everlasting burning, but the righteous into life eternal."

Third Book.
Cyprian to his son Quirinus, greeting. Of your faith and devotion which you manifest to the Lord God, beloved son, you asked me to gather out for your instruction from the Holy Scriptures some heads bearing upon the religious teaching of our school; seeking for a

succinct course of sacred reading, so that your mind, surrendered to God, might not be wearied with long or numerous volumes of books, but, instructed with a summary of heavenly precepts, might have a wholesome and large compendium for nourishing its memory. And because I owe you a plentiful and loving obedience, I have done what you wished. I have labored for once, that you might not always labor. Therefore, as much as my small ability could embrace, I have collected certain precepts of the Lord, and divine teachings, which may be easy and useful to the readers, in that a few things digested into a short space are both quickly read through and are frequently repeated. I bid you, beloved son, ever heartily farewell.

Heads.
1. On the benefit of good works and mercy.
2. In works and alms, even if by smallness of power less be done, that the will itself is enough.
3. That charity and brotherly love must be religiously and steadfastly practiced.
4. That we must boast in nothing, since nothing is our own.
5. That humility and quietness is to be maintained in all things.
6. That all good and righteous men suffer more, but ought to endure because they are proved.
7. That we must not grieve the Holy Spirit whom we have received.
8. That anger must be overcome, lest it constrain us to sin.
9. That brethren ought to sustain one another.
10. That we must trust in God only, and in Him

we must glory.

11. That he who has attained to faith, having put off the former man, ought to regard only celestial and spiritual things, and to give no heed to the world which he has already renounced.

12. That we must not swear.

13. That we are not to curse.

14. That we must never murmur, but bless God concerning all things that happen.

15. That men are tried by God for this purpose, that they may be proved.

16. Of the benefit of martyrdom.

17. That what we suffer in this world is of less account than is the reward which is promised.

18. That nothing must be preferred to the love of God and of Christ.

19. That we must not obey our own will, but that of God.

20. That the foundation and strength of hope and faith is fear.

21. That we must not rashly judge of another.

22. That when we have received a wrong, we must remit and forgive it.

23. That evil is not to be returned for evil.

24. That it is impossible to attain to the Father but by Christ.

25. That unless a man have been baptized and born again, he cannot attain to the kingdom of God.

26. That it is of small account to be baptized and to receive the Eucharist, unless one profits by it both in deeds and works.

27. That even a baptized person loses the grace which he has attained, unless he keeps innocency.

28. That remission cannot in the Church be granted unto him who has sinned against God.

29. That it was before predicted concerning the hatred of the Name.

30. That what any one has vowed to God, he must quickly pay.

31. That he who does not believe is judged already.

32. Of the benefit of virginity and of continency.

33. That the Father judges nothing, but the Son; and the Father is not honored by him by whom the Son is not honored.

34. That the believer ought not to live like the Gentiles.

35. That God is patient for this end, that we may repent of our sin and be reformed.

36. That a woman ought not to be adorned in a worldly manner.

37. That the believer ought not to be punished for other offences but for the name he bears only.

38. That the servant of God ought to be innocent, lest he fall into secular punishment.

39. That the example of living is given to us in Christ.

40. That we must not labor boastfully or noisily.

41. That we must not speak foolishly and offensively.

42. That faith is of advantage altogether, and that we can do as much as we believe.

43. That he who truly believes can immediately obtain.

44. That the believers who differ among themselves ought not to refer to a Gentile judge.

45. That hope is of future things, and therefore that faith concerning those things which are promised ought to be patient.

46. That a woman ought to be silent in the church.

47. That it arises from our fault and our desert that we suffer, and do not perceive God's help in everything.

48. That we must not take usury.

49. That even our enemies are to be loved.

50. That the sacrament of the faith must not be profaned.

51. That no one should be uplifted in his doing.

52. That the liberty of believing or of not believing is placed in free choice.

53. That the secrets of God cannot be seen through, and therefore that our faith ought to be simple.

54. That none is without filth and without sin.

55. That we must not please men, but God.

56. That nothing that is done is hidden from God.

57. That the believer is amended and reserved.

58. That no one should be made sad by death, since in living is labor and peril, in dying peace and the certainty of resurrection.

59. Of the idols which the Gentiles think gods.

60. That too great lust of food is not to be desired.

61. That the lust of possessing, and money, are not to be desired.

62. That marriage is not to be contracted with Gentiles.

63. That the sin of fornication is grievous.

64. What are those carnal things which beget death, and what are the spiritual things which lead to life.

65. That all sins are put away in baptism.

66. That the discipline of God is to be observed in

Church precepts.

67. That it was foretold that men would despise sound discipline.

68. That we must depart from him who lives irregularly and contrary to discipline.

69. That the kingdom of God is not in the wisdom of the world, nor in eloquence, but in the faith of the cross and in virtue of conversation.

70. That we must obey parents.

71. And that fathers ought not to be bitter against their children.

72. That servants, when they believe, ought the more to be obedient to their fleshly masters.

73. Likewise that masters ought to be more gentle.

74. That every widow that is approved ought to be honored.

75. That every person ought to have care rather of his own people, and especially of believers.

76. That one who is older must not rashly be accused.

77. That the sinner is to be publicly reproved.

78. That we must not speak with heretics.

79. That innocency asks with confidence, and obtains.

80. That the devil has no power against man unless God have allowed it.

81. That wages be quickly paid to the hireling.

82. That divination must not be used.

83. That a tuft of hair is not to be worn on the head.

84. That the beard must not be plucked.

85. That we must rise when a bishop or a presbyter comes.

86. That a schism must not be made, even although he who withdraws should remain in one faith and in the same tradition.

87. That believers ought to be simple with prudence.

88. That a brother must not be deceived.

89. That the end of the world comes suddenly.

90. That a wife must not depart from her husband; or if she departs, she must remain unmarried.

91. That everyone is tempted so much as he is able to bear.

92. That not everything is to be done which is lawful.

93. That it was foretold that heresies would arise.

94. That the Eucharist is to be received with fear and honor.

95. That we are to live with the good, but to avoid the evil.

96. That we must labor with deeds, not with words.

97. That we must hasten to faith and to attainment.

98. That the catechumen ought to sin no more.

99. That judgment will be in accordance with the terms, before the law, of equity; after Moses, of the law.

100. That the grace of God ought to be gratuitous.

101. That the Holy Spirit has often appeared in fire.

102. That all good men ought willingly to hear rebuke.

103. That we must abstain from much speaking.

104. That we must not lie.

105. That they are frequently to be corrected who do wrong in domestic service.

106. That when a wrong is received, patience is to be maintained, and that vengeance is to be left to God.

107. That we must not use detraction.

108. That we must not lay snares against our neighbor.

109. That the sick are to be visited.

110. That talebearers are accursed.

111. That the sacrifices of evil men are not acceptable.

112. That those are more severely judged who in this world have more power.

113. That widows and orphans ought to be protected.

114. That while one is in the flesh, he ought to make confession.

115. That flattery is pernicious.

116. That God is more loved by him who has had many sins forgiven in baptism.

117. That there is a strong conflict to be waged against the devil, and that therefore we ought to stand bravely, that we may be able to conquer.

118. Of Antichrist, that he will come as a man.

119. That the yoke of the law was heavy, which is cast off by us; and that the Lord's yoke is light, which is taken up by us.

120. That we are to be urgent in prayers.

Testimonies.

1. Of the benefit of good works and mercy.

In Isaiah: "Cry aloud," saith He, "and spare not; lift up thy voice like a trumpet; tell my people their sins, and the house of Jacob their wickedness. They seek me from day to day, and desire to know my ways, as a people which did righteousness, and did not forsake the judgment of God. They ask of me now a righteous judgment, and desire to approach to God, saying, What! because we have fasted, and Thou hast not seen: we have humiliated our souls, and Thou hast not known. For in the days of fasting are found your own wills; for either ye torment those who are subjected to you, or ye fast for strife and judgments, or ye strike your neighbors with fists. For what do you fast unto me, that to-day your voice should be heard in clamor? This fast I have not chosen, save that a man should humble his soul. And if thou shalt bend thy neck like a ring, and spread under thee sackcloth and ashes, neither thus shall it be called an acceptable fast. Not such a fast have I chosen, saith the Lord; but loose every knot of unrighteousness, let go the chokings of impotent engagements. Send away the harassed into rest and scatter every unrighteous contract. Break thy bread to the hungry and bring the houseless poor into thy dwelling. If thou sees the naked, clothe him; and despise not them of thy own seed in thy house. Then shall thy seasonable light break forth, and thy garments shall quickly arise; and righteousness shall go before thee: and the glory of God shall surround thee. Then thou shalt cry out, and God shall hear thee; while thou art yet speaking, He shall say, Here I am." Concerning this same thing in Job: "I have preserved the needy from the hand of the mighty; and I have helped the orphan, to whom there was no helper. The mouth of the widow blessed me, since I was the eye of the blind; I was also the foot of the lame, and the father of the weak." Of this same matter in Tobit: "And I said to Tobias, My son, go and bring whatever poor man thou shalt find out of our brethren, who still has God in mind with his whole heart. Bring him hither, and he shall eat my dinner together with me. Behold, I attend thee, my son, until thou come." Also in the same place: "All the days of thy life, my son, keep God in mind, and transgress not His precepts. Do justice all the days of thy life, and do not walk in the way of unrighteousness; because if thou act truly, there will be respect of thy works. Give alms of thy substance and turn not thy face from any poor man. So shall it come to pass that the face of God shall not be turned away from thee. Even as thou hast, my son, so do: if thou hast abundant substance, give the more alms therefrom; if thou hast little, communicate even of that little. And do not fear when thou give alms: thou lays up for thyself a good reward against the day of need; because alms delivers from death, and does not suffer to go into darkness. Alms is a good office for all who do it in the sight of the most high God." On this same subject in Solomon in Proverbs: "He that hath pity on the poor lends unto the Lord." Also in the same place: "He that giveth to the poor shall never want; but he who turns away his eye shall be in much penury." Also in the same place: "Sins are purged away by almsgiving and faith." Again, in the same place: "If thine enemy hunger, feed him; and if he thirst, give him to drink: for by doing this thou shalt scatter live coals upon his head." Again, in the same place: "As water extinguishes fire, so almsgiving extinguishes sin." In the same in Proverbs: "Say not, Go away, and return, tomorrow I will give; when you can do good immediately. For thou knows not what may happen on the coming day." Also in the same place: "He who stopped his ears that he may not hear the weak, shall himself call upon God, and there shall be none to hear him." Also in the same place: "He who has his conversation without reproach in righteousness, leaves blessed children." In the same in Ecclesiasticus: "My son, if thou hast, do good by thyself, and present worthy offerings to God; remember that death delays not." Also in the same place: "Shut up alms in the heart of the poor, and this will entreat for thee from all evil." Concerning this thing in the thirty-sixth Psalm, that mercy is beneficial also to one's posterity: "I have been young, and I have also grown old; and I have not seen the righteous forsaken, nor his seed begging their bread. The whole day he is merciful, and lends; and his seed is in blessing." Of this same thing in the fortieth Psalm: "Blessed is he who considers over the poor and needy: in the evil day God will deliver him." Also in the cxith Psalm: "He hath distributed, he hath given to the poor; his righteousness shall remain from generation to generation." Of this same thing in Hosea: "I desire mercy rather than sacrifice, and the knowledge of God more than whole burnt offerings." Of this same thing also in the Gospel according to Matthew: "Blessed are they who hunger and thirst after righteousness: for they shall be satisfied." Also in the same place: "Blessed are the merciful: for they shall obtain mercy." Also in the same place: "Lay up for yourselves treasures in heaven, where neither moth nor rust doth corrupt, and where thieves do not dig through and steal: for where your treasure is, there will your heart be also." Also in the same place: "The kingdom of heaven is like unto a merchantman seeking goodly pearls: and when he hath found a precious pearl, he went away and sold all that he had, and bought it." That even a small work is of advantage, also in the same place: "And whoever shall give to drink to one of the least of these a cup of cold water in the name of a disciple, verily I say unto you, His reward shall not perish." That alms are to be denied to none, also in the same place: "Give to everyone that asks thee; and from him who would wish to borrow, be not turned away." Also in the same place: "If thou wilt enter into life, keep the commandments. He saith, Which? Jesus saith unto him, Thou shalt not kill, Thou shalt not commit adultery, Thou shalt not bear false witness, Honor thy father and mother: and, Thou shalt love thy neighbor as thyself. The young man saith unto Him, All these things have I observed: what lack I yet? Jesus saith unto him, If thou wilt be perfect, go and sell all that thou hast, and give to the poor, and thou shalt have treasure in heaven; and come, follow me." Also in the same place: "When the Son of man shall come in His majesty, and all the angels with Him, then He shall sit on the throne of His glory: and all nations shall be gathered together before Him; and He shall separate them one from another, even as a shepherd separates the sheep from the goats: and He shall place the sheep on the right hand, but the goats on the left hand. Then shall the King say unto them that are on His right hand, Come, ye blessed of my Father, receive the kingdom prepared for you from the beginning of the world. For I was hungry, and ye gave me to eat: I was thirsty, and ye gave me to drink: I was a stranger, and ye took me in: naked, and ye clothed me: I was sick, and ye visited me: I was in prison, and ye came unto me. Then shall the righteous answer Him, and say, Lord, when saw we Thee a stranger, and took Thee in: naked, and clothed Thee? And when saw we Thee sick, and in prison, and came to Thee? And the King, answering, shall say unto them, Verily I say unto you, Inasmuch as ye did it to one of the least of these my brethren, ye did it unto me. Then shall He say unto them who are on His left hand, Depart from me, ye cursed, into everlasting fire, which my Father hath prepared for the devil and his angels: for I was hungry, and ye gave me not to eat: I was thirsty, and ye gave me not to drink: I was a stranger, and ye took me not in: I was naked, and ye clothed me not: sick, and in prison, and ye visited me not. Then shall they also answer, and say, Lord, when saw we Thee hungry, or thirsty, or a stranger, or naked, or sick, or in prison, and did not minister unto Thee? And He shall answer them, Verily I say unto you, Inasmuch as ye did it not to one of the least of these, ye did it not unto me. And these shall go away into everlasting burning: but the righteous into life eternal." Concerning this same matter in the Gospel according to Luke: "Sell your possessions and give alms." Also in the same place: "He who made that which is within, made that which is without also. But give alms, and behold, all things are pure unto you." Also in the same place: "Behold, the half of my substance I give to the poor; and if I have defrauded any one of anything, I restore him fourfold. And Jesus said unto him, that salvation has this day been wrought for this house, since he also is a son of Abraham." Of this same thing also in the second Epistle to the Corinthians: "Let your abundance supply their want, that their abundance also may be the supplement of your want, that there may be equality: as it is written, He who had much had not excess; and he who had little had no lack." Also in the same place: "He who soweth sparingly shall reap also sparingly; and he who soweth in blessing shall reap also of blessing. But let everyone do as he has proposed in his heart: not as if sorrowfully, or of necessity: for God loveth a cheerful giver." Also in the same place: "As it is written, He hath dispersed abroad; he hath given to the poor: his righteousness remains forever." Likewise in the same place: "Now he who ministered seed to the Sower, shall both supply bread to be eaten, and shall multiply your seed, and shall increase the growth of the fruits of your righteousness: that in all things ye may be made rich." Also in the same place: "The administration of this service has not only supplied that which is lacking to the saints, but has abounded by much giving of thanks unto God." Of this same matter in the Epistle of John: "Whoso hath this world's substance, and sees his brother desiring, and shut up his bowels from him, how dwells the love of God in him?" Of this same thing in the Gospel according to Luke: "When thou makes a dinner or a supper, call not thy friends, nor brethren, nor neighbors, nor the rich; lest haply they also invite thee again, and a recompense be made thee. But when thou makes a banquet, call the poor, the weak, the blind, and lame: and thou shalt be blessed; because they have not the means of rewarding thee: but thou shalt be recompensed in the resurrection of the just."

2. In works and alms, even if by smallness of power less be done, that the will itself is sufficient.

In the second Epistle of Paul to the Corinthians: "If there be a ready will, it is acceptable according to what a man hath, not according to that which he hath not; nor let there be to others a mitigation, but to you a burdening.

3. That charity and brotherly affection are to be religiously and steadfastly practiced.

In Malachi: "Hath not one God created us? Is there not one Father of us all? Why have ye certainly deserted everyone his brother?" Of this same thing according to John: "Peace I leave with you, my peace I give unto you." Also in the same place: "This is my commandment, That ye love one another, even as I have loved you. Greater love than this has no man, than that one should lay down his life for his friends." Also in the same place: "Blessed are the peacemakers, for they shall be called the sons of God." Also in the same place: "Verily I say unto you, That if two of you shall agree on earth concerning everything, whatever you shall ask it shall be given you from my Father which is in heaven. For wherever two or three are gathered together in my name, I am with them." Of this same thing in the first Epistle to the Corinthians: "And I indeed, brethren, could not speak unto you as to spiritual, but as to carnal, as to babes in Christ. I have given you milk for drink, not meat: for while ye were yet little ye were not able to bear it, neither now are ye able. For ye are still carnal: for where there are in you emulation, and strife, and dissensions, are ye not carnal, and walk after man?" Likewise in the same place: "And if I should have all faith, so that I can remove mountains, but have not charity, I am nothing. And if I should distribute all my goods for food, and if I should deliver up my body to be burned, but have not charity, I avail nothing. Charity is great-souled; charity is kind; charity envies not; charity deals not falsely; is not puffed up; is not irritated; thinketh not evil; rejoices not in injustice, but rejoices in the truth. It loves all things, believeth all things, hopes all things, bears all things. Charity shall never fail." Of this same thing to the Galatians: "Thou shalt love thy neighbor as thyself. But if ye bite and accuse one another, see that ye be not consumed one of another." Of this same thing in the Epistle of John: "In this appear the children of God and the children of the devil. Whosoever is not righteous is not of God, and he who loveth not his brother. For he who hates his brother is a murderer; and ye know that no murderer hath eternal life abiding in him." Also in the same place: "If anyone shall say that he loves God, and hates his brother, he is a liar: for he who loveth not his brother whom he sees, how can he love God whom he sees not?" Of this same thing in the Acts of the Apostles: "But the multitude of them that had believed acted with one soul and mind: nor was there among them any distinction, neither did they esteem as their own anything of the possessions that they had; but all things were common to them." Of this same thing in the Gospel according to Matthew: If thou would offer thy gift at the altar, and there remembers that thy brother hath ought against thee; leave thou thy gift before the altar, and go; first be reconciled to thy brother, and then come and offer thy gift at the altar." Also in the Epistle of John: "God is love and he that dwelleth in love dwelleth in God, and God in him." Also in the same place: "He who saith he is in the light, and hates his brother, is a liar, and walketh in darkness even until now."

4. That we must boast in nothing, since nothing is our own.

In the Gospel according to John: "No one can receive anything, except it were given him from heaven." Also in the first Epistle of Paul to the Corinthians: "For what have you that you have not received? But if you have received it, why boast, as if you had not received it?" Also in the first of Kings: "Boast not, neither speak lofty things, and let not great speeches proceed out of your mouth, for the Lord is a God of knowledge." Also in the same place: "The bow of the mighty men has been made weak, and the weak are girt about with strength." Of this same thing in the Maccabees: "It is just to be subjected to God, and that a mortal should not think things equal to God." Also in the same place: "And fear not the words of a man that is a sinner, because his glory shall be filth and worms. Today he shall be lifted up, and to-morrow he shall not be found; because he is turned into his earth, and his thought has perished."

5. That humility and quietness are to be maintained in all things.

In Isaiah: "Thus saith the Lord God, The heaven is my throne, and the earth is the stool of my feet. What seat will ye build for me, or what is the place for my rest? For all those things hath my hand made, and all those things are mine. And upon whom else will I look, except upon the lowly and quiet man, and him that trembles at my words?" On this same thing in the Gospel according to Matthew: "Blessed are the meek, for they shall inherit the earth." Of this same thing, too, according to Luke: "He that shall be least among you all, the same shall be great." Also in the same place: "Whosoever exalted himself shall be made low, and whosoever abases himself shall be exalted." Of this same thing to the Romans: "Be not high-minded, but fear; for if God spared not the natural branches, (take heed) lest He also spare not thee." Of this same thing in the thirty-third Psalm: "And He shall save the lowly in spirit." Also to the Romans: "Render to all what is due: tribute to whom tribute is due, custom to whom custom, fear to whom fear, honor to whom honor; owe no man anything, except to love another." Also in the Gospel according to Matthew: "They love the first place of reclining at feasts, and the chief seat in the synagogues, and salutations in the market, and to be called of men Rabbi. But call not ye Rabbi, for One is your Master." Also in the Gospel according to John: "The servant is not greater than his lord, nor the apostle greater than He that sent himself. If ye know these things, blessed shall ye be if ye shall do them." Also in the eighty-first Psalm: "Do justice to the poor and lowly."

6. That all good and righteous men suffer more, but ought to endure because they are proved.

In Solomon: "The furnace proves the vessels of the potter, and the trial of tribulation righteous men." Also in the fiftieth Psalm: "The sacrifice to God is a contrite spirit; a contrite and humbled heart God will not despise." Also in the thirty-third Psalm: "God is nearest to them that are contrite in heart, and He will save the lowly in spirit." Also in the same place: "Many are the afflictions of the righteous, but out of them all the Lord will deliver them." Of this same matter in Job: "Naked came I out of my mother's womb, naked also shall I go under the earth: the Lord gave, and the Lord hath taken away: as it hath pleased the Lord, so it is done; blessed be the name of the Lord. In all these things which happened to him Job sinned in nothing with his lips in the sight of the Lord." Concerning this same thing in the Gospel according to Matthew: "Blessed are they that mourn, for they shall be comforted." Also according to John: "These things have I spoken unto you, that in me ye may have peace. But in the world ye shall have affliction; but have confidence, for I have overcome the world." Concerning this same thing in the second Epistle to the Corinthians: "There was given to me a thorn in the flesh, a messenger of Satan to buffet me, that I should not be exalted. For which thing I thrice besought the Lord, that it should depart from me. And He said unto me, My grace is sufficient for thee; for strength is perfected in weakness." Concerning this same thing to the Romans: "We glory in hope of the glory of God. And not only so, but we also glory in afflictions: knowing that affliction worketh patience; and patience, experience; and experience, hope: and hope does not confound; because the love of God is infused in our hearts by the Holy Spirit, which is given unto us." On this same subject, according to Matthew: "How broad and spacious is the way which leadeth unto death, and many there are who go in thereby: how straight and narrow is the way that leadeth to life, and few there are that find it!" Of this same thing in Tobias: "Where is your righteousness? behold what you suffer." Also in the Wisdom of Solomon: "In the places of the wicked the righteous groan; but at their ruin the righteous will abound."

7. That we must not grieve the Holy Spirit, whom we have received.

Paul the apostle to the Ephesians: "Grieve not the Holy Spirit of God, in which ye were sealed in the day of redemption. Let all bitterness, and wrath, and indignation, and clamor, and blasphemy, be taken away from you."

8. That anger must be overcome, lest it constrain us to sin.

In Solomon in the Proverbs: "Better is a patient man than a strong man; for he who restrains his anger is better than he who taketh a city." Also in the same place: "The imprudent man declares his anger on the same day, but the crafty man hides away his dishonor." Of this same thing to the Ephesians: "Be ye angry, and sin not. Let not the sun set upon your wrath." Also in the Gospel according to Matthew: "Ye have heard that it was said by the ancients, Thou shalt not kill; and whoever shall kill shall be guilty of the judgment. But I say unto you, That everyone who is angry with his brother without cause shall be guilty of the judgment."

9. That brethren ought to support one another.

To the Galatians: "Each one having others in consideration, lest ye also should be tempted. Bear ye one another's burdens, and so ye shall fulfil the law of Christ."

10. That we must trust in God only, and in Him we must glory.

In Jeremiah: "Let not the wise man glory in his wisdom, neither let the strong man glory in his strength, nor let the rich man glory in his riches; but let him that glories, glory in this, that he understands and knows that I am the Lord, who do mercy, and judgment, and righteousness upon the earth, because in them is my pleasure, saith the Lord." Of the same thing in the fifty-fourth Psalm: "In the Lord have I hoped; I will not fear what man can do unto me." Also in the same place: "To none but God alone is my soul subjected." Also in the cxviith Psalm: "I will not fear what man can do unto me; the Lord is my helper." Also in the same place: "It is good to trust in the Lord rather than to trust in man; it is good to hope in the Lord rather than to hope in princes." Of this same thing in Daniel: "But Shadrach, Meshach, and Abednego answered and said to king Nebuchadnezzar, O king, there is no need to answer thee concerning this word. For God, whom we serve, is able to deliver us from the furnace of burning fire; and He will deliver us from thine hand, O king. And if not, be it known unto thee that we serve not thy gods, and we adore not the golden image which thou hast set up." Likewise in Jeremiah: "Cursed is the man who hath hope in man; and blessed is the man who trusts in the Lord, and his hope shall be in God." Concerning this same thing in Deuteronomy: "Thou shalt worship the Lord thy God, and Him only shalt thou serve." Of this same thing to the Romans: "And they worshipped and served the creature, forsaking the Creator. Wherefore also God gave them up to ignominious passions." Of this thing also in John: "Greater is He who is in you than he who is in this world."

11. That he who has attained to trust, having put off the former man, ought to regard only celestial and spiritual things, and to give no heed to the world which he has already renounced.

In Isaiah: "Seek ye the Lord; and when ye have found Him, call upon Him. But when He hath come near unto you, let the wicked forsake his ways, and the unrighteous man his thoughts: and let him be turned unto the Lord, and he shall obtain mercy, because He will plentifully pardon your sins." Of this same thing in Solomon: "I have seen all the works which are done under the sun; and, lo, all are vanity." Of this same thing in Exodus: "But thus shall ye eat it; your loins girt, and your shoes on your feet, and your staves in your hands: and ye shall eat it in haste, for it is the Lord's Passover." Of this same thing in the Gospel according to Matthew: "Take no thought, saying, What shall we eat? or, What shall we drink? or, Wherewith shall we be clothed? for these things the nations seek after. But your Father knows that ye have need of all these things. Seek first the kingdom of God, and His righteousness; and all these things shall be added unto you." Likewise in the same place: "Think not for the morrow, for the morrow shall take thought for itself. Sufficient unto the day is its own evil." Likewise in the same place: "No one looking back, and putting his hands to the plough, is fit for the kingdom of God." Also in the same place: "Behold the fowls of the heaven: for they sow not, nor reap, nor gather into barns; and your heavenly Father feeds them. Are not ye of more value than they?" Concerning this same thing, according to Luke: "Let your loins be girded, and your lamps burning; and ye like unto men that wait for their lord, when he comes from the wedding; that, when he comes and knocks, they may open to him. Blessed are those servants, whom their lord, when he cometh, shall find watching." Of this same thing in Matthew: "The foxes have holes, and the birds of the heaven have nests; but the Son of man hath not where He may lay His head." Also in the same place: "Whoso forsakes not all that he has, cannot be my disciple." Of this same thing in the first to the Corinthians: "Ye are not your own, for ye are bought with a great price. Glorify and bear God in your body." Also in the same place: "The time is limited. It remains, therefore, that both they who have wives be as though they have them not, and they who lament as they that lament not, and they that rejoice as they that rejoice not, and they who buy as they that buy not, and they who possess as they who possess not, and they who use this world as they that use it not; for the fashion of this world passes away." Also in the same place: "The first man is of the clay of the earth, the second man from heaven. As he is of the clay, such also are they who are of the clay; and as is the heavenly, such also are the heavenly. Even as we have borne the image of him who is of the clay, let us bear His image also who is from heaven." Of this same matter to the Philippians: "All seek their own, and not those things which are Christ's; whose end is destruction, whose god is their belly, and their glory is to their confusion, who mind earthly things. For our conversation is in heaven, whence also we expect the Savior, our Lord Jesus Christ, who shall transform the body of our humiliation conformed to the body of His glory." Of this very matter to Galatians: "But be it far from me to boast, except in the cross of our Lord Jesus Christ, by whom the world is crucified unto me, and I unto the world." Concerning this same thing to Timothy: "No man that wars for God binds himself with worldly annoyances, that he may please Him to whom he hath approved himself. But and if a man should contend, he will not be crowned unless he fights lawfully." Of this same thing to the Colossians: "If ye be dead with Christ from the elements of the world, why still, as if living in the world, do ye follow vain things?" Also concerning this same thing: "If ye have risen together with Christ, seek those things which are above, where Christ is sitting on the right hand of God. Give heed to the things that are above, not to those things which are on the earth; for ye are dead, and your life is hidden with Christ in God. But when Christ your life shall appear, then shall ye also appear with Him in glory." Of this same thing to the Ephesians: Put off the old man of the former conversation, who is corrupted, according to the lusts of deceit. But be ye renewed in the spirit of your mind, and put on the new man, him who according to God is ordained in righteousness, and holiness, and truth." Of this same thing in the Epistle of Peter: "As strangers and pilgrims, abstain from fleshly lusts, which war against the soul; but having a good conversation among the Gentiles, that while they detract from you as if from evildoers, yet, beholding your good works, they may magnify God." Of this same thing in the Epistle of John: "He who says he abides in Christ, ought himself also to walk even as He walked." Also in the same place: "Love not the world, neither the things that are in the world. If any man loveth the world, the love of the Father is not in him. Because everything which is in the world is lust of the flesh, and lust of the eyes, and the ambition of this world, which is not of the Father, but of the lust of this world. And the world shall pass away with its lust. But he that doeth the will of God abides forever, even as God abides forever." Also in the first Epistle of Paul to the Corinthians: "Purge out the old leaven, that ye may be a new dough, as ye are unleavened. For also Christ our Passover is sacrificed. Therefore let us celebrate the feast, not in the old leaven, nor in the leaven of malice and wickedness, but in the unleavened bread of sincerity and truth."

12. That we must not swear.

In Solomon: "A man that swears much shall be filled with iniquity, and the plague shall not depart from his house; and if he swear vainly, he shall not be justified." Of this same matter, according to Matthew: "(Again, ye have heard that it was said to them of old, Thou shalt not swear falsely, but shalt perform unto the Lord thine oaths.) I say unto you, Swear not at all: (neither by heaven, because it is God's throne; nor by the earth, because it is His footstool; nor by Jerusalem, because it is the city of the great King; neither shalt thou swear by thy head, because thou canst not make one hair white or black.) But let your discourse be, Yea, yea; Nay, nay: (for whatever is fuller than these is of evil.") Of this same thing in Exodus: "Thou shalt not take the name of the Lord thy God in vain."

13. That we must not curse.
In Exodus: "Thou shalt not curse nor speak ill of the ruler of thy people." Also in the thirty-third Psalm: "Who is the man who desires life, and loveth to see good days? Restrain thy tongue from evil, and thy lips that they speak no guile." Of this same thing in Leviticus: "And the Lord spoke to Moses, saying, Bring forth him who hath cursed abroad outside the camp; and all who heard him shall place their hands upon his head, and all the assembly of the children of Israel shall stone him." Of this same thing in Paul's Epistle to the Ephesians: "Let no evil discourse proceed out of your mouth, but that which is good for the edification of faith, that it may give grace to the hearers." Of this same thing to the Romans: "Blessing, and not cursing." Of this same thing in the Gospel according to Matthew: "He who shall say to his brother, Thou fool! shall be liable to the Gehenna of fire." Of this same matter, according to the same Matthew: "But I say unto you, That every idle word which men shall speak, they shall give account for it in the day of judgment. For by thy words thou shalt be justified, and by thy words thou shalt be condemned."

14. That we must never murmur, but bless God concerning all things that happen.
In Job: "Say some word against the Lord, and die. But he, looking upon her, said, You speak as one of the

foolish women. If we have received good things from the Lord's hand, why shall we not endure evil things? In all these things which happened unto him, Job sinned not with his lips in the sight of the Lord." Also in the same place: "Hast thou regarded my servant Job? for there is none like unto him in the earth: a man without complaint: a true worshipper of God, restraining himself from all evil." Of the same thing in the thirty-third Psalm: "I will bless the Lord at all times: His praise shall ever be in my mouth." Of this same thing in Numbers: "Let their murmuring cease from me, and they shall not die." Of this same thing in the Acts of the Apostles: "But about the middle of the night Paul and Silas prayed and gave thanks to God, and the prisoners heard them." Also in the Epistle of Paul to the Philippians: "But doing all things for love, without murmurings and reviling, that ye may be without complaint, and spotless sons of God."

15. That men are tried by God for this purpose, that they may be proved.

In Genesis: "And God, tempted Abraham, and said to him, Take thy only son whom thou loves, Isaac, and go into the high land, and offer him there as a burnt offering on one of the mountains of which I will tell thee." Of this same thing in Deuteronomy: "The Lord your God proves you, that He may know if ye love the Lord your God with all your heart, and with all your soul." Of this same thing in the Wisdom of Solomon: "Although in the sight of men they suffered torments, their hope is full of immortality; and having been in few things distressed, yet in many things they shall be happily ordered, because God tried them, and found them worthy of Himself. As gold in the furnace He proved them, and as a burnt offering He received them. And in their time there shall be respect of them; they shall judge the nations, and shall rule over the people; and their Lord shall reign forever." Of this same thing in the Maccabees: "Was not Abraham found faithful in temptation, and it was accounted unto him for righteousness?"

16. Of the benefits of martyrdom.

In the Proverbs of Solomon: "The faithful martyr delivers his soul from evils." Also in the same place: "Then shall the righteous stand in great boldness against them who have afflicted them, and who took away their labors. When they see them, they shall be disturbed with a horrible fear; and they shall wonder at the suddenness of their unhoped-for salvation, saying among themselves, repenting and groaning with distress of spirit, These are they whom some time we had in derision, and in the likeness of a proverb; we fools counted their life madness, and their end without honor. How are they reckoned among the children of God, and their lot among the saints! Therefore we have wandered from the way of truth, and the light of righteousness has not shined upon us, and the sun has not risen upon us. We have been wearied in the way of iniquity and of perdition, and we have walked through difficult solitudes; but we have not known the way of the Lord. What hath pride profited us? or what hath the boasting of riches brought to us? All these things have passed away as a shadow." Of this same thing in the cxvth Psalm: "Precious in the sight of the Lord is the death of His saints." Also in the cxxvth Psalm: "They who sow in tears shall reap in joy. Walking they walked, and wept as they cast their seeds; but coming they shall come in joy, raising up their laps." Of this same thing in the Gospel according to John: "He who loves his life shall lose it; and he that hates his life in this world shall find it to life eternal." Also in the same place: "But when they shall deliver you up, take no thought what ye shall speak; for it is not ye who speak, but the Spirit of your Father which speaks in you." Also in the same place: "The hour shall come, that everyone that kills you shall think he does service to God; but they shall do this also because they have not known the Father nor me." Of this same matter, according to Matthew: "Blessed are they which shall suffer persecution for righteousness' sake; for theirs is the kingdom of heaven." Also in the same place: "Fear not them which kill the body, but are not able to kill the soul; but rather fear Him which is able to kill the soul and body in Gehenna." Also in the same place: "Whosoever shall confess me before men, him also will I confess before my Father which is in heaven; but he who shall deny me before men, him also will I deny before my Father which is in heaven. And he that shall endure to the end, the same shall be saved." Of this same thing, according to Luke: "Blessed shall ye be when men shall hate you, and shall separate you (from their company), and shall drive you out, and shall speak evil of your name, as wicked, for the Son of man's sake. Rejoice in that day, and exult; for, lo, your reward is great in heaven." Also in the same place: "Verily I say unto you, There is no man that leaves house, or parents, or brethren, or wife, or children, for the sake of the kingdom of God, and does not receive seven times as much in this present time, but in the world to come life everlasting." Of this same thing in the Apocalypse: "And when he had opened the fifth seal, I saw under the altar of God the souls of them that were slain on account of the word of God and His testimony. And they cried with a loud voice, saying, How long, O Lord, holy and true, dost Thou not judge and avenge our blood on them that dwell on the earth? And unto every one of them were given white robes; and it was said to them, that they should rest still for a short time, until the number of their fellow-servants, and of their brethren, should be fulfilled, and they who shall afterwards be slain, after their example."4298 Also in the same place: "After these things I saw a great crowd, which no one among them could number, from every nation, and from every tribe, and from every people and tongue, standing before the throne and before the Lamb; and they were clothed with white robes, and palms were in their hands. And they said with a loud voice, Salvation to our God, that sits upon the throne, and to the Lamb. And one of the elders answered and said to me, What are these which are clothed with white robes? who are they, and whence have they come? And I said unto him, My lord, thou knows. And he said unto me, These are they who have come out of great tribulation, and have washed their robes, and made them white in the blood of the Lamb. Therefore they are before the throne of God, and serve Him day and night in His temple; and He who sits upon the throne shall dwell among them. They shall neither hunger nor thirst ever; and neither shall the sun fall upon them, nor shall they suffer any heat: for the Lamb who is in the midst of the throne shall protect them, and shall lead them to the fountains of the waters of life; and God shall wipe away every tear from their eyes." Also in the same place: "He who shall overcome I will give him to eat of the tree of life, which is in the paradise of my God." Also in the same place: "Be thou faithful even unto death, and I will give thee a crown of life." Also in the same place: "Blessed shall they be who shall watch, and shall keep their garments, lest they walk naked, and they see their shame." Of this same thing, Paul in the second Epistle to Timothy: "I am now offered up, and the time of my assumption is at hand. I have fought a good fight, I have finished my course, I have kept the faith. There now remains for me a crown of righteousness, which the Lord, the righteous Judge, will give me in that day; and not only to me, but to all also who love His appearing." Of this same thing to the Romans: "We are the sons of God: but if sons and heirs of God, we are also joint heirs with Christ; if we suffer together, that we may also be magnified together." Of this same thing in the cxviiith Psalm: "Blessed are they who are undefiled in the way, and walk in the law of the Lord. Blessed are they who search into His testimonies."

17. That what we suffer in this world is of less account than is the reward which is promised.

In the Epistle of Paul to the Romans: "The sufferings of this present time are not worthy of comparison with the glory that is to come after, which shall be revealed in us." Of this same thing in the Maccabees: "O Lord, who hast the holy knowledge, it is manifest that while I might be delivered from death, I am suffering most cruel pains of body, being beaten with whips; yet in spirit I suffer these things willingly, because of the fear of thine own self." Also in the same place: "Thou indeed, being powerless, destroys us out of this present life; but the King of the world shall raise us up who have died for His laws into the eternal resurrection of life." Also in the same place: "It is better that, given up to death by men, we should expect hope from God to be raised again by Him. For there shall be no resurrection to life for thee." Also in the same place: "Having power among men, although thou art corruptible, thou does what thou wilt. But think not that our race is forsaken of God. Sustain, and see how His great power will torment thee and thy seed." Also in the same place: Do not err without cause; for we suffer these things on our own accounts, as sinners against our God. But think not thou that thou shalt be unpunished, having undertaken to fight against God."

18. That nothing is to be preferred to the love of God and Christ.

In Deuteronomy: "Thou shalt love the Lord thy God with all thy heart, and with all thy soul, and with all thy might." Also in the Gospel according to Matthew: "He that loveth father or mother above me, is not worthy of me; and he that loveth son or daughter above me, is not worthy of me; and he that takes not up his cross and follows me, is not my disciple." Also in the Epistle of Paul to the Romans: "Who shall separate us from the love of Christ? shall tribulation, or distress, or persecution, or famine, or nakedness, or peril, or sword? As it is written, Because for thy sake we are killed all the day long, we are counted as sheep for the slaughter. But in all these things we are more than conquerors for His sake who loved us."

19. That we are not to obey our own will, but the will of God.

In the Gospel according to John: "I came not down from heaven to do mine own will, but the will of

Him that sent me." Of this same matter, according to Matthew: "Father, if it be possible, let this cup pass from me; nevertheless, not what I will, but what Thou wilt." Also in the daily prayer: "Thy will be done, as in heaven, so in earth." Also according to Matthew: "Not everyone who saith unto me, Lord, Lord, shall enter into the kingdom of heaven; but he who doeth the will of my Father which is in heaven, he shall enter into the kingdom of heaven." Also according to Luke: "But that servant which knows his Lord's will, and obeyed not His will, shall be beaten with many stripes." In the Epistle of John: "But he that does the will of God abides forever, even as He Himself also abides forever."

20. That the foundation and strength of hope and faith is fear.

In the cxth Psalm: "The fear of the Lord is the beginning of wisdom." Of the same thing in the Wisdom of Solomon: "The beginning of wisdom is to fear God." Also in the Proverbs of the same: "Blessed is the man who reverences all things with fear." Of the same thing in Isaiah: "And upon whom else will I look, except upon him that is lowly and peaceful, and that trembles at my words?" Of this same thing in Genesis: "And the angel of the Lord called him from heaven, and said unto him, Abraham, Abraham: and he said, Here am I. And he said, Lay not thine hand upon the lad, neither do anything unto him: for now I know that thou fears thy God, and hast not spared thy beloved son for my sake." Also in the second Psalm: "Serve the Lord in fear, and rejoice unto Him in trembling." Also in Deuteronomy, the word of God to Moses: "Call the people together to me, and let them hear my words, that they may learn to fear me all the days that they themselves shall live upon the earth." Also in Jeremiah: "Behold, the days come, saith the Lord, that I will perfect upon the house of Israel, and in the house of Judah, a new covenant: not according to the covenant that I had ordered with their fathers in the day when I laid hold of their hand to bring them out of the land of Egypt; because they have not abode in my covenant, and I have been unmindful of them, saith the Lord; because this is the covenant which I will ordain for the house of Israel; After those days, saith the Lord, I will give my law, and will write it in their mind and I will be to them for a God, and they shall be to me for a people. And they shall not teach every man his brother, saying, Know the Lord: because all shall know me, from the least even to the greatest of them: because I will be favorable to their iniquities, and their sins I will not remember any more. If the heaven should be lifted up on high, saith the Lord, and if the earth should be made low from beneath, yet I will not cast away the people of Israel, saith the Lord, for all the things which they have done. Behold, I will gather them together from every land in which I have scattered them in anger, and in my fury, and in great indignation; and I will grind them down into that place, and I will leave them in fear; and they shall be to me for a people, and I will be to them for a God: and I will give them another way, and another heart, that they may fear me all their days in prosperity with their children: and I will perfect for them an everlasting covenant, which I will not turn away after them; and I will put my fear into their heart, that they may not depart from me: and I will visit upon them to do them good, and to plant them in their land in faith, and with all the heart, and with all the mind." Also in the Apocalypse: "And the four and twenty elders which sit on their thrones in the sight (of God), fell upon their faces, and worshipped God, saying, We give Thee thanks, O Lord God omnipotent, which art and which was; because Thou hast taken Thy great power, and hast reigned. And the nations were angry, and Thy wrath is come, and the time in which it should be judged concerning the dead, and the reward should be given to Thy servants the prophets, and the saints that fear Thy name, small and great; and to disperse those who have corrupted the earth." Also in the same place: "And I saw another angel flying through the midst of the heaven, having the everlasting Gospel to preach to those who dwell upon the earth, and to all the nations, and tribes, and tongues, and peoples, saying with a loud voice, Fear God, and give Him honor, because the hour of His judgment is come; and adore Him who made the heaven, and the earth, and the sea, and the fountains of waters." Also in the same place: "And I saw as it were a sea of glass mingled with fire; and the beasts were feeding with His lambs; and the number of His name a hundred and forty and four, standing upon the sea of glass, having the harps of God; and they sing the song of Moses, the servant of God, and the song of the Lamb, saying, Great and marvelous are Thy works, O Lord God Almighty; just and true are Thy ways, Thou King of the nations. Who would not fear Thee and give honor to Thy name? for Thou only art holy: and because all nations shall come and worship in Thy sight, because Thy righteousness have been made manifest." Also in Daniel: "There was a man dwelling in Babylon whose name was Joachim; and he took a wife by name Susanna, the daughter of Helchias, a very beautiful woman, and one that feared the Lord. And her parents were righteous, and taught their daughter according to the law of Moses." Moreover, in Daniel: "And we are lowly this day in all the earth because of our sins, and there is not at this time any prince, or prophet, or leader, or burnt-offering, or oblation, or sacrifice, or incense, or place to sacrifice before Thee, and to find mercy from Thee. And yet in the soul and spirit of lowliness let us be accepted as the burnt offerings of rams and bulls, and as it were many thousands of lambs which are fattest. If our offering may be made in Thy presence this day, their power shall be consumed, for they shall not be ashamed who put their trust in Thee. And now we follow with our whole heart, and we fear and seek Thy face. Give us not over unto reproach, but do with us according to Thy tranquility, and according to the multitude of Thy mercy deliver us." Also in the same place: "And the king exceedingly rejoiced, and commanded Daniel to be taken up out of the den of lions; and the lions had done him no hurt, because he trusted and had believed in his God. And the king commanded, and they brought those men who had accused Daniel; and they cast them in the den of lions, and their wives and their children. And before they had reached the pavement of the den they were seized by the lions, and they broke all their bones in pieces. Then Darius the king wrote, To all peoples, tribes, and languages which are in my kingdom, peace be unto you from my face. I decree and ordain that all those who are in my kingdom shall fear and tremble before the most high God whom Daniel serves, because He is the God who lives and abides forever, and His kingdom shall not pass away, and His dominion goes on forever; and He alone doeth signs, and prodigies, and marvelous things in the heaven and the earth, who snatched Daniel from the den of lions." Also in Micah: "Wherewith shall I approach the Lord, and lay hold upon Him? in sacrifices, in burnt offerings, in calves of a year old? Does the Lord favor and receive me with thousands of fat goats? or shall I give my first fruits of unrighteousness, the fruit of my belly, the sin of my soul? It is told thee, O man, what is good; or what else the Lord doth require, save that thou should do judgment and justice, and love mercy, and be ready to go with the Lord thy God. The voice of the Lord shall be invoked in the city, and He will save those who fear His name." Also in Micah: "Feed Thy people with Thy rod, the sheep of Thine inheritance; and pluck up those who dwell separately in the midst of Carmel. They shall prepare Bashan and Gilead according to the days of the age; and according to the days of their going forth from the land of Egypt I will show them wonderful things. The nations shall see, and be confounded at all their might; and they shall place their hand upon their mouth. Their ears shall be deafened, and they shall lick the dust as do serpents. Dragging the earth, they shall be disturbed, and they shall lick the dust: in their end they shall be afraid towards the Lord their God, and they shall fear because of Thee. Who is a God as Thou art, raising up unrighteousness, and passing over impiety?" And in Nahum: "The mountains were moved at Him, and the hills trembled; and the earth was laid bare before His face, and all who dwell therein. From the face of His anger who shall bear it, and who withstand in the fury of His soul? His rage causes the beginnings to flow, and the rocks were melted by Him. The Lord is good to those who sustain Him in the day of affliction, and knows those who fear Him." Also in Haggai: "And Zerubbabel the son of Salathiel, of the tribe of Judah, and Jesus the son of Josedech, the high priest, and all who remained of the people, obeyed the voice of the Lord their God, because the Lord sent him to them, and the people feared from the face of God." Also in Malachi: "The covenant was with life and peace; and I gave to them the fear to fear me from the face of my name." Also in the thirty-third Psalm: "Fear the Lord, all ye His saints: for there is no want to them that fear Him." Also in the eighteenth Psalm: "The fear of the Lord is chaste, abiding forever."

21. That we must not rashly judge of another.

In the Gospel according to Luke: "Judge not, that ye be not judged: condemn not, that ye be not condemned." Of this same subject to the Romans: "Who art thou that judges another man's servant? to his own master he stands or falls. But he shall stand; for God is able to make him stand." And again: "Wherefore you are without excuse, O every man that judges: for in that in which you judge another, you condemn yourself; for you do the same things which you judge. But do you hope, who judges those who do evil, and does the same, that you yourself shall escape the judgment of God?" Also in the first Epistle of Paul to the Corinthians: "And let him that thinks he stand take heed lest he fall." And again: "If any man thinks that he knows anything, he knows not yet in what manner he ought to know."

22. That when we have received a wrong, we must remit and forgive it.

In the Gospel, in the daily prayer: "Forgive us our debts, even as we forgive our debtors." Also according to Mark: "And when ye stand for prayer, forgive, if ye have ought against anyone; that also your Father who is in heaven may forgive you your sins. But if ye do not forgive, neither will your Father which is in heaven forgive you your sins." Also in the same place: "In what measure ye mete, in that shall it be measured to you again."

23. That evil is not to be returned for evil.
In the Epistle of Paul to the Romans: "Rendering to no man evil for evil." Also in the same place: "Not to be overcome of evil, but overcome evil with good." Of this same thing in the Apocalypse: "And He said unto me, Seal not the words of the prophecy of this book; because now the time is at hand. And let those who persist in hurting, hurt: and let him who is filthy, be filthy still: but let the righteous do still more righteousness: and in like manner, let him that is holy do still more holiness. Behold, I come quickly; and my reward is with me, to render to every man according to his deeds."

24. That it is impossible to attain to the Father but by His Son Jesus Christ.
In the Gospel according to John: "I am the way, the truth, and the life: no man cometh unto the Father, but by me." Also in the same place: "I am the door: by me if any man enter in, he shall be saved."

25. That unless a man have been baptized and born again, he cannot attain unto the kingdom of God.
In the Gospel according to John: "Except a man be born again of water and the Spirit, he cannot enter into the kingdom of God. For that which is born of the flesh is flesh; and that which is born of the Spirit is spirit." Also in the same place: "Unless ye eat the flesh of the Son of man, and drink His blood, ye shall not have life in you."

26. That it is of small account to be baptized and to receive the Eucharist, unless one profit by it both in deeds and works.

In the first Epistle of Paul to the Corinthians: "Know ye not, that they which run in a race run indeed all, although one receives the prize? So run, that ye may obtain. And those indeed that they may receive a corruptible crown, but we an incorruptible." In the Gospel according to Matthew: "Every tree that bringeth not forth good fruit shall be cut down, and cast into the fire." Also in the same place: "Many shall say unto me in that day, Lord, Lord, have we not prophesied in Thy name, and in Thy name have cast out devils, and in Thy name have done great works? And then shall I say to them, I never knew you; depart from me, ye who work iniquity." Also in the same place: "Let your light shine before men, that they may see your good works, and glorify your Father which is in heaven." Also Paul to the Philippians: "Shine as lights in the world."

27. That even a baptized person loses the grace that he has attained, unless he keep innocency.

In the Gospel according to John: "Lo, thou art made whole: sin no more, lest a worse thing happen unto thee." Also in the first Epistle of Paul to the Corinthians: "Know ye not that ye are the temple of God, and the Spirit of God abides in you? If anyone violate the temple of God, him will God destroy." Of this same thing in the Chronicles: "God is with you, while ye are with Him: if ye forsake Him, He will forsake you."

28. That remission cannot in the Church be granted unto him who has sinned against God (i.e., the

Holy Ghost).

In the Gospel according to Matthew: "Whosoever shall say a word against the Son of man, it shall be forgiven him; but whosoever shall speak against the Holy Ghost, it shall not be forgiven him, neither in this world nor in the world to come." Also according to Mark: "All sins shall be forgiven, and blasphemies, to the sons of men; but whoever shall blaspheme against the Holy Ghost, it shall not be forgiven him, but he shall be guilty of eternal sin." Of this same thing in the first book of Kings: "If a man sin by offending against a man, they shall pray the Lord for him; but if a man sin against God, who shall pray for him?"

29. That it was before predicted, concerning the hatred of the Name,

In the Gospel according to Luke: "And ye shall be hated of all men for my name's sake." Also according to John: "If the world hate you, know ye that it first hated me. If ye were of the world, the world would love what would be its own: but because ye are not of the world, and I have chosen you out of the world, therefore the world hates you. Remember the word which I said unto you, The servant is not greater than his lord. If they have persecuted me, they will also persecute you." Also in Baruch: "For the time shall come, and ye shall seek me, both ye and those who shall be after you, to hear the word of wisdom and of understanding; and ye shall not find me. But the nations shall desire to see the wise man, and it shall not happen to them; not because the wisdom of this world shall be wanting, or shall fail to the earth; but neither shall the word of the law be wanting to the world. For wisdom shall be in a few who watch, and are silent and quiet, and who hold converse with one another; because some shall dread them, and shall fear them as evil. But some do not believe the word of the law of the Highest. But some who are amazed in their countenance will not believe; and they also who contradict will believe, and will be contrary to and hindering the spirit of truth. Moreover, others will be wise to the spirit of error, and declaring the edicts, as if of the Highest and the Strong One. Moreover, others are possessors of faith. Others are mighty and strong in the faith of the Highest, and hateful to the stranger."

30. That what any one has vowed to God, he must quickly repay.

In Solomon: "According as thou hast vowed a vow to God, delay not to pay it." Concerning this same thing in Deuteronomy: "But if thou hast vowed a vow to the Lord thy God, thou shalt not delay to pay it: because the Lord thy God inquiring shall seek it of thee; and it shall be for a sin. Thou shalt observe those things that shall go forth out of thy lips, and shalt perform the gift which thou hast spoken with thy mouth." Of this same matter in the forty-ninth Psalm: "Sacrifice to God the sacrifice of praise, and pay thy vows to the Most High. Call upon me in the day of trouble, and I will deliver thee, and thou shalt glorify me." Of this same thing in the Acts of the Apostles: "Why hath Satan filled thine heart, that thou should lie to the Holy Ghost, when thy estate was in thine own power? Thou hast not lied unto men, but unto God." Also in Jeremiah: "Cursed is he who doeth the work of God negligently."

31. That he who does not believe is judged

already.

In the Gospel according to John: "He that believeth not is already judged, because he hath not believed in the name of the only Son of God. And this is the judgment, that light has come into the world, and men have loved darkness rather than light." Of this also in the first Psalm: "Therefore the ungodly shall not rise up in judgment, nor sinners in the council of the righteous."

32. Of the benefit of virginity and of continency.

In Genesis: "Multiplying I will multiply thy sorrows and thy groanings, and in sorrow shalt thou bring forth children; and thy turning shall be to thy husband, and he shall rule over thee." Of this same thing in the Gospel according to Matthew: "All men do not receive the word, but they to whom it is given: for there are some eunuchs who were born so from their mother's womb, and there are eunuchs who have been constrained by men, and there are eunuchs who have made themselves eunuchs for the kingdom of heaven's sake. He who can receive it, let him receive it." Also according to Luke: "The children of this world beget, and are begotten. But they who have been considered worthy of that world, and the resurrection from the dead, do not marry, nor are married: for neither shall they begin to die: for they are equal to the angels of God, since they are the children of the resurrection. But, that the dead rise again, Moses intimates when he says in the bush, The Lord, the God of Abraham, and the God of Isaac, and the God of Jacob. He is not the God of the dead, but of the living: for all live unto Him." Also in the first Epistle of Paul to the Corinthians: "It is good for a man not to touch a woman. But, on account of fornication, let every man have his own wife, and every woman have her own husband. Let the husband render what is due to the wife, and similarly the wife to the husband. The wife hath not power over her own body, but the husband. And in like manner, the husband hath not power over his own body, but the wife. Defraud not one the other, except by agreement for a time, that ye may have leisure for prayer; and again return to the same point, lest Satan tempt you on account of your incontinency. This I say by way of allowance, not by way of command. But I wish that all men should be even as I am. But everyone has his proper gift from God; one in one way, but another in another way." Also in the same place: "An unmarried man thinks of those things which are the Lord's, in what way he may please God; but he who has contracted marriage thinks of those things that are of this world, in what way he may please his wife. Thus also, both the woman and the unmarried virgin thinketh of those things which are the Lord's, that she may be holy both in body and in spirit; but she that hath married thinks of those things which are of this world, in what way she may please her husband." Also in Exodus, when the Lord had commanded Moses that he should sanctify the people for the third day, he sanctified them, and added: "Be ye ready, for three days ye shall not approach to women." Also in the first book of Kings: "And the priest answered to David, and said, There are no profane loaves in my hand, except one sacred loaf. If the young men have been kept back from women, they shall eat." Also in the Apocalypse: "These are they who have not defiled themselves with women, for they have continued virgins; these are they who follow the Lamb whithersoever He shall go."

33. That the Father judges nothing, but the Son; and that the Father is not glorified by him by whom the Son is not glorified.

In the Gospel according to John: "The Father judges nothing, but hath given all judgment unto the Son, that all may honor the Son as they honor the Father. He who honored not the Son, honored not the Father who hath sent Him." Also in the seventy-first Psalm: "O God, give the king Thy judgment, and Thy righteousness to the king's son, to judge Thy people in righteousness." Also in Genesis: "And the Lord rained upon Sodom and Gomorrah sulfur, and fire from heaven from the Lord."

34. That the believer ought not to live like the Gentile.

In Jeremiah: "Thus saith the Lord, Walk ye not according to the way of the Gentiles." Of this same thing, that one ought to separate himself from the Gentiles, lest he should be a companion of their sin, and become a partaker of their penalty, in the Apocalypse: "And I heard another voice from heaven, saying, Go forth from her, my people, lest thou be partaker of her crimes, and lest thou be stricken with her plagues; because her crimes have reached even to heaven, and the Lord God hath remembered her iniquities. Therefore He hath returned unto her double, and in the cup which she hath mixed double is mingled for her; and in how much she hath glorified herself and possessed of delights, in so much is given unto her both torment and grief. For in her heart she says, I am a queen, and cannot be a widow, nor shall I see sorrow. Therefore in one hour her plagues shall come on her, death, grief, and famine; and she shall be burned with fire, because the Lord God is strong who shall judge her.

And the kings of the earth shall weep and lament themselves for her, who have committed fornication with her, and have been conversant in her sins."4394 Also in Isaiah: "Go forth from the midst of them, ye who bear the vessels of the Lord."

35. That God is patient for this end, that we may repent of our sin, and be reformed.

In Solomon, in Ecclesiasticus: "Say not, I have sinned, and what sorrow hath happened to me? For the Highest is a patient repayer." Also Paul to the Romans: "Or despises thou the riches of His goodness, and forbearance, and patience, not knowing that the goodness of God leadeth thee to repentance? But, according to thy hardness and impenitent heart, thou treasures up to thyself wrath in the day of wrath and of revelation of the just judgment of God, who will render to every man according to his deeds."

36. That a woman ought not to be adorned in a worldly fashion.

In the Apocalypse: "And there came one of the seven angels having vials, and approached me, saying, Come, I will show thee the condemnation of the great whore, who sits upon many waters, with whom the kings of the earth have committed fornication. And I saw a woman who sate upon a beast. And that woman was clothed with a purple and scarlet robe; and she was adorned with gold, and precious stones, and pearls, holding a golden cup in her hand full of curses, and impurity, and fornication of the whole earth." Also to Timothy: "Let your women be such as adorn themselves with shamefacedness and modesty, not with twisted hair, nor with gold, nor with pearls, or precious garments, but as becometh women professing chastity, with a good conversation." Of this same thing in the Epistle of Peter to the people at Pontus: "Let there be in a woman not the outward adorning of ornament, or of gold, or of apparel, but the adorning of the heart." Also in Genesis: "Thamar covered herself with a cloak, and adorned herself; and when Judah beheld her, she appeared to him to be a harlot."

37. That the believer ought not to be punished for other offences, except for the name he bears.
In the Epistle of Peter to them of Pontus: "Nor let any of you suffer as a thief, or a murderer, or as an evil-doer, or as a minder of other people's business, but as a Christian."

38. That the servant of God ought to be innocent, lest he fall into secular punishment.
In the Epistle of Paul to the Romans: "Wilt thou not be afraid of the power? Do that which is good, and thou shalt have praise of it."

39. That there is given to us an example of living in Christ.
In the Epistle of Peter to them of Pontus: "For Christ suffered for us, leaving you an example, that ye may follow His steps; who did no sin, neither was guile found in His mouth; who, when He was reviled, reviled not again; when He suffered, threatened not, but gave Himself up to him that judges unrighteously." Also Paul to the Philippians: "Who, being appointed in the figure of God, thought it not robbery that He was equal with God;

but emptied Himself, taking the form of a servant, He was made in the likeness of man, and was found in fashion as a man. He humbled Himself, becoming obedient even unto death, and the death of the cross. For which cause also God hath exalted Him, and hath given Him a name, that it may be above every name, that in the name of Jesus every knee should be bowed, of things heavenly, and earthly, and infernal; and that every tongue should confess that the Lord Jesus Christ is in glory of God the Father." Of this same thing in the Gospel according to John: "If I have washed your feet, being your Master and Lord, ye also ought to wash the feet of others. For I have given you an example, that as I have done, ye also should do to others."

40. That we must not labor noisily nor boastfully.

In the Gospel according to Matthew: "Let not thy left hand know what thy right hand doeth, that thine alms may be in secret; and thy Father, which sees in secret, shall render to thee." Also in the same place: "When thou does an alms, do not sound a trumpet before thee, as the hypocrites do in the streets and in the synagogues, that they may be glorified of men. Verily I say unto you, They have fulfilled their reward."

41. That we must not speak foolishly and offensively.

In Paul's Epistle to the Ephesians: "Foolish speaking and scurrility, which are not fitting for the occasion, let them not be even named among you."

42. That faith is of advantage altogether, and that we can do as much as we believe.

In Genesis: "And Abraham believed God, and it was counted unto him for righteousness." Also in Isaiah: "And if ye do not believe, neither shall ye understand." Also in the Gospel according to Matthew: "O thou of little faith, wherefore didst thou doubt?" Also in the same place: "If you have faith as a grain of mustard seed, ye shall say to this mountain, Pass over from here to that place, and it shall pass over; and nothing shall be impossible unto you." Also according to Mark: "All things whatsoever ye pray and ask for, believe that ye shall receive them, and they shall be yours." Also in the same place: "All things are possible to him that believeth." In Habakkuk: "But the righteous live by my faith." Also in Daniel: "Ananias, Azarias, and Misael, trusting in God, were delivered from the fiery flame."

43. That he who believes can immediately obtain (i.e., pardon and peace).

In the Acts of the Apostles: "Lo, here is water; what is there which hinders me from being baptized? Then said Philip, If thou believes with all thine heart, thou mayest."

44. That believers who differ among themselves ought not to refer to a Gentile judge.

In the first Epistle of Paul to the Corinthians: "Dares any of you, having a matter against another, to discuss it among the unrighteous, and not among the saints? Know ye not that the saints shall judge this world?" And again: "Now indeed there is altogether a fault among you, because ye have judgments one against another. Wherefore do ye not rather suffer injury? or wherefore are ye not rather defrauded? But ye do wrong, and defraud, and this your brethren. Know ye not that the unrighteous shall not obtain the kingdom of God?"

45. That hope is of future things, and therefore that our faith concerning those things which are promised ought to be patient.

In the Epistle of Paul to the Romans: "We are saved by hope. But hope that is seen is not hope; for what a man sees, why doth he hope for? But if we hope for what we see not, we hope for it in patience."

46. That a woman ought to be silent in the church.

In the first Epistle of Paul to the Corinthians: "Let women be silent in the church. But if any wish to learn anything, let them ask their husbands at home." Also to Timothy: "Let a woman learn with silence, in all subjection. But I permit not a woman to teach, nor to be set over the man, but to be in silence. For Adam was first formed, then Eve; and Adam was not seduced, but the woman was seduced."

47. That it arises from our fault and our desert that we suffer, and do not perceive God's help in everything.

In Hosea: "Hear ye the word of the Lord, ye children of Israel: because judgment is from the Lord against the inhabitants of the earth, because there is neither mercy nor truth, nor acknowledgment of God upon the earth; but cursing, and lying, and slaughter, and theft, and adultery is scattered abroad upon the earth: they mingle blood to blood. Therefore the land shall mourn, with all its inhabitants, with the beasts of the field, with the creeping things of the earth, with the birds of heaven; and the fishes of the sea shall fail: so that no man may judge, no man may refute." Of this same thing in Isaiah: "Is not the Lord's hand strong to save, or has He weighed down His ear that He may not hear? But your sins separate between you and God; and on account of your iniquities He turns away His face from you, lest He should pity. For your hands are polluted with blood, and your fingers with sins; and your lips have spoken wickedness, and your tongue devises unrighteousness. No one speaks true things, neither is judgment true. They trust in vanity, and speak emptiness, who conceive sorrow, and bring forth wickedness." Also in Zephaniah: "In failing, let it fail from the face of the earth, saith the Lord. Let man fail, and cattle; let the birds of heaven fail, and the fishes of the sea; and I will take away the unrighteous from the face of the earth."

48. That we must not take usury.

In the thirteenth Psalm: "He that hath not given his money upon usury, and has not received gifts concerning the innocent. He who doeth these things shall not be moved for ever." Also in Ezekiel: "But the man who will be righteous, shall not oppress a man, and shall return the pledge of the debtor, and shall not commit rapine, and shall give his bread to the hungry, and shall cover the naked, and shall not give his money for usury." Also in Deuteronomy: "Thou shalt not lend to thy brother with usury of money, and with usury of victuals."

49. That even our enemies must be loved.

In the Gospel according to Luke: "If ye love those

who love you, what thank have ye? For even sinners love those who love them." Also according to Matthew: "Love your enemies, and pray for those who persecute you, that ye may be the children of your Father who is in heaven, who makes His sun to rise upon the good and the evil, and giveth rain upon the righteous and the unrighteous."

50. That the sacrament of faith must not be profaned.
In Solomon, in the Proverbs: "Say not anything in the ears of a foolish man; lest, when he hears it, he may mock at thy wise words." Also in the Gospel according to Matthew: "Give not that which is holy to dogs; neither cast ye your pearls before the swine, lest perchance they trample them down with their feet, and turn again and crush you."

51. That no one should be uplifted in his labor.
In Solomon, in Ecclesiasticus: "Extol not thyself in doing thy work." Also in the Gospel according to Luke: "Which of you, having a servant ploughing, or a shepherd, says to him when he cometh from the field, Pass forward and recline? But he says to him, Make ready somewhat that I may sup, and gird thyself, and minister to me, until I eat and drink; and afterwards thou shalt eat and drink? Does he thank that servant because he has done what was commanded him? So also ye, when ye shall have done that which is commanded you, say, We are unprofitable servants; we have done what we had to do."

52. That the liberty of believing or of not believing is placed in free choice.
In Deuteronomy: "Lo, I have set before thy face

life and death, good and evil. Choose for thyself life, that thou mayest live." Also in Isaiah: "And if ye be willing, and hear me, ye shall eat the good of the land. But if ye be unwilling, and will not hear me, the sword shall consume you. For the mouth of the Lord hath spoken these things." Also in the Gospel according to Luke: "The kingdom of God is within you."

53. That the secrets of God cannot be seen through, and therefore that our faith ought to be simple.

In the first Epistle of Paul to the Corinthians: "We see now through the glass in an enigma, but then with face to face. Now I know partly; but then I shall know even as also I am known." Also in Solomon, in Wisdom: "And in simplicity of heart seek Him." Also in the same: "He who walketh with simplicity, walketh trustfully." Also in the same: "Seek not things higher than thyself, and look not into things stronger than thyself." Also in Solomon: "Be not excessively righteous, and do not reason more than is required." Also in Isaiah: "Woe unto them who are convicted in themselves." Also in the Maccabees: "Daniel in his simplicity was delivered from the mouth of the lions." Also in the Epistle of Paul to the Romans: "Oh the depth of the riches of the wisdom and knowledge of God! How incomprehensible are His judgments, and how unsearchable are His ways! For who has known the mind of the Lord? or who has been His counsellor? or who has first given to Him, and it shall be recompensed to him again? Because from Him, and through Him, and in Him, are all things: to Him be glory for ever and ever." Also to Timothy: "But foolish and unlearned questions avoid, knowing that they generate strife. But the servant of God ought not to strive, but to be gentle towards all men."

54. That no one is without filth and without sin.
In Job: "For who is pure from filth? Not one; even if his life be of one day on the earth." Also in the fiftieth Psalm: "Behold, I was conceived in iniquities, and in sins hath my mother conceived me." Also in the Epistle of John: "If we say that we have no sin, we deceive ourselves, and the truth is not in us."

55. That we must not please men, but God.
In the fifty-second Psalm: "They that please men are confounded, because God hath made them nothing." Also in the Epistle of Paul to the Galatians: "If I wished to please men, I should not be the servant of Christ."

56. That nothing that is done is hidden from God.
In the Wisdom of Solomon: "In every place the eyes of God look upon the good and evil." Also in Jeremiah: "I am a God at hand, and not a God afar off. If a man should be hidden in the secret place, shall I not therefore see him? Do not I fill heaven and earth? saith the Lord." Also in the first of Kings: "Man looks on the face, but God on the heart." Also in the Apocalypse: "And all the churches shall know that I am the searcher of the reins and heart; and I will give to every one of you according to his works." Also in the eighteenth Psalm: "Who understands his faults? Cleanse Thou me from my secret sins, O Lord." Also in the second Epistle of Paul to the Corinthians: "We must all be manifested before the tribunal of Christ, that everyone may bear again the things which belong to his own body, according to what he hath done, whether good or evil."

57. That the believer is amended and reserved.

In the cxviith Psalm: "The Lord amending hath amended me, and hath not delivered me to death." Also in the eighty-eighth Psalm: "I will visit their transgressions with a rod, and their sins with scourges. But my mercy will I not scatter away from them." Also in Malachi: "And He shall sit melting and purifying, as it were, gold and silver; and He shall purify the sons of Levi." Also in the Gospel: "Thou shalt not go out thence until thou pay the uttermost farthing."

58. That no one should be made sad by death; since in living is labor and peril, in dying peace and the certainty of resurrection.

In Genesis: "Then said the Lord to Adam, Because thou hast hearkened to the voice of thy wife, and hast eaten of that tree of which alone I commanded thee that thou shouldest not eat, cursed shall be the ground in all thy works; in sadness and groaning shalt thou eat of it all the days of thy life: thorns and thistles shall it cast forth to thee; and thou shalt eat the herb of the field in the sweat of thy brow. Thou shalt eat thy bread until thou return unto the earth from which also thou was taken; because earth thou art, and to earth thou shalt go." Also in the same place: "And Enoch pleased God, and was not found afterwards: because God translated him." And in Isaiah: "All flesh is grass, and all the glory of it as the flower of grass. The grass withered, and the flower hath fallen away; but the word of the Lord abides forever." In Ezekiel: "They say, Our bones are become dry, our hope hath perished: we have expired. Therefore prophesy, and say, Thus saith the Lord, Behold, I open your monuments, and I will bring you forth from your monuments, and I will bring you into the land of Israel; and I will put my Spirit upon you, and ye shall live; and I will place you into your land: and ye shall know that I the Lord have spoken, and will do it, saith the Lord." Also in the Wisdom of Solomon: "He was taken away, lest wickedness should change his understanding; for his soul was pleasing to God." Also in the eighty-third Psalm: "How beloved are thy dwellings, Thou Lord of hosts? My soul desires and hastes to the courts of God." And in the Epistle of Paul to the Thessalonians: "But we would not that you should be ignorant, brethren, concerning those who sleep, that ye sorrow not as others which have no hope. For if we believe that Jesus died and rose again, so also them which have fallen asleep in Jesus will God bring with Him." Also in the first Epistle to the Corinthians: "You fool, that which you sow is not quickened except it have first died." And again: "Star differs from star in glory: so also the resurrection. The body is sown in corruption, it rises without corruption; it is sown in ignominy, it rises again in glory; it is sown in weakness, it rises again in power; it is sown an animal body, it rises again a spiritual body." And again: "For this corruptible must put on incorruption, and this mortal put on immortality. But when this corruptible shall have put on incorruption, and this mortal shall have put on immortality, then shall come to pass the word that is written, Death is absorbed into striving. Where, O death, is thy sting? Where, O death, is thy striving?" Also in the Gospel according to John: "Father, I will that those whom Thou hast given me be with me where I shall be, and may see my glory which Thou hast given me before the foundation of the world." Also according to Luke: "Now let Thou Thy servant depart in peace, O Lord, according to the word; for mine eyes have seen Thy salvation." Also according to John: "If ye loved me, ye would rejoice because I go to the Father; for the Father is greater than I."

59. Of the idols which the Gentiles think to be gods.

In the Wisdom of Solomon: "All the idols of the nations they counted gods, which neither have the use of their eyes for seeing, nor their nostrils to receive breath, nor their ears for hearing, nor the fingers on their hands for handling; but their feet also are slow to walk. For man made them; and he who has borrowed his breath, he fashioned them. But no man will be able to fashion a god like to himself. For since he is mortal, he fashioned a dead thing with wicked hands. But he himself is better than they whom he worships, since he indeed lived, but they never." On this same matter: "Neither have they who have regarded the works known who was the artificer, but have thought that either fire, or wind, or the rapid air, or the circle of the stars, or the abundant water, or the sun and moon, were the gods that rule over the world; and if, on account of the beauty of these, they have thought thus, let them know how much more beautiful than these is the Lord; or if they have admired their powers and operations, let them perceive from these very things that He who has established these mighty things is stronger than they." Also in the cxxxivth Psalm: "The idols of the nations are silver and gold, the work of men's hands. They have a mouth, and speak not; they have eyes, and see not; they have ears, and hear not; and neither is there any breath in their mouth. Let them who make them become like unto them, and all those who trust in them." Also in the ninety-fifth Psalm: "All the gods of the nations are demons, but the Lord made the heavens." Also in Exodus: "Ye shall not make unto yourselves gods of silver nor of gold." And again: "Thou shalt not make to thyself an idol, nor the likeness of anything." Also in Jeremiah: "Thus saith the Lord, Walk not according to the ways of the heathen; for they fear those things in their own persons, because the lawful things of the heathen are vain. Wood cut out from the forest is made the work of the carpenter, and melted silver and gold are beautifully arranged: they strengthen them with hammers and nails, and they shall not be moved, for they are fixed. The silver is brought from Tharsis, the gold comes from Moab. All things are the works of the artificers; they will clothe it with blue and purple; lifting them, they will carry them, because they will not go forward. Be not afraid of them, because they do no evil, neither is there good in them. Say thus, The gods that have not made the heaven and the earth perish from the earth, and from under this heaven. The heaven hath trembled at this, and hath shuddered much more vehemently, saith the Lord. These evil things hath my people done. They have forsaken the fountain of living water, and have dug out for themselves worn-out wells, which could not hold water. Thy love hath smitten thee, and thy wickedness shall accuse thee. And know and see that it shall be a bitter thing for thee that thou hast forsaken me, saith the Lord thy God, and thou hast not hoped in me, saith thy Lord. Because of old time thou hast resented my yoke, and hast broken thy bonds, and hast said, I will not serve, but I will go upon every lofty mountain, and upon every high hill, and upon every shady tree: there I will be confounded with fornication. To the wood and to the stone they have said, Thou art my father; and to the stone, Thou hast begotten me: and they turned to me their back, and not their face." In Isaiah: "The dragon hath fallen or is dissolved; their carved works have become as beasts and cattle. Laboring and hungry, and without strength, ye shall bear them bound upon your neck as a heavy burden." And again: "Gathered together, they shall not be able to be saved from war; but they themselves have been led captive with thee." And again: "To whom have ye likened me? See and understand that ye err in your heart, who lavish gold out of the bag, and weigh silver in the balance, bringing it up to the weight. The workmen have made with their hand the things made; and, bowing themselves, they have adored it, and have raised it on their shoulders: and thus they walked. But if they should place them down, they will abide in their place, and will not be moved; and they will not hear those who cry unto them: they will not save them from evils." Also in Jeremiah: "The Lord, who made heaven and earth, in strength hath ordered the world, in His wisdom hath stretched forth the heaven, and the multitude of the waters in the heaven. He hath brought out the clouds from the end of the earth, the lightning in the clouds; and He hath brought forth the winds from His treasures. Every man is made foolish by his knowledge, every artificer is confounded by his graven images; because he hath molten a falsehood: there is no breath in them. The works shut up in them are made vain; in the time of their consideration they shall perish." And in the Apocalypse: "And the sixth angel sounded with his trumpet. And I heard one of the four corners of the golden ark, which is in the presence of God, saying to the sixth angel who had the trumpet, Loose the four angels which are bound upon the great river

Euphrates. And the four angels were loosed, which were prepared for an hour, and a day, and a month, and a year, to slay the third part of men; and the number of the army of the horsemen was two hundred thousand of thousand: I heard the number of them. And then I saw the horses in the vision, and those that sate upon them, having breastplates of fire, and of hyacinth, and of sulfur: and the heads of the horses (as the heads of lions); and out of their mouth went fire, and smoke, and sulfur. By these three plagues the third part of men was slain, by the fire, and the smoke, and the sulfur which went forth from their mouth, and is in their tails: for their tails were like unto eels; for they had heads, and with them they do mischief. And the rest of the men who were not slain by these plagues, nor repented of the works of the deeds of their hands, that they should not worship demons and idols, that is, images of gold, and of silver, and of brass, and of stone, and of wood, which can neither see nor walk, repented not also of their murders." Also in the same place: "And the third angel followed them, saying with a loud voice, If any man worship the beast and his image, and hath received his mark in his forehead or upon his hand, the same shall drink of the wine of His wrath, and shall be punished with fire and sulfur, under the eyes of the holy angels, and under the eyes of the Lamb; and the smoke of their torments shall ascend up for ever and ever."

60. That too great lust of food is not to be desired.

In Isaiah: "Let us eat and drink, for tomorrow we shall die. This sin shall not be remitted to you even until ye die." Also in Exodus: "And the people sate down to eat and drink, and rose up to play." Paul, in the first to the

Corinthians: "Meat commended us not to God; neither if we eat shall we abound, nor if we eat not shall we want." And again: "When ye come together to eat, wait one for another. If any is hungry, let him eat at home, that ye may not come together for judgment." Also to the Romans: "The kingdom of God is not meat and drink, but righteousness, and peace, and joy in the Holy Ghost." In the Gospel according to John: "I have meat which ye know not of. My meat is, that I should do His will who sent me, and should finish His work."

61. That the lust of possessing, and money, are not to be sought for.

In Solomon, in Ecclesiasticus: "He that loveth silver shall not be satisfied with silver." Also in Proverbs: "He who holds back the corn is cursed among the people; but blessing is on the head of him that communicates it." Also in Isaiah: "Woe unto them who join house to house, and lay field to field, that they may take away something from their neighbor. Will ye dwell alone upon the earth?" Also in Zephaniah: "They shall build houses, and shall not dwell in them; and they shall appoint vineyards, and shall not drink the wine of them, because the day of the Lord is near." Also in the Gospel according to Luke: "For what does it profit a man to make a gain of the whole world, but that he should lose himself?" And again: "But the Lord said unto him, Thou fool, this night thy soul is required of thee. Whose, then, shall those things be which thou hast provided?" And again: "Remember that thou hast received thy good things in this life, and likewise Lazarus evil things. But now he is besought, and thou grieves." And in the Acts of the Apostles: "But Peter said unto him, Silver and gold indeed I have not; but what

I have I give unto you: In the name of Jesus Christ of Nazareth, rise up and walk. And, taking hold of his right hand, he lifted him up." Also in the first to Timothy: "We brought nothing into this world, but neither can we take anything away. Therefore, having maintenance and clothing, let us with these be content. But they who will become rich fall into temptation and a snare, and many and hurtful lusts, which drown man in perdition and destruction. For the root of all evils is covetousness, which some coveting, have made shipwreck from the faith, and have plunged themselves in many sorrows."

62. That marriage is not to be contracted with Gentiles.

In Tobias: "Take a wife from the seed of thy parents, and take not a strange woman who is not of the tribe of thy parents." Also in Genesis, Abraham sends his servant to take from his seed Rebecca, for his son Isaac. Also in Esdras, it was not sufficient for God when the Jews were laid waste, unless they forsook their foreign wives, with the children also whom they had begotten of them. Also in the first Epistle of Paul to the Corinthians: "The woman is bound so long as her husband lives; but if he die, she is freed to marry whom she will, only in the Lord. But she will be happier if she abides thus." And again: "Know ye not that your bodies are the members of Christ? Shall I take the members of Christ, and make them the members of a harlot? Far be it from me. Or know ye not that he who is joined together with a harlot is one body? for two shall be in one flesh. But he who is joined to the Lord is one spirit." Also in the second to the Corinthians: "Be not joined together with unbelievers. For what participation is there between righteousness and unrighteousness? or what communication hath light with darkness?" Also concerning Solomon in the third book of Kings: "And foreign wives turned away his heart after their gods."

63. That the sin of fornication is grievous.
In the first Epistle of Paul to the Corinthians: "Every sin whatsoever a man doeth is outside the body; but he who commits fornication sins against his own body. Ye are not your own, for ye are bought with a great price. Glorify and bear the Lord in your body."

64. What are those carnal things which beget death, and what are the spiritual things which lead to life.
Paul to the Galatians: "The flesh lusted against the Spirit, and the Spirit against the flesh: for these are contrary the one to the other, that ye cannot do even those things which ye wish. But the deeds of the flesh are manifest, which are: adulteries, fornications, impurities, filthiness, idolatries, sorceries, murders, hatreds, strife, emulations, animosities, provocations, hatreds, dissensions, heresies, envying, drunkenness, reveling, and such like: with respect to which I declare, that they who do such things shall not possess the kingdom of God. But the fruit of the Spirit is charity, joy, peace, magnanimity, goodness, faith, gentleness, continency, chastity. For they who are Christ's have crucified their flesh, with its vices and lusts."

65. That all sins are put away in baptism.
In the first Epistle of Paul to the Corinthians: "Neither fornicators, nor those who serve idols, nor adulterers, nor effeminate, nor the lusters after mankind,

nor thieves, nor cheaters, nor drunkards, nor revilers, nor robbers, shall obtain the kingdom of God. And these things indeed ye were: but ye are washed, but ye are sanctified in the name of our Lord Jesus Christ, and in the Spirit of our God."

66. That the discipline of God is to be observed in Church precepts.

In Jeremiah: "And I will give to you shepherds according to my own heart; and they shall feed the sheep, feeding them with discipline." Also in Solomon, in the Proverbs: "My son neglect not the discipline of God, nor fail when rebuked by Him. For whom God loves, He rebukes." Also in the second Psalm: "Keep discipline, lest perchance the Lord should be angry, and ye perish from the right way, when His anger shall burn up quickly against you. Blessed are all they who trust in Him." Also in the forty-ninth Psalm: "But to the sinner saith God, For what dost thou set forth my judgments, and takes my covenant into thy mouth? But thou hates discipline, and hast cast my words behind thee." Also in the Wisdom of Solomon: "He who casts away discipline is miserable."

67. That it was foretold that men should despise sound discipline.

Paul, in the second to Timothy: "There will be a time when they will not endure sound doctrine; but according to their own lusts will heap to themselves teachers itching in hearing, tickling their ears; and shall turn away their hearing indeed from the truth, but they shall be converted unto fables."

68. That we must depart from him who lives

irregularly and contrary to discipline.

Paul to the Thessalonians: "But we have commanded you, in the name of Jesus Christ, that ye depart from all brethren who walk disorderly, and not according to the tradition which they have received from us." Also in the forty-ninth Psalm: "If you see a thief, at once you run with him, and place your portion with the adulterers."

69. That the kingdom of God is not in the wisdom of the world, nor in eloquence, but in the faith of the cross, and in virtue of conversation.

In the first Epistle of Paul to the Corinthians: "Christ sent me to preach, not in wisdom of discourse, lest the cross of Christ should become of no effect. For the word of the cross is foolishness to those who perish; but to those who are saved it is the power of God. For it is written, I will destroy the wisdom of the wise, and I will reprove the prudence of the prudent. Where is the wise? where is the scribe? where is the disputer of this world? Hath not God made foolish the wisdom of this world? Since indeed, in the wisdom of God, the world by wisdom knew not God, it pleased God by the foolishness of preaching to save them that believe. Because the Jews desire signs, and the Greeks seek for wisdom: but we preach Christ crucified, to the Jews indeed a stumbling-block, and to the Gentiles foolishness; but to them that are called, Jews and Greeks, Christ the power of God, and the wisdom of God." And again: "Let no man deceive himself. If any man think that he is wise among you, let him become a fool to this world, that he may be wise. For the wisdom of this world is foolishness with God. For it is written, Thou shalt rebuke the wise in their own craftiness." And again: "The Lord knows the thoughts of the wise, that they are foolish."

70. That we must obey parents.

In the Epistle of Paul to the Ephesians: "Children, be obedient to your parents: for this is right. Honor thy father and thy mother (which is the first command with promise), that it may be well with thee, and thou mayest be long-lived on the earth."

71. And that fathers also should not be harsh in respect of their children. Also in the same place: "And, ye fathers, drive not your children to wrath: but nourish them in the discipline and rebuke of the Lord."

72. That servants, when they have believed, ought to serve their carnal masters the better.

In the Epistle of Paul to the Ephesians: "Servants, obey your fleshly masters with fear and trembling, and in simplicity of your heart, as to Christ; not serving for the eye, as if you were pleasing men; but as servants of God."

73. Moreover, that masters should be the more gentle.

Also in the same place: "And, ye masters, do the same things to them, forbearing anger: knowing that both your Master and theirs is in heaven; and there is no choice of persons with Him."

74. That all widows that are approved are to be held in honor.

In the first Epistle of Paul to Timothy: "Honor widows which are truly widows. But the widow that is wanton, is dead while she lives." And again: "But the younger widows pass by: for when they shall be wanton in Christ, they wish to marry; having judgment, because they have cast off their first faith."

75. That every person ought to have care rather of his own people, and especially of believers.

The apostle in his first Epistle to Timothy: "But if any take not care of his own, and especially of those of his own household, he denies the faith, and is worse than an infidel." Of this same thing in Isaiah: "If thou shalt see the naked, clothe him; and despise not those who are of the household of thine own seed." Of which members of the household it is said in the Gospel: "If they have called the master of the house Beelzebub, how much rather them of his household!"

76. That an elder must not be rashly accused.

In the first to Timothy: "Against an elder receive not an accusation."

77. That the sinner must be publicly reproved.

In the first Epistle of Paul to Timothy: "Rebuke them that sin in the presence of all, that others also may be afraid."

78. That we must not speak with heretics.

To Titus: "A man that is a heretic, after one rebuke avoid; knowing that one of such sort is perverted, and sins, and is by his own self condemned." Of this same thing in the Epistle of John: "They went out from among us, but they were not of us; for if they had been of us, they would doubtless have remained with us." Also in the second to Timothy: "Their word doth creep as a canker."

79. That innocency asks with confidence, and obtains.

In the Epistle of John: "If our heart blame us not, we have confidence towards God; and whatever we ask, we shall receive from Him." Also in the Gospel according to Matthew: "Blessed are they of a pure heart, for they shall see God." Also in the twenty-third Psalm: "Who shall ascend into the hill of the Lord? or who shall stand in His holy place? The innocent in hands and of a pure heart."

80. That the devil has no power against man unless God have allowed it.

In the Gospel according to John: "Jesus said, Thou could have no power against me, unless it were given thee from above." Also in the third of Kings: "And God stirred up Satan against Solomon himself." Also in Job, first of all God permitted, and then it was allowed to the devil; and in the Gospel, the Lord first permitted, by saying to Judas, "What thou does, do quickly." Also in Solomon, in the Proverbs: "The heart of the king is in God's hand."

81. That wages be quickly paid to the hireling.

In Leviticus: "The wages of thy hireling shall not sleep with thee until the morning."

82. That divination must not be used.

In Deuteronomy: "Do not use omens nor auguries."

83. That a tuft of hair is not to be worn on the head.

In Leviticus: "Ye shall not make a tuft from the hair of your head."

84. That the beard must not be plucked.
"Ye shall not deface the figure of your beard."

85. That we must rise when a bishop or a presbyter comes.

In Leviticus: "Thou shalt rise up before the face of the elder, and shall honor the person of the presbyter."

86. That a schism must not be made, even although he who withdraws should remain in one faith, and in the same tradition.

In Ecclesiasticus, in Solomon: "He that cleaves firewood shall be endangered by it if the iron shall fall off." Also in Exodus: "In one house shall it be eaten: ye shall not cast forth the flesh abroad out of the house." Also in the cxxxiid Psalm: "Behold how good and how pleasant a thing it is that brethren should dwell in unity!" Also in the Gospel according to Matthew: "He that is not with me is against me; and he that gathered not with me scatters." Also in the first Epistle of Paul to the Corinthians: "But I beseech you, brethren, by the name of our Lord Jesus Christ, that ye all say the same thing, and that there be no schisms among you; but that ye be all joined together in the same mind and in the same opinion." Also in the sixty-seventh Psalm: "God, who makes men to dwell with one mind in a house."

87. That believers ought to be simple, with prudence.

In the Gospel according to Matthew: "Be ye prudent as serpents, and simple as doves." And again: "Ye are the salt of the earth. But if the salt has lost its savor, in what shall it be salted? It is good for nothing, but to be cast out abroad, and to be trodden under foot of men."

88. That a brother must not be deceived.

In the first Epistle of Paul to the Thessalonians: "That a man do not deceive his brother in a matter, because God is the avenger for all these."

89. That the end of the world comes suddenly.

The apostle says: "The day of the Lord shall so come as a thief in the night. When they shall say, Peace and security, then on them shall come sudden destruction." Also in the Acts of the Apostles: "No one can know the times or the seasons which the Father has placed in His own power."

90. That a wife must not depart from her husband; or if she should depart, she must remain unmarried.

In the first Epistle of Paul to the Corinthians: "But to them that are married I command, yet not I, but the Lord, that the wife should not be separated from her husband; but if she should depart, that she remain unmarried or be reconciled to her husband: and that the husband should not put away his wife."

91. That everyone is tempted so much as he is able to bear.

In the first Epistle of Paul to the Corinthians: "No temptation shall take you, except such is human. But God is faithful, who will not suffer you to be tempted above that ye are able; but will with the temptation also make a way to escape, that ye may be able to bear it."

92. That not everything is to be done which is lawful.
Paul, in the first Epistle to the Corinthians: "All things are lawful, but all things are not expedient: all things are lawful, but all things edify not."

93. That it was foretold that heresies would arise.
In the first epistle of Paul to the Corinthians: "Heresies must needs be, in order that they which are approved may be made manifest among you."

94. That the Eucharist is to be received with fear and honor.
In Leviticus: "But whatever soul shall eat of the flesh of the sacrifice of salvation, which is the Lord's, and his uncleanness is still upon him, that soul shall perish from his people." Also in the first to the Corinthians: "Whosoever shall eat the bread or drink the cup of the Lord unworthily, shall be guilty of the body and blood of the Lord."

95. That we are to live with the good, but to avoid the evil.
In Solomon, in the Proverbs: "Bring not the impious man into the habitation of the righteous." Also in

the same, in Ecclesiasticus: "Let righteous men be thy guests." And again: "The faithful friend is a medicine of life and of immortality." Also in the same place: "Be thou far from the man who has the power to slay, and thou shalt not suspect fear." Also in the same place: "Blessed is he who finds a true friend, and who speaks righteousness to the listening ear." Also in the same place: "Hedge thine ears with thorns, and hear not a wicked tongue." Also in the seventeenth Psalm: "With the righteous Thou shalt be justified; and with the innocent man Thou shalt be innocent; and with the froward man Thou shalt be froward." Also in the first Epistle of Paul to the Corinthians: "Evil communications corrupt good dispositions."

96. That we must labor not with words, but with deeds.

In Solomon, in Ecclesiasticus: "Be not hasty in thy tongue, and in thy deeds useless and remiss." And Paul, in the first to the Corinthians: "The kingdom of God is not in word, but in power." Also to the Romans: "Not the hearers of the law are righteous before God, but the doers of the law shall be justified." Also in the Gospel according to Matthew: "He who shall do and teach so, shall be called greatest in the kingdom of heaven." Also in the same place: "Everyone who heareth my words, and doeth them, I will liken him to a wise man who built his house upon a rock. The rain descended, the floods came, the winds blew, and beat upon that house, and it fell not: for it was founded upon a rock. And everyone who heareth my words, and doeth them not, I will liken him to the foolish man, who built his house upon the sand. The rain descended, the floods came, the winds blew, and beat upon that house; and it fell: and its ruin became great."

97. That we must hasten to faith and to attainment.

In Solomon, in Ecclesiasticus: "Delay not to be converted to God, and do not put off from day to day; for His anger cometh suddenly."

98. That the catechumen ought now no longer to sin.

In the Epistle of Paul to the Romans: "Let us do evil until the good things come; whose condemnation is just."

99. That judgment will be according to the times, either of equity before the law, or of law after Moses.

Paul to the Romans: "As many as have sinned without law, shall perish without law; and as many as have sinned in the law, shall be judged also by the law."

100. That the grace of God ought to be without price.

In the Acts of the Apostles: "Thy money be in perdition with thyself, because thou hast thought that the grace of God is possessed by money." Also in the Gospel: "Freely ye have received, freely give." Also in the same place: "Ye have made my Father's house a house of merchandise; and ye have made the house of prayer a den of thieves." Also in Isaiah: "Ye who thirst, go to the water, and as many as have not money: go, and buy, and drink without money." Also in the Apocalypse: "I am Alpha and Omega, the beginning and the end. I will give to him that thirsts from the fountain of the water of life freely. He who shall overcome shall possess these things, and their inheritance; and I will be his God, and he shall be my son."

101. That the Holy Spirit has frequently appeared in fire.

In Exodus: "And the whole of Mount Sinai smoked, because God had come down upon it in fire." Also in the Acts of the Apostles: "And suddenly there was made a sound from heaven, as if a vehement blast were borne along, and it filled the whole of that place in which they were sitting. And there appeared to them cloven tongues as if of fire, which also settled upon each of them; and they were all filled with the Holy Ghost." Also in the sacrifices, whatsoever God accounted accepted, fire descended from heaven, which consumed what was sacrificed. In Exodus: "The angel of the Lord appeared in a flame of fire from the bush."

102. That all good men ought willingly to hear rebuke.

In Solomon, in the Proverbs: "He who reproves a wicked man shall be hated by him. Rebuke a wise man, and he will love you."

103. That we must abstain from much speaking.

In Solomon: "Out of much speaking thou shalt not escape sin; but sparing thy lips, thou shalt be wise."

104. That we must not lie.

"Lying lips are an abomination to the Lord."

105. That they are frequently to be corrected who do wrong in domestic duty.

In Solomon: "He who spare the rod, hated his son." And again: "Do not cease from correcting the child."

106. That when a wrong is received, patience is to be maintained, and vengeance to be left to God.

"Say not, I will avenge me of mine enemy; but wait for the Lord, that He may be thy help." Also elsewhere: "To me belongs vengeance; I will repay, saith the Lord." Also in Zephaniah: "Wait on me, saith the Lord, in the day of my rising again to witness; because my judgment is to the congregations of the Gentiles, that I may take kings, and pour out upon them my anger."

107. That we must not use detraction.

In Solomon, in the Proverbs: "Love not to detract, lest you be taken away." Also in the Fiftieth Psalm: You sit and speak against thy brother; and against the son of your mother you place a stumbling-block." Also in the Epistle of Paul to the Colossians: "To speak ill of no man, nor to be litigious."

108. That we must not lay snares against our neighbor.

In Solomon, in the Proverbs: "He who digs a pit for his neighbor, himself shall fall into it."

109. That the sick are to be visited.

In Solomon, in Ecclesiasticus: "Be not slack to visit the sick man; for from these things thou shalt be strengthened in love." Also in the Gospel: "I was sick, and ye visited me; I was in prison, and ye came unto me."

110. That talebearers are accursed.

In Ecclesiasticus, in Solomon: "The talebearer and the double-tongued is accursed; for he will disturb many who have peace."

111. That the sacrifices of the wicked are not acceptable.

In the same: "The Highest approves not the gifts of the unrighteous."

112. That those are more severely judged, who in this world have had more power.

In Solomon: "The hardest judgment shall be made on those who govern. For to a mean man mercy is granted; but the powerful shall suffer torments mightily." Also in the second Psalm: "And now, ye kings, understand; be amended, ye who judge the earth."

113. That the widow and orphans ought to be protected.

In Solomon: "Be merciful to the orphans as a father, and as a husband to their mother; and thou shalt be the son of the Highest if thou shalt obey." Also in Exodus: "Ye shall not afflict any widow and orphan. But if ye afflict them, and they cry out and call unto me, I will hear their crying, and will be angry in mind against you; and I will destroy you with the sword, and your wives shall be widows, and your children orphans." Also in Isaiah: "Judge for the fatherless and justify the widow; and come let us reason, saith the Lord." Also in Job: "I have preserved the poor man from the hand of the mighty, and I have helped the fatherless who had no helper: the mouth of the widow hath blessed me." Also in the sixty-seventh Psalm: "The Father of the orphans, and the Judge of the widows."

114. That one ought to make confession while he is in the flesh.

In the fifth Psalm: "But in the grave who will confess unto Thee?" Also in the twenty-ninth Psalm: "Shall the dust make confession to Thee?" Also elsewhere that confession is to be made: "I would rather have the repentance of the sinner than his death." Also in Jeremiah: "Thus saith the Lord, Shall not he that falls arise? or shall not he that is turned away be converted?"

115. That flattery is pernicious.

In Isaiah: "They who call you blessed, lead you into error, and trouble the paths of your feet."

116. That God is more loved by him who has had many sins forgiven in baptism.

In the Gospel according to Luke: "To whom much is forgiven, he loveth much; and to whom little is forgiven, the same loveth little."

117. That there is a strong conflict to be waged against the devil, and that therefore we ought to stand bravely, that we may be able to conquer.

In the Epistle of Paul to the Ephesians: "Our wrestle is not against flesh and blood, but against the powers and princes of this world, and of this darkness; against the spiritual things of wickedness in the heavenly places. Because of this, put on the whole armor of God, that ye may be able to resist in the most evil day; that when ye have accomplished all, ye may stand, having your loins girt in the truth of the Gospel, putting on the breastplate of righteousness, and having your feet shod with the preparation of the Gospel of peace; in all things taking the shield of faith, in which ye may extinguish all the fiery darts of the most wicked one; and take the helmet of salvation, and the sword of the Spirit, which is the word of God."

118. Also of Antichrist, that he will come as a man.

In Isaiah: "This is the man who arouses the earth, who disturbs kings, who makes the whole earth a desert."

119. That the yoke of the law was heavy, which is cast off by us, and that the Lord's yoke is easy, which is taken up by us.

In the second Psalm: "Wherefore have the heathen been in tumult, and the people meditated vain things? The kings of the earth have stood up, and their princes have been gathered together against the Lord, and against His Christ. Let us break their bonds asunder and cast away from us their yoke." Also in the Gospel according to Matthew: "Come unto me, ye who labor and are burdened, and I will make you to rest. Take my yoke upon you and learn of me: for I am meek and lowly of heart, and ye shall find rest for your souls. For my yoke is good, and my burden is light." Also in the Acts of the Apostles: "It seemed good to the Holy Ghost, and to us, to impose upon you no other burden than those things which are of necessity, that you should abstain from idolatries, from shedding of blood, and from fornication. And whatsoever you would not to be done unto you, do not to others."

120. That we are to be urgent in prayers.

In the Epistle of Paul to the Colossians: "Be instant in prayer and watch therein." Also in the first Psalm: "But in the law of the Lord is his will, and in His law will he meditate day and night."

**Find this and other great works of the
early Church Fathers at
lighthousechristianpublishing.com.**

St. Cyprian

Our Father who art in heaven, hallowed be thy name.
Thy kingdom come, Thy will be done, on earth as it is in heaven.
Give us this day our daily bread and forgive us our trespasses as we forgive those who trespass against us.
And lead us not into temptation, but deliver us from evil, for Thy is the kingdom, the power and the glory.

Amen

Hail Mary full of grace, the Lord is with thee.
Blessed art thou amongst women and blessed is the fruit
of thy womb Jesus. Holy Mary mother of God, pray for us
sinners, now and the hour of our death.

St. Michael the Arch Angel,
Defend us in battle.
Be our protection against the wickedness and
snares of the devil.
May God rebuke him we humbly pray
And do thou Prince of the heavenly host, by the
power of God, cast into hell Satan and all the evil spirits
who prowl about the world seeking the ruin of souls.

www.ingramcontent.com/pod-product-compliance
Lightning Source LLC
Chambersburg PA
CBHW071228070526
44583CB00017B/2090